Money
and
Divorce

The First 90 Days and After

James J. Gross
Michael F. Callahan
Attorneys at Law

SPHINX® PUBLISHING
AN IMPRINT OF SOURCEBOOKS, INC.®
NAPERVILLE, ILLINOIS
www.SphinxLegal.com

Published by: **Sphinx® Publishing, An Imprint of Sourcebooks, Inc.®**

Naperville Office
P. O. Box 4410
Naperville, Illinois 60567-4410
630-961-3900
Fax: 630-961-2168
www.sourcebooks.com
www.SphinxLegal.com

This publication is designed to provide accurate and authoritative information in regard to the subject matter covered. It is sold with the understanding that the publisher is not engaged in rendering legal, accounting, or other professional service. If legal advice or other expert assistance is required, the services of a competent professional person should be sought.

From a Declaration of Principles Jointly Adopted by a Committee of the American Bar Association and a Committee of Publishers and Associations

This product is not a substitute for legal advice.

Disclaimer required by Texas statutes.

Library of Congress Cataloging-in-Publication Data

Gross, James J.
  Money and divorce : the first 90 days and after-- / by James Gross and Michael Callahan.-- 1st ed.
      p. cm.
  ISBN-13: 978-1-57248-524-2 (pbk. : alk. paper)
  ISBN-10: 1-57248-524-8 (pbk. : alk. paper)
  1. Divorced people--Finance, Personal--Handbooks, manuals, etc. I. Callahan, Michael. II. Title.

HG179.G753 2006
332.0240086'53--dc22
                                                                2005033871

Printed and bound in the United States of America.
SB — 10 9 8 7 6 5 4 3 2 1

Dedication

To our mothers, Lucille Gross and Agnes Callahan, who both left us last year, but gave us a legacy of love and family that is much more valuable than money.

Acknowledgment

We wish to thank paralegals Alison Hoover and Amanda Dunlap for their invaluable research and assistance in preparing this book.

I'd never divorce you,
because I love you, I cherish you, I honor you
and I don't want to lose half my stuff.

—Steve Martin

Contents

SECTION TWO: BEGINNING YOUR DIVORCE (THE SECOND NINETY DAYS)

SECTION THREE: SETTLEMENT (THE THIRD NINETY DAYS)

SECTION FOUR: LITIGATION AS THE LAST RESORT (THE FOURTH NINETY DAYS AND AFTER)

Introduction

People who are getting a divorce want to know what to do. It is such an overwhelming and daunting task that it is easy to feel confused and helpless. This book helps by laying out a timeline for the things you need to do if you are facing a divorce, and serves as an essential guide through the legal and financial process of divorce. It is a step-by-step plan with an action timeline for the things you need to do if you are facing a divorce.

This book is about your legal and financial divorce. It is about time and money. You need to look at your divorce as a financial restructuring. You are best served if you can view it as a business deal. A business deal requires a cool head, careful planning, organization, and attention to detail. In this business deal, you are going to have to gather records, deal with your attorney, negotiate with your spouse, and appear in court.

The main issues in a divorce can be counted on one hand. They are grounds for divorce, children, alimony, property, and legal fees. However, the devil is in the details, and the details of those issues are exceedingly complex. Most of the problems with these main issues involve time and money.

A divorce can take a little time and a little money, or a lot of both. One case took a couple of hours to settle and cost about $500. Another case was in litigation for five years and it cost over $100,000 in legal fees.

After all, divorce is not a single event—it is a process. The process has a beginning, middle, and end. There are things you need to think about before you decide to get a divorce, and preplanning for a divorce to do once you make the decision. There are things you need to know during the negotiation and litigation phase of your divorce. There are even actions to take after the divorce—even when the best action to take is no action at all.

You may find yourself in a divorce that is not your idea at all. While it takes two people to get married, it only takes one to get a divorce. You can slow a divorce down with court-ordered marital counseling or by making your spouse prove the grounds claimed—but if one spouse wants a divorce, he or she can usually get it.

Divorce has a huge emotional cost. There is hurt, anger, anxiety, depression, confusion, frustration, fear, and despair about the future. You need to deal with your emotions with a therapist, a friend, a support group, or in any other way that you can. Think about those issues as part of your emotional divorce. Your lawyer cannot help you with your emotional divorce. You will need to get your emotions under control so they do not get in the way of your legal and financial divorce.

More than 90% of all divorces settle before trial, making the marital settlement agreement a big part of a divorce. If you try your case, it will cost a lot more money and it will take a lot more time.

Most families live on a budget. It may be very informal and the family may not always stay within it, but usually there is one. There is a certain amount of income every month and certain expenses that must be paid. Divorce affects the family's finances in many ways. There are new expenses, such as attorney's fees, court costs and other costs of litigation, therapist or counselor fees, and the costs of moving and setting up a new household. Financial advice from a good accountant or financial planner can be very helpful. Some financial professionals specialize in counseling people involved in divorce and are certified divorce planners.

A divorce can affect income and restructure wealth in dramatic ways. The biggest change in your financial situation is usually that there will be two households to maintain where there was one before the divorce. While two people may be able to live as cheaply as one in a marriage, they certainly cannot do so in a divorce, when there are two households to support with the same income that previously supported one household.

This book breaks down the issues and tells you what steps to take in what order, and when to take them. Every divorce is different, so yours may vary a little from the divorce timeline described. For the most part, divorces tend to fall into certain patterns and the issues come at you in a specific order. This book takes you through a year of divorce, starting with the decision of whether to stay or go and ending with what happens after the divorce trial. The year is broken down into four ninety-day sections.

We have tried to give you practical and useful information. The hope is that if you have this knowledge about money and time, the process will be easier to understand, and your divorce will be less painful and confusing.

Section One:

Pre-Divorce
(The First Ninety Days)

Chapter One

Stay or Go

When two people get married, the emphasis is usually on the romantic and religious aspects of the relationship. Unfortunately, romance is not always enough to save a marriage. There are many reasons for conflict in a marriage and many reasons for a divorce.

Do You Really Want a Divorce?

If you do have a choice in the matter, then the first question you have to ask yourself is if you really want a divorce. The answer may not be clear to you right now. The decision to stay in your marriage or leave it is a significant one. It frequently takes time—sometimes years—to make this decision. It is perfectly acceptable to stay in the inquiry stage for a while. Here are some of the things you need to think about before you decide to get a divorce.

 ◆ Sometimes the devil you know is better than the devil you don't. Although you may not get along with your spouse, you may dislike being alone even more. Eating by yourself, watching television alone, and sleeping by yourself can be difficult.

 ◆ If you have been away from the singles' scene for awhile, you may find it to be an uncomfortable situation. You are older now, and you may have the responsibility of children to deal with. Dating is a hard thing to get back into after being married for a number of years.

◆ Two may be able to live as cheaply as one when they are married, but in a divorce, you are trying to pay for two separate households with the same money that previously supported one. Sacrifices must be made and your standard of living might go down.

◆ Divorces involving custody fights over children are the worst of all, because the stakes are the highest. The children are right in the middle of the conflict between their parents, knowing their lives will change forever and their family is breaking up. Children usually bounce back from divorce with time, but that does not mean the bounce does not hurt. Children experience regret, blame, depression, anxiety, guilt, and anger during a divorce. Also, remember that visitation and child support have to be established.

Reasons for Divorce

There are many reasons for conflict in a marriage and many reasons for a divorce.

Infidelity is involved in roughly one in five divorces. Some marriages survive infidelity, but if there is another man or woman in your life (or in your spouse's life), then you are not in a committed relationship. There is a problem with your marriage.

Verbal or physical violence is another reason for divorce. Everyone has the right to be free from unwanted touching and physical harm. Even words alone can be threatening and painful. No one should endure verbal or physical violence. Sometimes control is the issue. A husband may find success in the business world by exerting control, but running his house the same way may cause his wife to stifle her emotional needs until she leaves.

Disagreement over finances may cause conflict. Opposites attract, but different financial strategies and philosophies can cause conflict in a marriage. A wife who is a saver might marry a spender. The wife might feel like she is rescuing the husband by providing order and a budget, and the husband might enjoy the structure that the wife brings. However, after a while, the restrictions are too binding and the husband rebels, then the wife reacts by being even more strict than she normally would be on her own.

People have different approaches to parenting. The wife may feel that her husband is too strict with the children and that the children need to learn independence. The husband may feel that his wife is too lenient. A husband may feel his wife is lax about the children's weight or medical problems, while his wife sees her husband as overprotective and perhaps even a hypochondriac.

Alternatives to Try

There are alternatives to divorce. By the time people get to the lawyer's office, they have usually made up their minds to get a divorce. However, a few change their minds or want to give their marriage one last chance. In that case, there are a few things you can try.

First, talk to each other. It is difficult to discuss these issues with your spouse, especially if you have reached the point where there is no communication at all. However, if you both can listen and acknowledge what the other person is saying, talking about your problems may actually solve them.

If you cannot talk it out, you may find that a trained mediator can help you resolve your problems. *Mediators* are trained professionals who remain neutral and help you reach agreements. It may be possible to negotiate an agreement to resolve some of the conflicts that have arisen in your marriage. You can even negotiate details such as who will cook meals and who will carry out the trash.

Counseling is a good way to figure out what to do. The marriage counselor will ask questions that help you think more clearly about your situation and what you want. The marriage counselor will help the two of you communicate better with each other and provide ways for you to resolve your conflicts. Sometimes all a couple needs is a good conflict resolution mechanism.

Accepting Reality

Divorce creates an enormous amount of stress. It requires great amounts of energy, time, and money. It is not unusual to experience anxiety, depression, or even thoughts of suicide during a divorce. It is difficult and unpleasant, and should be avoided if possible. However, sometimes you have no choice. It takes two people to get married, but only one to get divorced. If your spouse wants a divorce, then you can slow it down, but you cannot prevent it. Someone determined to get a divorce is allowed by law to get one, even if the other party does not want a divorce. If you want the divorce the same holds true. Your spouse cannot prevent it from ultimately happening.

Marriage creates legal rights and obligations that involve finances and property. For example, spouses have the duty to support each other and their children. Since divorce is the end of a marriage, it must be obtained through the court. All of this is governed by the legislature and the courts, and is set out in writing in a body of law called *domestic relations*. Many people only learn about these laws for the first time from their lawyer when they are getting a divorce.

The decision to obtain a divorce is a difficult one. There are more decisions to make as you move through the process, and some will be hard to make. While these decisions are important, you will survive your divorce and move on with your life.

Chapter Two

Researching Your Divorce

It is important for you to learn everything you can about divorce early in the process. If you know little or nothing about the process, you may not make the best decisions or choices. You can raise your odds of success by finding out what is going to happen before it happens.

Our legal system is complicated, and can be confusing and confounding. If you have an overview about the laws that the judge will apply, it will be helpful in navigating your case. This chapter discusses the legal system, how it came to be, its limitations, how laws are made, and where to find the law. It also discusses how to find a good lawyer.

It used to be that the law was not very accessible to anyone except lawyers. People would hire a lawyer, and the lawyer would go off and handle the case. All that has changed with the Internet. There is a wealth of information available about divorce and the law.

You can use a search engine like Google to get started. You may want to start by typing "divorce" or "divorce [your state]," and reading whatever strikes your interest.

It is a good idea to learn about the basics of divorce law in your state early in the process. You can learn about divorce law by looking up your state's statutes on the Internet, checking law firm websites, or looking into other helpful sites. The Internet is a convenient way to obtain summary and detailed information about divorce.

Of course, there are other ways to research the subject. You can start your research at a library or bookstore. There are seminars and support groups you can look into. You may want to talk to friends who have been through divorce, but keep in mind that every divorce is different.

You will want to know the answers to many questions, including the following.

- ◆ Do I have grounds for divorce?
- ◆ How will property be divided?
- ◆ How much support will I receive or have to pay?
- ◆ How does the court decide questions of child custody and visitation?
- ◆ What court can or must I file in?
- ◆ How long does it take?
- ◆ What alternatives are there to a contested divorce trial?
- ◆ Where can I get in contact with support and peer groups?

This book will answer these questions in general terms. Then, you will have the concepts and knowledge necessary to do further research concerning the specific details for your state on the Internet, or at the library or bookstore.

Overview

Our laws have developed over hundreds of years, and can be said to consist of three categories. *Substance* is the basic meaning of the law. Substance determines how the judge is supposed to decide your case. *Procedure* is a series of rules for dealing with the court. For example, procedure tells you what pleadings are to be filed by what dates. *Evidence* is a series of rules for how to present facts at trial.

The law is supposed to be rational, reasoned, and logical. It is designed to be a codification of human behavior. It is studied, considered, and debated.

However, human beings are imperfect, and since our legal system is designed by human beings, it is not perfect. Realizing that may save you some frustration in dealing with your case.

Although it may seem that two lawyers and a judge will arrive at a fair result, this is not always the case.

Our legal system is based on an adversarial model. The theory is that each side marshals the facts, presents evidence, and argues the law most favorably to their side. In theory, the judge or jury is supposed to sort out the truth and render a just result.

Lawyers are taught to kick the other side when they are down. This does not work very well when there are families and children involved.

Judges

In most states, a divorce trial is heard by a judge, who hears the evidence and testimony in the case and makes a decision. The judge is in charge of courtroom procedure, and makes rulings on issues that must be decided by *motions* or other pleadings.

The important thing to know about judges is that they resolve disputes. They are decision-makers, not all-wise and all-knowing. Judges are human, and therefore fallible, and they do not always get it right. Remember that they have heard thousands of cases, so behavior by the other side that seems shocking to you may not seem so shocking to the judge, who has heard the same and worse before. In divorce, there is usually something in the decision that each side does not like.

Finding the Law

The law helps those who help themselves. Judges do not get out from behind the bench to go investigate a case. Instead, the burden is on the parties to do all of the investigation and presentation of proof themselves. Luckily, the law is freely available to the public on the Internet, and every law school and most courts have law libraries. Most of the law is written down and organized for retrieval of important information.

The United States and each state has a written constitution that sets forth essential rights of the people. This is the supreme law of the land and provides the framework for all other laws passed. All new laws are supposed to be consistent with the constitution of each state and the United States Constitution.

The legislature, elected by and representing the people, passes laws (also called *statutes*) each year. These statutes are published in books called *codes* for each state. Laws are meant to codify human behavior, and they reflect the will of the majority in our society. They are intended to be logical and practical, but you may not always find this to be true.

The appellate court for each jurisdiction reviews the records of trial courts on a case-by-case basis when appeals are brought by one of the parties in a case. The appellate court either affirms, vacates, modifies, or reverses the trial court. It usually explains its decision in writing, and many decisions are published in books called *reporters* and summarized in books called *digests*. (You can find reporters and digests in a law library.) These cases form a *precedent* for later trials and appeals. The court can interpret or even invalidate laws if they are unconstitutional. While the legislature reflects the will of the majority in writing general laws, the court can look at the facts of individual cases and make exceptions for the minority when the law would create an unjust result.

Courts are run by rules, which are published in a rule book and must be followed. The rules are published by private companies. You can find them in a law library and sometimes on the Internet. The rules are very detailed and cover how pleadings must be presented and signed, deadlines, how information is obtained from the other side, how evidence is to be presented at trial, and many other subjects. In addition, some courts and some judges publish what are called *local rules*, which may be available only on a memorandum from the clerk. There are also what lawyers refer to as *unpublished rules*— the local customs and practices of various courts and judges that you can only know from experience.

There are various legal encyclopedias, digests, treatises, practice manuals, and other books available at law libraries to help you sort out and make sense of the law. Many court houses have law libraries that are open to the public. While there are general books on the law, you may want to start with a specific book on divorce law in your jurisdiction. The librarian can be helpful in deciding which books to use. Further, most court files are public records. Go to the file clerk at the local courthouse. There will be an index of cases there. Divorce cases usually have two last names that are alike, such as, "Smith vs. Smith." The clerk will let you check out a file. See how lawyers have drafted pleadings similar to yours. In addition, some courts provide forms, help desks, and seminars to assist you in your case.

Chapter Three

Gathering Information

Knowledge is power—especially in divorce. The person with command of the facts has an advantage in negotiation of a divorce settlement or litigation of a contested divorce. You want to gather as many facts about your family finances as you can.

You can hand over a shopping bag full of thrown-together documents to your attorney and let him or her sort through the papers. If you have an unlimited budget, this might be a convenient way to handle it. Your attorney will happily bill you for the time it takes to organize your financial information. Besides, with all the stress a divorce brings—including relocation, dealing with the children, financial problems, emotional upheaval, and confusing legal issues—the last thing you want to deal with is paperwork. However, the more you can organize your own financial documents, the more you will reduce your attorney's fee and improve your chances of success.

You are going to have to gather and organize a lot of information for your case. A good way of organizing the information you find is a *financial statement*. A financial statement consists of a *balance sheet* and an *income and expense statement*. Blank forms for a balance sheet and expense statement can be found on pages 19–21.

You can use the financial statement as a checklist for gathering the information you need to collect. Once you fill it out, it will help you organize your financial information in a way that makes sense and is easily understandable. Give it to your lawyer at the first meeting to save time and expense. Many courts have a financial statement form available at the court clerk's office, and some courts have them online. You can go to the clerk's office at the courthouse to see if the court has a form that you must use. If one is not provided by your court clerk, use the example on pages 19–21 to create your own financial statement. The court may require you to file a financial statement with your complaint for divorce.

Balance Sheet

The *balance sheet* is a snapshot of your financial picture on a particular day. It consists of your *assets*, which are things you own, and your *liabilities*, meaning what you owe. The balance sheet is dated, and the items are listed with their values on that date. In standard business accounting, assets are listed at historical cost, but that is not the practice in completing financial statements in divorce cases.

You will want to indicate how property is titled—*jointly* with your spouse or *solely* by husband or wife. Put this information in the "Comments" column on the balance sheet at the end of this chapter. Do the best you can, using estimates when necessary and footnotes if explanations are required. You can write "unknown" if you have no idea of the amount for some items, and then revise the balance sheet as you obtain more information.

Assets can be broken down into *real property* and *personal property*.

Real property means land and any buildings on that land. For real property, list your marital residence if you own your own home. Also include any condominium, cooperative apartment, vacation property, rental property, or undeveloped land that you own.

Personal property includes *tangible personal property* and *intangible personal property*. Tangible personal property means you can touch it; for example, household furniture, furnishings, clothing, jewelry, gold, automobiles, boats, airplanes, and other vehicles. It also includes furs, guns, stamp collections, coin collections, artwork, books, china, crystal, sterling, and antiques. Intangible personal property is property that you cannot touch. Examples include business interests, retirement funds, stock options, country club memberships, frequent flyer miles, contracts, tax refunds, royalties, patents, cash value of life insurance, gift certificates, notes receivable, prizes, awards, and lawsuits.

Liabilities are the things you owe, including your mortgage, home equity line, automobile loan, personal loans, credit cards, taxes due, and other debts.

Once you have listed your assets and liabilities either in the above categories or on the court form, you can use a three-ring binder to collect and organize supporting documents. Place your balance sheet in the front of the binder. Then, place a number by each line item on your balance sheet and make a corresponding tab in your notebook for the documents that support each item. For example, put copies of current statements in the tabs for your bank accounts, brokerage accounts, retirement accounts, and credit cards. Put an appraisal, assessment, or information on comparable sales in the tab for real estate. Put your mortgage statement in the mortgage tab.

Income and Expense Statement

The *income and expense statement* shows your finances over a particular period of time, such as a year or a month. You should show your income and your spouse's income separately. Income includes salary, bonuses, overtime pay, interest, dividends, business income, rental income, and all other sources of income. Supporting documents to verify income will include pay stubs, IRS returns and forms, and bank and brokerage statements. When filling out the income statement at the end of this chapter, first put your monthly gross or total income in the far right column. Then, put deductions from that figure in the middle column. Subtotal your deductions in the middle column and repeat this number as a negative to the right. The difference between gross income and total deductions is your net income. Do the same for other income to obtain your total monthly income.

When first examining you expenses, it is important to consider your history. Look at your living expenses over the past year and categorize them. Use the court form categories or those that you would use in setting up a budget. The court forms sometimes ask you to divide each item between you and your children. For example, you might put down two-thirds of the car payment for you and one-third for the children. There are no rules for dividing expenses between you and the children, but if you are unreasonable, the court may reallocate your expenses in a different fashion. There may also be strategy involved in this division, depending on whether you are trying to focus the court more on alimony or child support. Supporting documents for expenses include your bank statements, canceled checks, receipts, and credit card statements.

Next, you may need to adjust your expenses for the future if they will be different after a separation or divorce. You can explain the adjustments you have made with footnotes on your income and expense statement.

Supporting Documents

If you are the spouse who handles the family's finances, then it will take some time, but you will be able to obtain all of the supporting documents. If you do not handle the family's finances, then it may take considerably more effort, especially if you are faced with a spouse who is not forthcoming with the information or is trying to conceal it from you. If you cannot find everything, do not despair. The court has discovery rules that will help you obtain information later. (See pages 223–224 for more information on discovery.) However, finding it in advance saves time and legal fees, and prevents concealment.

You want to make copies of everything, including scraps of paper and handwritten notes, that may lead you to more information. Check open briefcases, desk drawers, safes, safe-deposit boxes, and automobiles. Print out any information that you find on the family computer. Ivana Trump once said that every man keeps a little piece of paper somewhere on which he writes down everything he owns.

Tax Returns

Try to obtain tax returns for the last five years. If you do not have copies, you can request them from the IRS. An accountant can review the returns and find information that may not be readily apparent to you. In particular, you will want to pay attention to the following IRS forms and schedules.

◆ Individual Tax Returns (Form 1040)
  • Schedule A—Itemized Deductions
  • Schedule B—Interest and Dividends (this form will list bank and brokerage accounts)
  • Schedule C—Profit or Loss from Business
  • Schedule D—Capital Gains and Losses (this form will tell you about stock sales)
  • Schedule E—Supplemental Income and Loss (this form will tell you about income from rents, royalties, partnerships, estates, trusts, and so on)
  • Schedule K-1—Partnership, Estates, Trusts
  • Form 2106—Employee Business Expense (look for perks such as vehicle, travel, meals)
  • Form 4684—Casualties and Thefts
  • Form 5043—Retirement Assets
  • Form 5500, 5500C, and 5500EZ—Retirement Assets (including detailed amounts)
  • Supporting documentation—W-2s, 1099s, etc.
◆ Corporate Tax Returns (Form 1120 and Form 1120S for Subchapter S corporations)
  • Schedule A—Cost of Goods Sold
  • Schedule D—Capital Gains and Losses
  • Schedule E—Compensation of Officers
  • Schedule K—Other Information
  • Schedule K-1—Allocation of Profit and Loss among Shareholders
  • Schedule L—Balance Sheets
  • Schedule M-1—Reconciliation of Books of Company with Income Tax Return
  • Schedule M-2—Analysis of Unappropriated Retained Earnings

- Form 4562—Depreciation and Amortization
- Form 4797—Sales of Business Property
- Form 5500—Annual Return/Report of Employee Benefit Plan
- ◆ Partnership Tax Returns (Form 1065)
- ◆ Gift and Estate Tax Returns

Business and Employment Records

Pay can include deferred income, commissions, bonuses, royalties, vacations, sick pay, and severance pay. Income can include perks such as a company car, auto expenses, meals, entertainment, travel, and loans. Pension plan contributions by an employer are income as well, even though they are not taxable. They show up as a separate item from wages on W-2s and 1099s. You should obtain copies of pay stubs, employee benefit brochures, employment contracts, and related documents.

If a spouse owns a business, income can be manipulated. Expenses can be prepaid, income and receivables can be deferred, inventory can be bought or sold down, and friends can be hired. An accountant can help you review and understand the tax returns.

If your spouse owns a business, you will want to see the legal and financial records for that business. If it is incorporated, there will be a corporate record book with dates of formation, articles of incorporation, bylaws, minutes, and a stock transfer ledger. The business will also have checkbooks, journals, ledgers, and financial statements. Try to obtain any expense statements, loan applications, leases, contracts, business plans, projections, marketing literature, websites, and any other records that are available.

Bank, Stock, and Credit Card Accounts

You will want to copy all bank, stock, and credit card statements. If you find canceled checks written by your spouse that are suspicious, such as large payments to "Cash" or persons you do not recognize, copy both front and back of the check. Credit card statements can indicate needs and expenses, or a lifestyle that may be used to establish alimony and child support. They might show expenses related to adultery or the dissipation of marital assets.

Other Personal Property Records
Bills of sale, appraisals, royalty statements, life insurance statements, wills, trust agreements, home inventories, vehicle titles, homeowners insurance policies and riders, pension plan documents, and loan applications are examples of records that may show the existence and value of personal property. However, be aware that appraisals for insurance purposes may be higher than appraisals for replacement value, and tax assessments may understate the real value of property.

Address Books
Address books contain important names and numbers for your case. You can use telephone numbers to find addresses and names with a cross directory on the Internet. This may lead you to additional information for your case, and it is helpful to give your lawyer information that can be used to subpoena testimony and documents. Items to look for in an address book include:

- ◆ bank account numbers, codes, and PIN numbers;
- ◆ accountants;
- ◆ bookkeepers;
- ◆ financial planners;
- ◆ stock brokers;
- ◆ bankers;
- ◆ investment advisors;
- ◆ business associates;
- ◆ computer consultants;
- ◆ lawyers;
- ◆ private detectives;
- ◆ paramours;
- ◆ escort and dating services;
- ◆ doctors;
- ◆ therapists;
- ◆ travel agents;
- ◆ storage companies;
- ◆ record storage companies;

- real estate agents;
- appraisers;
- post office boxes;
- telephone answering services;
- voice mail passwords;
- email accounts, user names, and passwords; and,
- mystery numbers.

Real Estate Records

Real estate records you will want to gather include deeds, leases, mortgages, mortgage statements, tax bills and assessments, sales contracts, utility bills, and related documents.

Miscellaneous Documents

Some miscellaneous documents that may prove helpful in your case include diaries, calendars, emails, telephone bills, investigative reports, photographs, videos, education records, wills, trust documents, computer records, business and personal Internet home pages, and professional licenses.

The Personal Computer

If you have a family personal computer that is not password-protected, you can search through the files to find useful information. The courts have compared this to searching an unlocked file cabinet. You will be able to use what you find, such as financial records, incriminating emails, and so on. Be aware that your spouse may be able to do the same thing—so take steps to protect your information. The law in your state may prohibit you from using information retrieved from a personal computer if it is password-protected or belongs solely to your spouse or his or her employer. Some states have criminal statutes prohibiting computer invasion of privacy.

BALANCE SHEET
(Date _____)

ASSETS	VALUE	DATE	COMMENTS
Real Estate			
Bank Accounts			
Stock/Investments			
Pension Plans			
Automobiles			
Household Items			
Other Assets			
TOTAL ASSETS			
LIABILITIES			
Home Mortgages			
Automobile Loans			
Credit Cards			
Loans to Relatives			
Bank Loans			
Accrued Taxes			
Other Debts			
TOTAL LIABILITIES			
NET WORTH			

INCOME STATEMENT

GROSS MONTHLY WAGES:		
Deductions		
Federal		
State		
Medicare		
FICA		
Retirement		
Total Deductions:		
NET INCOME FROM WAGES:		
OTHER GROSS INCOME:		
Deductions		
1.		
2.		
3.		
Total Other Deductions:		
NET OTHER INCOME:		
TOTAL MONTHLY INCOME:		

EXPENSE BUDGET

EXPENSE	SELF	CHILDREN	TOTAL	NOTES
Housing				
Mortgage or Rent				
Real Estate Taxes				
Homeowners Insurance				
Utilities				
Electric				
Heat				
Water/Sewer				
Telephone				
Cable Television				
Food				
Groceries				
Eating Out				
School Lunches				
Clothes				
Transportation				
Medical				
Entertainment				
Other Expenses				
TOTAL EXPENSES				

Chapter Four

Planning for Divorce

There are necessary steps in preparing and planning for any divorce. If you have decided to get a divorce, completed your research, and collected and organized your financial information, then you have already taken many of these steps. However, there are several more crucial items that will need your attention next.

Start a Separate Bank Account

You are going to need your own money for a divorce. You will have to be able to maintain yourself and your children for a while if you are dependent on your spouse and your spouse decides to cut off support. You will also probably need funds to hire a lawyer.

If there is any way to start a separate account to guard against future financial contingencies, now is the time to do it. There are several ways to start your own account. You can withdraw funds from a joint account. You can start depositing your pay into a separate account. If you pay the bills, you may be able to divert a small amount of money to your separate account. An attorney can help you plan the best way to set up a separate account.

If you have to borrow money from a relative or friend, be sure to sign a promissory note so the court will look at this as a loan that you have to repay and not as a gift. A promissory note is an "IOU" in which you agree to repay any money loaned to you. An example of a promissory note is found on page 29.

Set Up a Divorce Calendar

If you are currently using a desk calendar or day planner, you will now need to include your divorce events. You will need to keep track of meetings with your lawyer and court deadlines. It may be used as evidence in your case when your spouse did not keep an appointment, or violated an agreement or court order in some fashion. It may be helpful to keep track of discussions with your spouse.

Visitation dates with children need to be calendared. You will also want to keep track of appointments with your children's teachers, doctors, coaches, and tutors. This may become evidence of your participation in your children's lives if it is questioned in your divorce.

Review your calendar once a week (on Sunday or Monday) during your divorce. That way, you will know what is coming up for the week and what items are due or court appearances are scheduled in your divorce. Then, check your calendar every morning for that day's divorce events.

Judges tend to think that their schedules trump everything else, including your job. Use the calendar to know in advance when you will need to take time off.

Make a To-Do List

You will need to stay organized and set your priorities during a divorce. List all the items you have to accomplish and mark them off as you go through them. For example, collect documents, fill out financial forms, contact a lawyer, and have the house appraised. A sample to-do list is provided on page 30.

Keep a Divorce Notebook

A divorce produces a lot of paperwork. It comes at you in a blizzard. The simplest way to keep track of all these papers is with a three-ring binder and a three-hole punch. You can put papers in chronological order and make an index. You may prefer to set up various categories of divorce papers, such as correspondence with your attorney, drafts of agreements, financial information, and pleadings. You can use dividers in your binder for each category, or use individual folders with brads and a two hole punch. This will help you keep papers neat and organized.

Make Your Debt Payments

If you have debt in your name, like credit cards or student loans, you will want to pay those debts down as much as possible before a divorce. If you use marital assets to pay debt in your name, then it is like getting your spouse to pay half. Otherwise, you might get stuck with all these debts after the divorce.

Financial Planning

You, your spouse, and your children currently constitute one household. At the end of the separation and divorce process, there will be two households. This fundamental change will affect your budget, other financial planning, and the way you raise your children. Now is the time to think through these issues, think about what you want your postdivorce financial life to look like, and make a plan so that your vision can become a reality. There are three possible starting scenarios: you are the income earner, your spouse is the income earner, or you are both income earners.

You as the Income Earner

If you are the sole income earner, you must recognize that family expenses are going to increase as soon as you separate, and in most situations, your spouse's financial contribution is not going to increase immediately. Review your household income and expenses for the last year, and determine whether the household is running a surplus or a deficit. Next, project the post-separation expenses of the two households.

You will have the additional housing and utility expenses of the new household. Other expenses, such as commuting, food, entertainment, and the like, may also change. Your tax situation will change. You will incur attorney's fees and the other expenses of divorce litigation. If you have young children, there will be day care expenses once your spouse goes to work.

If your family is like most American families, you have already been spending close to your entire income, if not more, on living and entertainment expenses. When one household becomes two, there will not be enough money to pay the expenses of both, unless something changes. You may have to cut expenses, sell the car and get a less expensive model, or maybe sell the house. Your spouse may need to obtain employment right away.

The solution that appears obvious to you may turn out to be quite objectionable to your spouse. The point of planning is to think the situation through; identify what, if anything, the financial problem is likely to be; and, consider possible solutions. If you determine a course of action, you will want to act upon it now when agreement seems likely. At the very least, you will want to avoid any irrevocable actions now that will make your desired solution impossible later. For example, before you buy a car, rent an apartment, buy a residence, or co-sign for a spouse's purchase, you should be certain that you can afford it. Many agreements are lost before they can be finalized because one spouse does something that so angers the other that everything falls apart.

Your Spouse as the Income Earner

For planning purposes, if one spouse earns a disproportionate percentage of the family income, there is a primary earner spouse and a financially dependent spouse. If you are the financially dependent spouse, you have to consider the same issues as the primary earner, but from a different point of view. When you run the numbers for the post-separation households, there may be enough or almost enough money to go around.

However, you do not control any of that income. For the time being, you need to determine whether your spouse is likely to voluntarily support you for some period of time. You may not know this for certain until your spouse signs an agreement or writes that first post-separation check.

If your spouse does not voluntarily support you and the children, your remedy is to ask the court to order support. You will not have a good prediction of any of this, and you will not know the answers for sure until the agreement is signed or the judge makes a ruling. The point is to think about it, and iden-tify problems and possible solutions. Then, take the actions that you can take and avoid missteps. For example, do not agree to a division of cash and accounts that leaves you out of funds in the near future without a temporary support agree-ment. Similarly, do not wait until your cash and access to credit runs out before you go to court. Find out how long it takes to have a hearing on temporary support, and if your spouse will not agree to pay sufficient support, file your case early enough so that you will appear before the judge before you run out of cash.

Two Income Earners

If both you and your spouse are employed, you do not have the problem of not controlling any of the income. When you are both substantial earners, negotiations will take place on a more level financial playing field. When you calculate postdivorce finances, you may project that you will need support or that your spouse is likely to ask you for support.

If you have young children, you probably already have day care expenses. The cost and logistics of day care may change once you separate. Each parent's role in the day-to-day family transportation scheme may change. That may affect your work in important ways. If so, you should plan on how to have your employer on your side. Let your supervisor know well in advance that your family situation may require some time off or adjustments to your work schedule. Try not to allow divorce crises to unexpectedly interfere with your work.

Stick to a Routine

It will help if you try to keep things as normal as possible in your life. Do not skip meals or change sleeping habits. Positive routines like using your to-do list and calendar will help you keep focus. Exercise is always a great way to relieve stress. Avoid isolating yourself from your friends.

Try to maintain a positive outlook and do not let yourself be lured into needless conflicts with your spouse. Remember two things: you will need his or her signature on a settlement agreement before your divorce is over, and you will still be parents together for years after the divorce.

Take it one day at a time. Focus on the present and not the past. Try to control only those things within your control. Many things in a divorce are outside of your control. Try not to blow those things out of proportion. Make a plan. Then, keep working your plan. That is how you will take control of your divorce and not let it take control of you.

Finally, in planning for your divorce, the following are a few suggestions for dealing with the emotional disruption that comes with a divorce.

- ◆ It will help if you try to keep things as normal as possible in your life. Do not skip meals or change sleeping habits. Start or continue an exercise routine to relieve stress. Do not make the mistake of isolating yourself from your friends, even if you are feeling depressed.
- ◆ Take it one day at a time. Focus on the present and not the past.
- ◆ Try to control only those things within your control. Many things in a divorce are outside of your control. Try not to blow those things out of proportion.
- ◆ Try to maintain a positive outlook. Fear, depression, and anger will paralyze you. You will need to operate with confidence and tranquility to take the actions you need to take to have a successful outcome in your divorce.
- ◆ Do not let yourself be lured into needless conflicts with your spouse. Remember, you want his or her signature on a settlement agreement. If children are involved, you will still be parents together for years after the divorce.
- ◆ Make a divorce plan. Write it down. Use your to do list and calendar. Then, keep working on your plan. That is how you will take control of your divorce and not let it take control of you.

PROMISSORY NOTE

FOR VALUE RECEIVED, I _____, the undersigned Borrower, promise to pay to _____, Lender, or order the sum of _____dollars ($_____), together with interest thereon at the rate of _____ percent (_____%) per annum. The entire unpaid principal and accrued interest thereon, if any, shall become immediately due and payable on demand by the holder hereof. This Note may be prepaid in whole or in part at any time without premium or penalty. All prepayments shall be applied first to interest, then to principal payments in the order of their maturity. The undersigned agrees to pay all costs and expenses, including all reasonable attorney's fees, for the collection of this Note upon default. All payments shall be made at _____ _____, or at such other place as the holder hereof may from time to time designate in writing.

_____   _____
Witness   Borrower

Dated: _____

TO-DO LIST

(Date _____)

Section Two:

Beginning Your Divorce
(The Second Ninety Days)

Chapter Five

Defensive Actions

People hope their divorce will be amicable. Ideally, you and your spouse will be able to discuss your financial situation, come to some agreement, and put that agreement in writing. However, sometimes people find out too late that their spouse is not being honest or agreeable.

You must plan for the worst case scenario. If your spouse has an attorney, that attorney is advising your spouse to take protective actions. It is important to take reasonable steps to guard your interests in the event of a divorce. They may be viewed by your spouse as aggressive and offensive tactics, but they are really defensive actions.

You are on your own now and you must learn to protect yourself and your children. Once you have decided to file for divorce or are served with legal documents, you will need to protect your financial interests by taking the following defensive actions discussed in this chapter.

Protect the Cash

It is a good idea to keep some cash on hand in case your spouse freezes the bank accounts and credit cards. You will need money to survive until you can get access to credit or open another bank account.

Safeguard any joint bank accounts. If an account is in joint names, then either spouse can withdraw part or all of the account. You can protect yourself from your spouse withdrawing all the money in several ways. The best way to protect your money is to divide accounts by agreement, but this cannot always be accomplished, because your spouse may not agree. You can instead remove one-half of the balance of the account, but be sure to inform your spouse in writing that you have done so. Otherwise, your spouse may overdraft the account without realizing that the funds were not available, which might adversely affect your credit. You also have the option of asking your bank to freeze the account, which means that money cannot be removed from or deposited into the account without permission from both parties listed on the account. Another option is to close all of the joint accounts and deposit them into one frozen account that will be dealt with in the same way. If you do not address this issue, you are giving your spouse the chance to liquidate the accounts without your knowledge.

You should have a bank account in your name to establish your own credit and financial standing. You may need access to your own money in the beginning of your divorce if your spouse stops access to other family money.

Divide the Credit

When you have joint credit cards, the credit card company will hold both of you responsible for any debt, even if you did not charge anything. If your spouse does not pay or goes bankrupt, the credit card company will come after you for the entire amount.

To prevent your spouse from being able to accumulate more debt that could potentially become your responsibility, close any joint credit cards as soon as possible and open new cards in your own name. The balance on the joint account will still have to be paid, and will accrue interest until paid. You can deal with this by each spouse agreeing to transfer a portion of the balance to new cards in individual names, or you can ask the credit card company to freeze the account until you can decide in your divorce who will be responsible for the debt.

It is a good idea to inform your spouse that you intend to cancel the credit cards to prevent him or her from being caught by surprise when the card is denied. You do not want your spouse and children stranded at a gas station without cash or credit.

The best way to close the account is to write a certified, return receipt letter to the credit card company to notify them of the impending divorce and that you are no longer responsible for any charges to the account. If your credit card accounts remain open in both your name and your spouse's name, then you are still liable for any charges your spouse makes. Ask the credit card company to provide separate accounts or apply for an account in your name only.

Like credit cards, you can also close any equity credit lines immediately. An equity credit line is an open-ended loan in which your marital property (i.e., your house) is used as security. The lending institution will put a lien against your house, and the lien is recorded on the title. If you are unsure as to whether or not there is an equity credit line on your house, contact a title insurance company and have them perform a search. This service might cost over $100, but the title company will deliver a complete list of liens against your property. If you do not close any equity lines of credit, you run the risk of losing your home.

Your credit reports are a fast way to check mortgage, loan, and credit card balances. It is also a good way to get a quick picture of your overall debt if you are not the spouse handling the house-hold finances. You can also see if your spouse has obtained any credit in joint names or in your name that you did not know about. There are three credit reporting agencies. You will want to obtain a copy of your credit history from each of them.

Equifax Credit Information Services, Inc.
P.O. Box 740241
Atlanta, GA 30374
800-685-1111
www.equifax.com

Experian
475 Anton Boulevard
Costa Mesa, CA 92626
888-397-3742
www.experian.com

TransUnion, LLC
P.O. Box 2000
Chester, PA 19022
800-888-4213
www.transunion.com

Reduce Expenses

Once you decide to divorce, try to reduce any unnecessary expenses. Cancel any utilities you do not need, such as cable television or extra phone lines. It is a good idea to meet with your spouse before cutting off any utilities, or to at least give your spouse notice.

If you have any personal property you do not want or need, this is the best time to sell it. Once a divorce is filed, you may find yourself in a dispute with your spouse over whether these items may be considered marital property, and you may no longer be able to sell them, even if they are yours.

Stop contributing to any IRAs, 401(k) accounts, pension plans, or any other type of retirement account. If you made contributions to these accounts during your marriage, then your spouse will generally receive at least a portion of the marital contribution to your account as part of the property settlement, so it is a good idea to stop putting money in these accounts. You can generally stop your contributions by signing a form at your workplace.

For any other investments you may have, contact your broker or financial officer, and let him or her know about the divorce. Ask that no stocks or any other types of investments be moved or transferred without written consent and approval of both parties. It is best to first call your broker, since stock transactions can take place within minutes over the phone or Internet. After you have notified your broker over the phone, you should also put this statement into a letter and send it to your broker.

Safeguard Possessions and Documents

Another important step to take during this initial period is to inventory all personal property—especially stored property. If you have a safe-deposit box or storage unit, remove whatever personal property is yours. This applies only to your personal property—not to common possessions or community property.

If you decide not to remove your personal property from a safe-deposit box or storage unit, it is a good idea to make a list of the stored property, or to use a camcorder to take a video recording of the property. A sample form to inventory contents of a safe-deposit box or a storage unit is included on page 40. If you use a camcorder, try to make sure the date function is working. This way, you will have a dated record of the property that was in the safe-deposit box or the storage unit, in case your spouse decides to clean you out.

As with the safe-deposit box or storage unit, you should also inventory everything in the house. The best way to do this is with photographs or videotape, but a sample form to inventory household items is included on page 41.

Move any personal papers and all of your records out of the family home. You should store the papers where your spouse cannot access them. Make copies of any joint records you have (such as bank statements, real estate records, and tax returns) and store these copies outside of the family home. These documents may also help your attorney prepare any necessary financial statements.

You may wish to open a post office box to ensure that your spouse does not open your mail. You do not want your spouse reading communications between you and your attorney.

Likewise, you will want to change and safeguard computer passwords to prevent your spouse from accessing email and other files on your computer. You also want to change passwords for accessing your ATM, online banking, and credit cards.

Your spouse probably has extra keys to your house and your car. He or she may also have keys to your office or your parent's house. There may be keys for a desk, file cabinet, or safe. Ask for the return of these keys as soon as possible.

Keep Separate Property Separate

If you came into the marriage with separate property or received property by an inheritance or gift from your relatives, then it is yours to take when you leave the marriage.

However, this is not the case if you have converted separate property to marital property by putting it in joint names with your spouse.

If you have money that is premarital, an inheritance, or a gift from a third party, keep it separate and do not put it in a joint account. Also, use marital funds—not your separate funds—to pay marital debts and expenses.

Consider Selling the House

Many people try to hang onto their houses at all costs for emotional reasons, and end up losing it in the long run because they cannot make the mortgage payments.

For example, a wife might trade her interest in the husband's pension plan for the house. However, if she cannot make the mortgage payments later, she loses the house and she has no pension. The equity in a house is not a liquid asset that you can use to pay for food and other living expenses. Give some thought to selling the house as soon as possible and downsizing by moving into something smaller and less expensive.

Review Wills, Insurance, and Other Instruments

Think about making a will if you do not have one or changing one that you do have. Most states give a spouse the right to take a portion of your estate, even if you change your will and take him or her out of it. This changes, however, after you sign a settlement agreement or divorce your spouse.

Revoke any powers of attorney that you have given your spouse to handle your financial or business affairs. Send a copy of the revocation to anyone who has a power of attorney on file. If you have a health care directive or living will that gives your spouse the power to make health care decisions for you, revoke it. Send a copy to any doctor or hospital that has a copy of your health care directive. If your spouse is the beneficiary of your life insurance policies, retirement funds, or other investments, you may want to fill out the appropriate change of beneficiary forms.

It is probably not wise to remove your spouse from your health insurance. If your spouse has a catastrophic illness or accident, the costs would consume marital assets and you might be responsible for some of the medical costs.

Automobile insurance ought to be divided up according to who will own and drive which automobile. Until this is done, make sure that you are insured on the car you are driving and that you have insurance on all the cars in your name, whether you are driving them or not.

You will want to keep your homeowners insurance in effect as long as your name is on the house. You may need renters insurance as well, if you have left the marital residence and are renting a separate residence.

If You Need a Protective Order

If you are being abused verbally or physically, then protect yourself first and worry about finances and assets later. You can obtain a protective order from the court and have your spouse put out of the house if you are in danger. If your spouse violates the protective order, you can call the police and they will respond immediately. The court can put a spouse in jail for violating a protective order.

If your spouse threatens or harms your children, obtain a protective order. If you are afraid your spouse will take the children, you can ask the court for an emergency custody order. Let their schools and day care know that they should only release the children to you. If your children have passports, keep them in a safe place.

Hire a Private Detective

You can hire a private detective if you want to determine whether your spouse is guilty of marital misconduct, such as adultery. The private detective will follow your spouse or conduct a stakeout and give you a report. Private detectives can also help locate or trace hidden assets.

Remember, though, that you will have the discovery rules of the court available once you file for divorce. You can ask your spouse about adultery under oath and penalty of perjury. You can also subpoena bank and payroll records.

INVENTORY OF SAFE-DEPOSIT BOX OR STORAGE UNIT
BOX/UNIT NO. _____
AT _____ BANK/FACILITY

_____
Date

Item #	Description

INVENTORY OF HOUSEHOLD ITEMS

Date

Item #	Description	Room	Value

Chapter Six

The Move-Out Decision

The decision to move out is an important one on many levels. It can have numerous consequences affecting the divorce proceedings. Once it is clear that the marriage is over, it can be unpleasant to remain in the residence with your spouse. In most situations, somebody will have to move in order for there to be a divorce. If it is not obvious who is going to move, you should consider all of the consequences of being the one who moves before you do it, because you cannot undo it once you go.

You may have heard the term *legal separation.* Usually, when people use this term they are referring to a legal change in status that is something less than a full divorce—legal recognition that the spouses are no longer living as husband and wife, without the right to remarry. This legal procedure is available in most states and goes by names like *legal separation, limited divorce,* and *divorce from bed and board.* Moving out does not require that you file for this legal procedure. Moving out and reaching a binding written agreement do not require that you file for this legal procedure. If you are eventually going to obtain a divorce, you do not generally need to file for a legal separation or whatever limited divorce procedure is available in your state.

Your Leverage Decreases
If you are not fortunate enough to have worked out an agreement with your spouse prior to leaving, and you are the spouse who leaves the residence, you must consider how it will affect you later during settlement discussions and the divorce proceedings. Exactly how much leverage you lose is determined by the laws of your state.

The marital home is usually the biggest asset associated with the marriage. When one spouse leaves the home, it can reduce the leverage that spouse has when it comes to settlement and property distribution discussions, particularly if children are involved. If you intend to request that you keep the house, perhaps it is not the best decision to move out and leave it with your spouse.

The leverage you have in custody proceedings can be negatively impacted if you leave the children in your spouse's care, if he or she is staying in the marital residence. If you intend to request that the court grant you physical custody of the children, your decision to move out and leave the children with the other parent can come back to haunt you. This decision tends to imply that you feel your spouse is a fit and proper person to care for your children. If this is not how you feel about your spouse, it would be wise to reconsider leaving the children with him or her.

Your Costs Increase

When one household becomes two, expenses invariably increase. It is crucial to consider the impact of this significant change in your budget and financial planning. Considering the fact that the budget for most households is calculated based on the combined income of both spouses, financial troubles can result when two separate households have to be maintained on that same combined income.

First, determine whether your spouse has the financial ability to maintain the expenses of the marital home. If there are children involved, and your spouse is unable to financially maintain the house and support the children, you must consider that you will probably need to provide financial support to your spouse's household after you move. This will help you determine what you will be able to afford.

Until there is a written separation agreement in place, both spouses usually remain financially liable for the mortgage, property taxes, and so on. If you do not have an agreement, you will have month-by-month or even bill-by-bill negotiations.

In some cases, this can result in games of financial "chicken," in which neither spouse pays the expense until the creditor begins threatening adverse credit reports, repossession, foreclosure, or utility cutoffs. Separation and divorce is stressful enough without engaging in this particular tactic. It can also be very expensive and damaging to your credit rating at a time when you may need to borrow money.

Try to reach and document an agreement with your spouse, stating who is responsible for each debt and expense, and how much support, if any, one spouse will pay the other. Generally, it is best to stop using a joint account once one spouse moves out.

In addition to the housing expenses and legal expenses you may incur during settlement or divorce proceedings, other unexpected costs may arise. The cost of your commute may increase if you move further from your job. Another important item to consider if you have children is child care expenses. While the children are in your care, you will need to coordinate and make arrangements for the times when you are at work. Since most child care providers charge by the week or month, it is not cost-effective to have two separate child care providers. However, if you and your spouse live a significant distance away from each other, you may need to arrange for your own child care provider.

The logistics of child care may also be disruptive to your work schedule. If you have to transport your child thirty miles out of your way to the child care provider before work every day, you may end up not getting to work on time. It may be a good idea to discuss these changes with your employer prior to moving out to determine how much flexibility you have in your schedule.

Establish What You are Doing

It is important to consider that the method you choose in leaving the residence can have a significant impact on the divorce proceedings to follow. That being said, it is necessary that you recognize the difference between deserting your spouse and separating from your spouse. Generally speaking, *desertion* is when one spouse abandons the other, and in doing so, ceases to cohabitate or engage in sexual relations with the other without justification or the other spouse's consent.

Keep in mind that desertion is a *fault ground* for divorce in many jurisdictions, whereas voluntary separation is a *no-fault ground* for divorce. Essentially, you do not want to provide fault grounds to your spouse on which to base his or her complaint for divorce. If you and your spouse mutually agree that it would be best for you to leave, grounds for divorce would generally fall under the voluntary separation category.

If you decide against moving out and your spouse does not move, you may be living separately in the same house for some period of time. In some states, this can count toward the required period of separation for divorce on no-fault grounds. Generally, you must leave a paper trail to establish the beginning date of the separation, indicate that you and your spouse have finally and irrevocably separated, and be able to prove these actions. Sometimes this takes the corroboration of a second witness other than your spouse. Typical factors that courts have examined in determining whether married couples have separated while still living in the same house are:

◆ no sexual relations between the spouses;
◆ separate finances;
◆ not taking meals together or doing household and personal tasks for each other;
◆ not going out together or otherwise holding themselves out as husband and wife; and,
◆ expressly telling people that they have separated and are going to be divorced.

This tactic can save money, but the cost in personal serenity may be high. You will want to be reasonably certain that this will work before you rely on a separation in the same house as grounds for divorce. If preliminary research indicates this is a possibility, consult a good family lawyer to find out what you have to do to establish that you and your spouse have separated while still living in the same household.

The Children

When dealing with custody issues, there are two components. The first is *physical custody*, or who the children are physically residing with. The second is *legal custody*, or who has the decision-making power when it comes to matters such as the children's education, health, and so forth.

When thinking about moving out, consider how it will affect your physical custody preference. Generally speaking, the farther away you move, the more difficult frequent visitation becomes, and the less likely you will be granted shared physical custody of your children. It is extremely difficult to maintain a shared physical custody arrangement if you move a long distance away. If you move to another school district, it may interfere with a weekday visitation schedule. Not being able to transport the children to school yourself may limit you to weekend, summer, and holiday visitation only. Consider how much time you would like to spend with your children, and factor that into your decision of how far away and where you move to when leaving the marital home. You should discuss and agree on how frequently the noncustodial parent may call, whether the calls will be at a set time, and so on. The rules should not be overly restrictive, but they should take usual meal times, bedtime, homework, etc. into account.

Discuss the logistics of the visitation schedule. For example, discuss who will pick the children up and drop them off, where you will pick them up and drop them off, and what time the pick-ups and drop-offs will occur. Decide how you will divide time around upcoming holidays. If you reach an agreement, it is best to have it put in writing and signed. Include the rules regarding telephone access in this agreement.

Assuming that, if you move out, you are leaving your children in the care of your spouse, it would be wise to seek an agreement with your spouse concerning a temporary schedule for time-sharing with the children. You might lose a little of your bargaining power if you do not have a schedule established prior to leaving. Even if you move without a temporary custody and access agreement, you are still the parent of your children. You have a right to be with and co-parent your children, subject to your spouse's right to do the same. The parent living with the children does not have the legal right to deny the other parent access to the children simply because there is no agreement or court order stating what the access shall be. The competing, undefined rights of the two parents to be with the children can lead to confrontation and ugly scenes that are not good for the children. If you cannot reach an agreement, you move out anyway, and your spouse unreasonably restricts your time with and access to the children, it is usually best to promptly go to court and obtain a court order to clarify the situation. Unfortunately, this will probably result in your incurring substantial attorney's fees early in the divorce process.

If you want to move and take the children with you, consider the effect that moving from their home, neighborhood, and possibly school, on top of their parent's separation, may have on them. If your spouse does not agree, there could be immediate court action needed. Generally, the judge will not approve of moving the children unless there is a safety issue. If you feel that you have to move for your own safety and take the children with you for their well-being, you should not deny your spouse access to the children—unless you fear for their safety. Otherwise, the judge may conclude that you are attempting to alienate your children from the other parent, and may rule in his or her favor on that basis.

Both Spouses Unwilling to Leave

If you and your spouse agree that you must separate and are at an impasse on who is to leave, you may want to consider a *nesting arrangement*. In these arrangements, the children stay in the house full-time, and the parents move in and out. These arrangements can be useful in breaking an impasse and minimizing disruption to the children. They can also save money if the parents share an apartment for their time out of the house. However, most professionals familiar with separation and divorce do not consider nesting a viable long-term solution for most divorcing couples.

In some states, it may be possible, while living in the same house, to obtain a court order resolving custody and granting exclusive possession of the home to one spouse. If this appears to be necessary in your case, consult a good family lawyer to determine your legal options.

In some jurisdictions, you can obtain a court order for exclusive use and possession of the home, custody, and support while both spouses still live in the same home only in a proceeding based on domestic violence. Do not hesitate to pursue this course if your spouse has used violence against you or your children. If there has been no violence, do not create an incident that provokes violence to obtain a legal solution to the problem of a spouse who will not move. It is a misuse of legal process and you would be putting yourself at legal and physical risk.

Crashing

"Crashing" at a friend's place is an option that you may want to consider if you need to leave the marital residence but are financially strapped. Your move to temporary housing will count towards the start of the separation for voluntary separation grounds, if your departure from the marital home is intended to ban and is permanent. Your move to a room at a friend's house can also constitute desertion if your spouse can establish that it was without consent or justification, just as an unconsented, unjustified move to more permanent quarters could.

If you have children, though, the move to a friend's is not equivalent to moving to a new place of your own. If you remain at a friend's for long and it is a place where your children cannot spend time with you, it could hurt your case for custody or significant time-sharing.

Effect on Equitable Distribution of Property

Another thing to consider is that, when it comes to the disposition of the marital home, the court tends to tip the scale in favor of the spouse who is caring for the children in the marital home. In some jurisdictions, the law specifically provides that, in determining an equitable distribution of marital property, the court will take into account that one spouse is living in the family home with the children. If so, the court will consider whether the best interests of the children require that they remain in the home for some specified period of time before the home is sold and the proceeds are equitably divided, or that title to the home be transferred to the spouse living in it with the children. The law in some states also extends this special treatment to home furnishings and other tangible personal property used by the family, such as vehicles, appliances, and furniture. The court can also rule on contributions to the expenses of the marital home.

Summary

The move of one spouse out of the marital residence is one of the most important events in the separation and divorce process. Sometimes the spouse that should move is obvious and it is not controversial. If who should move is causing controversy, you should consider all relevant factors and use good judgment in deciding what to do. The move-out decision may affect the ultimate custody determination and it has many financial ramifications. Now is not the time to make a rash decision. As with any major decision in life, consider the financial and other consequences in advance, and try to have all of your bases covered before you leave.

Chapter Seven

The Interim Agreement

In most divorces, there is a period of time between the decision to separate and the actual divorce. This may be a few months, or it could be a year or more. During this time, you will have to make decisions about who is going to live where, time-sharing of the children, and how to support two households. If you fail to reach agreement on these matters, then the economically dependent spouse can go to court and ask the judge to establish support, as well as order legal fees and other costs be paid.

It would be great if you could settle all the issues of your marriage and divorce right now and be done with it—but that rarely happens. It takes time, thought, and effort to negotiate a comprehensive marital settlement agreement. However, you may be able to agree on some critical issues for a short-term solution with an *interim agreement*. The interim agreement is a legally binding agreement that will be enforced by the court. The term of the agreement will usually be until superseded by a complete agreement on all issues, or if you are not able to agree, by the divorce decree of the court. You can negotiate new terms when you are ready to complete a final agreement, or you may decide to make some portions of the interim agreement controlling for the final agreement (for example, custody, division of bank accounts, or sale of the marital residence).

Some of the critical issues you may be able to decide with an interim agreement are discussed in this chapter. A sample interim agreement can be found on page 55.

Separation Date

If physical separation is one of the grounds for divorce in your state, you can establish the start date in the interim agreement. You can also acknowledge that the separation is mutual and that it will not be used to prove desertion or abandonment in your divorce. Further, you can say that the separation cannot be used later in court to prove that the person moving out of the marital home abandoned his or her rights to the house or the children.

Marital Residence

Your interim agreement might provide that one party will stay in the marital residence and the other party will move. Other arrangements can be made, such as a nesting agreement, in which the children stay in the marital residence and the parties alternate moving in and out. You may wish to respect each other's privacy and provide for exclusive use and possession of the marital home when it is the other party's respective time. You may also want to provide that the person moving out can come back during certain times to feed the children, help them with their homework, and put them to bed.

Personal Property

You can use the agreement to start dividing your property. You can decide which furniture will be moved to the other residence. You may want to provide a date by which furniture will be divided permanently or by which certain items of a marital residence will be moved. You can provide that any new furniture and furnishings will be the property of the party who purchased them. You can divide your clothing, jewelry, and other personal items now, or provide for a time when the leaving spouse may return to get these items. This is a good time to prepare an inventory of everything in the house, if you have not already done so, and begin to decide how you will eventually divide things up.

You may wish to decide who will drive which automobile and who will be responsible for insurance, repairs, loan payments, gasoline, and traffic tickets. This is a good time to look at the titles and see how the automobiles are owned. You may decide to transfer titles now or later.

It is probably too early to make final decisions about big assets like real estate, pensions, automobiles, bank accounts, and stock, but you may be able to start dividing some of the smaller items now.

Children

You can agree on which parent the children will live with most of the time, which is called *primary residential* or *physical custody*, or you can agree to shared custody, such as one week with one parent and the next week with the other. A temporary time-sharing arrangement will include a weekly holiday and summer schedule. You can go into some detail if you wish and provide pick-up and drop-off times, after-school activities, routines at each household, and the like. School and day care expenses may also be addressed. Temporary child support can be based on the guidelines that are contained in each state's laws. You can find calculators on the Internet for child support.

Spousal Support

If one spouse does not work or makes considerably less than the other, then you will need to make a plan about how to support two households on the income that formerly supported one. This usually requires some temporary spousal support by way of monthly support payments, or identifying who will be responsible for which expenses. The best way to do this is to prepare and agree on budgets for both households that fit within the available income. You may have to eliminate some expenses to accomplish this. You may also want to say that this payment will not be used later in court to establish a precedent for the amount of permanent support.

Legal Fees

If one of the spouses controls all of the family assets and income, then the other spouse will need some money to hire a lawyer. That spouse may also need money to hire experts to value real estate, pensions, or a business. If you can agree on where the money is coming from to pay lawyers and experts, then you can avoid litigating this issue.

Dispute Resolution

It is a good idea to include some form of dispute resolution in the agreement if you can, so that you do not have to go to court every time you disagree. An example would be that all disputes must be submitted first to mediation. You can establish how the fees for mediation will be paid and how many hours of mediation will be required. You may also put in your agreement that the parties will negotiate in good faith to reach a comprehensive marital settlement agreement in the future.

SAMPLE INTERIM AGREEMENT

THIS AGREEMENT is made as of the __6th__ day of __June__, __2006__, by and between __Samantha Green__ ("Wife") and __Stuart Green__ ("Husband").

WHEREAS, the parties were married on _____ __April 8, 1999__ _____ in __Jefferson City__, __Missouri__; and

WHEREAS, __two__ children were born of the marriage, namely __Ricardo Green__, born __October 7, 2001__; and __Amanda Green__, born __March 9, 2003__; and

WHEREAS, certain marital difficulties and differences have arisen between the parties, which they are attempting to resolve by good faith settlement negotiations; and in the meantime, they wish to enter into a voluntary and temporary interim separation agreement;

NOW, THEREFORE, in consideration of the mutual promises, agreements, and covenants expressed herein, it is hereby covenanted and agreed by each party hereto and with the other hereto as follows:

1. The parties agree to live separate and apart from one another, voluntarily and by mutual consent in separate abodes, without cohabitation, until such time as they may reconcile or enter into a permanent separation agreement.

2. In accordance therewith, the children shall stay in the marital home at **1613 Hillcrest Drive, Chevy Chase, Maryland, 20815,** and the parties will move in and out each week and alternative weekly living with the children.

3. The Wife will have exclusive use and possession of the **station wagon** until further agreement or court order.

4. The Husband will have use and possession of the **van** until further agreement or court order.

5. The parties will continue to pay all expenses related to the marital home and other family expenses, in the same fashion as the *status quo ante*, until further agreement or court order.

6. The Husband agrees to keep the Wife's name on all insurance policies, including health, life, home, and automobile, and pay the premiums on same, until further agreement or court order.

7. It is agreed by the parties that their separation is mutual and voluntary and it shall not be construed as desertion or abandonment in any court proceeding.

IN WITNESS WHEREOF, the parties hereto have hereunder set their hands and seals the date and year first above written.

Stuart Green	*Samantha Green*
Husband	Wife

Chapter Eight

Selecting a Lawyer

There is no law that requires you to hire a lawyer, so you may represent yourself if you wish. If you represent yourself, you are considered *pro se*, which means "by yourself" in Latin. Many divorce cases are decided by the courts every day with no lawyers involved, or with a lawyer only on one side. (A few states will permit one lawyer to represent both spouses, but that is not a very good idea.)

Many people want a lawyer in a divorce. You can save on legal fees if you represent yourself, but there are certain advantages to having a lawyer represent you. Family law is complicated. A good lawyer can help you get through the process, avoid mistakes, and save time. A lawyer can be an effective advocate for your interests.

A lawyer can worry about your case instead of you worrying about your case. Lawyers are trained to represent their clients. They have skills and experience from doing this over and over again. Lawyers know the rules, the laws, and the cases in which the courts have interpreted the laws. They are accustomed to appearing in court. When you represent yourself, you will be expected to know the rules, the laws, and the cases. Do not expect the judge to give you much leeway. If you represent yourself while your spouse hires a lawyer, you can bet that the spouse's lawyer will use the law and the rules against you. Opposing counsel is not permitted to give you help or advice.

Lawyers share a common language with other lawyers and judges. That language is full of terms, jargon, and phrases in Latin, English, and French that stand for certain principles of law. The lawyers and judges have studied and understand the underlying body of law that these terms represent. Because lawyers share a common bond and common language, the judge and the opposing attorney may give you more consideration and respect when you have an attorney.

Lawyers will know how to handle complications in your case. Lawyers with experience have seen trouble before—such as not being able to serve the other side or not being able to obtain information from your spouse—and they will know what to do.

Even if you decide not to hire a lawyer, you may still want to think about hiring one as a consultant. This is called a *limited scope of engagement.* It is possible to hire a lawyer on an hourly basis to answer your questions, help you obtain and marshal facts, guide your case, and review your pleadings. The engagement will not include the lawyer being your *counsel of record* or going to court with you. Hiring a lawyer as a consultant can keep you on track by allowing you access to his or her expertise and knowledge when you need it. You will still have to do all the work yourself and respond to the pleadings sent by the other side, but you will not have the expense of hiring a lawyer to handle the entire matter.

Even if you have researched the law and have a general idea of how it applies to your divorce, you may want to consult with an experienced divorce attorney before you make any irrevocable decisions in your case. It often takes a lawyer's special training and experience to determine how the law will be applied to your specific facts. You should at least think about hiring a lawyer if:

◆ you have a contested case with high stakes like alimony, property transfer, or children in dispute;

◆ your spouse has hired a lawyer; or,

◆ you do not know what to do next, or you simply do not have the time or patience to deal with all of the frustration and confusion that comes with the territory of our complex legal system.

Finding the Right Lawyer

Unlike criminal law, there is no constitutional right to counsel in family law. The court will not appoint one for you or provide you with a free attorney. The court might appoint counsel if you are charged with criminal contempt for failing to pay child support, but for matters not involving the threat of jail or termination of parental rights, you will have to hire and pay for your own attorney if you want one.

The level of service you will need from your lawyer will depend on whether your divorce is contested or uncontested. If your divorce is uncontested from the outset, you may be able to retain the services of a lawyer on a flat-fee basis. If not, your lawyer will probably charge you an hourly fee for his or her time, and perhaps for the time of paralegals and other assistants. Rates vary widely across the country, so you should do a little comparative research.

You should choose and use your lawyer carefully. Choosing a lawyer is in some respects much like making any other major consumer purchase—you must do your research. Ask your friends and colleagues for recommendations. Check the Internet and review lawyers' websites. Check with the local bar association and the state bar for disciplinary actions. You can check legal rating services such as Martindale-Hubbell at **www.martindale.com**.

There are all kinds of lawyers out there. Some are experienced and some are just starting out. A lawyer can practice as a sole practitioner, or as a partner or associate in a firm. Some are overworked and some do not have enough clients. Finding and evaluating your attorney may be the single most important thing you do in your case.

A good way to find a family lawyer is to check the Internet. One place to look is **www.lawyers.com**, which maintains a national directory with biographies, credentials, and ratings from other attorneys and judges. The highest rating is "AV," and only about 10% of all lawyers have this rating. You can also find good family lawyers at **www.divorcenet.com** and other websites.

Word of mouth is an excellent way to find an attorney. With half of all marriages ending in divorce, chances are that you know people who have been divorced. Ask your friends or relatives who have been divorced about their divorce lawyers.

There are other places you can go as well. The family law section of the county, state, or national bar associations can usually give you several recommendations. You can frequently find seminars on divorce given by lawyers, and you can go to see if you like the presenter. If you see a therapist, he or she probably knows a good divorce lawyer. (Therapists frequently recommend patients to divorce lawyers and vice versa.)

Interviewing Your Choices

When you have selected one or more candidates, call and schedule an interview. You may or may not be charged for the consultation, depending on the practice in your geographic area. Many family law attorneys charge for initial consultations because it disqualifies the lawyer and the law firm from representing the other spouse, and the lawyer is working at the initial consultation, gathering facts and giving advice. It is more than a sales call.

From your point of view, it is more than the lawyer's job interview. You will be telling a stranger the intimate details of your marriage and family life. It is not an experience most people want to repeat any more than absolutely necessary. You will be receiving advice regarding crucial decisions that will affect your family and property in important ways.

This will be an important meeting for which you should prepare well. Find out what the attorney is going to be asking about and what paperwork, if any, he or she wants you to bring to the conference. If the attorney or his or her staff will not tell you what you will be talking about, move on to your next candidate. You should also think about and write out all the questions you will want to ask the attorney at your conference.

Once you have retained counsel, use him or her wisely. Call your lawyer when you have important questions. Ask advice about the future course of proceedings, whether to accept or counter settlement proposals, and the likely ultimate outcome of the case. Cooperate with your counsel in matters such as responding to discovery requests and preparing for hearings. Do not use your lawyer as a therapist. If you want to complain to someone about the current state of your life (and you may want and need to do that), call someone who will not charge you $250 per hour (or more). Find someone at your lawyer's office to answer minor questions, such as the time of your hearing or what items on your bill mean. Your relationship with your lawyer will be important, so find a good one and let him or her guide you though the process. Always tell your lawyer the truth without embellishment. If you lose confidence in your lawyer, change lawyers.

Evaluating Lawyers

Once you have narrowed down your search, there are several things to look for when you are evaluating a prospective lawyer. You can learn a great many things about a lawyer from the Internet. You can also set up an initial conference where you can observe the lawyer and ask direct questions. This section explains some things you may want to think about and questions you may want to ask before hiring a lawyer.

Family law has become specialized and complex. It would be good for you to find someone with experience in this area of the law. In fact, you may want to hire someone with at least five years of experience as a divorce lawyer (ten to fifteen years is even better). However, not every lawyer with fifteen years of experience has the necessary knowledge, skills, and wisdom. You will still have to interview the lawyer and conduct your investigation to be sure.

Does your lawyer practice divorce full-time, or does he or she hold him- or herself out as skilled in other areas at the same time, such as personal injury law or real estate law? Is the lawyer a divorce attorney who only practices family law, or does he or she have a general practice that offers services of every type to every kind of client, only dabbling in family law from time to time? Is the lawyer recognized as an authority in family law, or is he or she still a relative unknown? If your research shows you that a lawyer has recently graduated from law school or just passed the bar exam in your state, the hourly fees may be lower, but it may end up costing you a lot more in the long run. All lawyers have to start somewhere, but you do not want to be their practice case. You are looking for an experienced, recognized authority who is a full-time divorce attorney.

Stability is also important. Ask if your lawyer has been in the same place or with the same firm for some years, or has been looking for new practice areas and opportunities by bouncing around from job to job.

While you do not want someone who is meek and mild and will cave to the other side, you also do not want a lawyer who is so aggressive and rude that everyone is alienated and nothing gets accomplished. Find someone with a reputation for taking a firm but polite approach toward the other side, opposing counsel, and the court. You do not want to win your divorce by destroying your family. Many people think they need a lawyer with a reputation as a shark, barracuda, or bomber. When the other side has hired such a lawyer, people think they need to fight fire with fire. Although the legal system is based on an adversarial model, it functions most efficiently when opposing lawyers are civil with one another. Attorneys who trade letters and pleadings full of attacks and insults will not win your case. Judges are not impressed by this, and it will increase your legal fees, prolong your case, and damage family relationships.

Other things to ask of your potential new lawyer include the following.

- ◆ Will your lawyer have time to handle your case, or does he or she seem overworked and harried with too many cases?
- ◆ Does the lawyer have an organized office and desk, or is it overflowing with papers and case files?
- ◆ Does this lawyer limit legal services to a few select clients who receive the best representation, or does he or she have so many cases he or she cannot give you personal time and attention?
- ◆ Do you get the feeling that the lawyer is interested in your case and wants to help you succeed with it, or is he or she only in it for the money?

- Will the lawyer handle your case personally, or pass it off to another lawyer or paralegal?
- Do you get the impression that your case is a small one to this attorney who is looking for bigger ones to take to trial?
- Is the lawyer easily accessible, or does he or she hide behind a wall of secretaries, associates, paralegals, administrative assistants, and receptionists?

While you cannot expect a lawyer to be at your beck and call because he or she has other cases, you do want a lawyer who is readily available to you by telephone, fax, and email. Small questions may be answered by a member of the lawyer's staff. However, when you do want to get in touch with your lawyer immediately on an urgent divorce matter, you do not want to receive a return call two or three days later. If you cannot get your lawyer on the phone, get another lawyer. When your case needs attention, will the lawyer be able to provide that attention?

If your lawyer is in a small firm or practices alone, make sure there is sufficient staff to handle your case. When the lawyer goes on vacation, gets sick, or is at trial, will anyone else be in charge of your case? Is the backup another lawyer, or will your case be delegated to a receptionist, secretary, paralegal, or associate who only takes messages and tries to relay them to the lawyer? If your lawyer is in a large firm, are you paying for that lawyer's abilities, experience, and skills, or are you paying for high rents, associate salaries, and perks for the partners?

Is your lawyer willing to keep your costs down by working efficiently with you? Does the lawyer provide out-of-pocket expenses (like copies, faxes, filing fees, transcripts, process servers, online research) at cost, or will you be paying a mark-up on those expenses?

Communication skills are essential for a lawyer in a divorce case. That lawyer will be communicating your position with your spouse's lawyer in settlement discussions and with the judge at trial. If your lawyer has published articles, you can sample his or her writing style. How does the lawyer communicate with you? That will be similar to the way he or she communicates with opposing counsel and the judge. Choose a lawyer with a communication style you can relate to.

Is this lawyer able to move your case along in a professional manner? There are some lawyers who just do not care about their work or their clients. They may be overworked or burned out. They may be having problems in their personal lives. Some lawyers do not particularly enjoy the practice of law, and some are not very good at it. There are lawyers who procrastinate, who mismanage cases, and who are disorganized. They may neglect your case and possibly cause you to suffer an adverse result.

Replacing Your Attorney

You can fire your lawyer any time for any reason. Your lawyer should turn over your files and any balance of your retainer promptly. The lawyer may keep his or her own notes, but letters, pleadings, and other documents belong to you, and should be returned to you. (If you owe any money, that should be paid.) Before your lawyer has filed any pleadings or made a court appearance in your case, it is fairly easy to fire your lawyer. You just write a letter explaining that you no longer need his or her services. Be sure to keep a copy for your records in case there is any question.

Once your attorney files a pleading or makes an appearance for you in court, then he or she is your counsel of record until the court orders otherwise. In addition to writing a letter of dismissal to the attorney, you will have to inform the court. You must notify the court clerk in writing that you intend to represent yourself or that you have new counsel. Until the court approves the withdrawal of your former attorney, pleadings will continue to go to that lawyer.

Legal Fees

At the end of the initial office conference, you and the lawyer will probably turn toward the fees you will be charged if you hire the attorney to handle your case. A *retainer* is an advance fee that most divorce lawyers require before they will begin work on your case. It is not unusual for a divorce retainer to be

$2,000–$5,000 or more. The retainer is placed in the lawyer's trust account. The lawyer bills his or her time against the retainer. Any part of the retainer that is not used is refundable.

The retainer is not a flat fee, a cap on fees, or even an estimate. If your retainer is exhausted, the lawyer will probably ask you for an additional retainer. If you cannot pay, then you and your lawyer have to discuss whether you can afford for him or her to keep representing you. The lawyer may withdraw unless you can pay the retainer or make other arrangements. Remember—while the lawyer cannot neglect your case, the lawyer may give priority to the paying client rather than the nonpaying client.

Lawyers charge by the hour for the work they do in your case. Legal fees will be the largest expense in a divorce case. The hourly rates are usually based on the lawyer's experience. The more experienced a lawyer is, the higher his or her fee may be, but he or she is more likely to have handled a case like yours before. As a result, he or she can accomplish the same work in less time than a less experienced lawyer. Paralegals are legal assistants who help lawyers do their work, and they are billed at a lower rate than the lawyer.

You will probably ask the lawyer how much all of this is going to cost. Any estimate of costs by a lawyer will be a guess. You and your lawyer have no control over many of the variables in any case. It all depends on the complexity of your case, what your spouse and his or her lawyer do, and what the judge decides.

You may wonder exactly what lawyers do for the money they charge you. They assemble and organize the facts in your case, help you establish strategy and tactics, and provide counsel concerning the law applicable to your case. Your lawyer will also draft and file pleadings with the court for you, interview your witnesses, and obtain information from the other side through the discovery process. He or she will participate in settlement discussions and draft a settlement agreement. If the case cannot be settled, then your lawyer will appear before the judge on your behalf, examine witnesses at trial, present documents, and make arguments in your favor. Naturally, your attorney's fees will be higher if you try your case than if you settle it.

Sometimes one party ends up paying some portion of the other spouse's legal fees, as well as the children's legal fees. If one spouse controls all the income and assets of a marriage, the judge will probably order that spouse to pay a portion of the attorney's fees and costs of the other.

Costs

Legal fees are not the only expenses associated with a divorce. There will be court costs for filing papers in your case. You will have to pay for transcripts of depositions and copies of documents produced by your spouse. If you choose to try to resolve your case without going to trial, there will be expenses related to hiring a mediator. If children are involved, a custody evaluator and guardian ad litem may become involved. You may have to hire real estate appraisers, or pension and business valuators. There may be costs for other experts like accountants, vocational rehabilitation experts, private investigators, psychologists, or other medical experts. These costs are in addition to legal fees, are usually required in advance, and can amount to thousands of dollars.

Filing Fee and Other Court Costs

You will usually be charged a fee for filing the initial complaint for divorce. There may also be other charges for filing motions and other pleadings. Your fees are also used to pay clerks and other courthouse employees to file and process the case. There are different clerks for different tasks at the courthouse. The first clerk you see will be the one that processes your complaint, starts a court file, and assigns your case a number. There is also a file clerk who keeps track of all the files. The judge may also have a courtroom clerk at the hearing, a law clerk to help research the law, and a secretary.

Sometimes there will be a fee for specialized court personnel, such as a master, magistrate, or commissioner. These people are lawyers who are sometimes appointed as special assistants to the court to hear uncontested divorces (and some contested divorces) to help move the case along. They will make recommendations to the judge, which are usually adopted by the judge.

Transcripts

When your attorney deposes your spouse or another witness, or when you are deposed by your spouse's attorney, a reporter will take down what is said and produce a written transcript. If the witness changes his or her testimony at trial, you can use the deposition to question the witness's credibility. Each transcript may cost a few hundred dollars. You may also need to order transcripts of court hearings if you need them in your case.

Service of Process

Different courts have different rules for *service of process*, which means notifying your spouse that you have filed a lawsuit by giving him or her a copy of the complaint and other documents from the court. Some courts permit service by mail, while others allow service by the sheriff's office. You can also hire a private process server to hand-deliver the documents to your spouse.

Alternative Dispute Resolution

Alternative dispute resolution means settlement discussions with a neutral third party who acts as a mediator or facilitator to help you reach an agreement out of court. If this third party is involved in your case—many courts order the parties to use the services of a mediator—you will have to pay for this service.

Custody Evaluator or Assessor

If you have a contested custody case, the court may order a custody evaluation or assessment. You may have to pay for the assessment, usually in advance. These are typically performed by a social worker who conducts an investigation, writes a report, and makes a recommendation on any custody issues. The evaluator will interview you, your spouse, your children, and third parties such as teachers and neighbors. In a *custody assessment*, the assessor only interviews one or both parents and the children. A custody evaluator determines the best parent for custody of the children, while a custody assessor recommends whether a parent is fit to have custody at all. The court places great weight on the custody recommendations of the evaluator or assessor. If the evaluation is not in your favor, you may have to hire your own evaluator at an additional expense to give a different opinion to the court.

Guardian Ad Litem
In a custody dispute, the court may require a lawyer for the children, often referred to as a *guardian ad litem*. This lawyer will represent the children and tell the court the children's wishes. The attorney can also give the court his or her own opinion of what is best for the children and make a custody recommendation. You may have to pay for this attorney, which will add to your costs.

Expert Witness Fees
Nonexpert witnesses cannot give opinions—they can only testify to facts. Expert witnesses are allowed to give opinions to help the court. You may want an expert witness to testify as to the value of real estate, a business, a pension plan, or some other asset. You may want a vocational rehabilitation expert to testify about potential income if alimony is in dispute. Psychologists and psychiatrists frequently give opinions in custody cases. All of these experts will expect to be paid for reports, depositions, and testimony in court by the party calling them as witnesses.

Private Investigator
A private investigator can help you prove marital misconduct, such as adultery. You may also hire a private investigator to find and interview witnesses, or conduct an asset search if you suspect your spouse is hiding assets.

Reducing Legal Expenses
Contested divorce cases are some of the most complex and costly of trials. The cost is comparable to a new car or paying for a year of a child's college tuition. Legal fees and other costs will be measured in the thousands of dollars. The average contested divorce costs somewhere between $15,000 and $30,000. When spouses are really determined to fight it out in court, legal fees and other costs can go over $100,000. The following are some ways that you can save some money.

Do your research and become knowledgeable about divorce. Bring yourself up to speed on the process. Go to the library or your local bookstore, consult the Internet, or take a class. There is plenty of information available about divorce. The more you know about divorce, the more comfortable you will feel with the process, and the less fear you will have as you go through it.

The best method to reach an amicable agreement about the future is to sit down at the kitchen table and make an attempt to work things out with your spouse. The more you can settle between yourselves without bringing in the court and lawyers, the more money you will save in legal expenses.

Try alternative dispute resolution. An *alternative dispute resolution* (ADR) is one that tries to avoid a final court trial. There are several forms of ADR and many courts make your participation in some mandatory. You and your spouse can hire a private mediator before the court orders you to mediation. Most times it is cost-effective, because you are splitting the cost of a mediator and working together instead of paying for two lawyers to fight with each other. You are also deciding the outcome of your case instead of letting a judge, who is a stranger to your marriage, make the decision. *Collaborative law* is another approach to alternative dispute resolution if you cannot work it out, in which all the participants agree to focus on settling the case instead of litigating it.

If you cannot work it out, hire a good divorce lawyer. This may be the most important decision in your case. If your spouse has hired a shark or barracuda for a lawyer, the temptation to fight fire with fire is great. However, some lawyers will exhaust all your resources and your spouse's resources, and accomplish little in your case. Ask yourself if this is how you want to spend your children's college tuition.

Do your own private investigation. After all, no one knows more about your marriage and your spouse than you do. List all your assets. Make copies of supporting statements and documents. Copy any records that are left around the house. Check the computer, day planner, address book, phone records, mail, desk, and trash as well.

Obtain financial forms from the court and complete them. The court financial forms will help you organize the necessary data for your case. You will begin to see if current income and assets can support your present lifestyle, or if you will need to make some changes for the future.

Get organized. Complete the divorce information questionnaire at the end of this chapter before your first meeting with a lawyer.

Begin putting together all the information you can on the marital residence. Make a copy of the mortgage documents. Ask a real estate agent to estimate the value and give you some comparable sales in the neighborhood, or have an appraiser give you a current appraisal.

If there is a family business, ask an accountant to give you its preliminary value. A business can have value beyond the bank accounts and other assets. It can have *goodwill value* or *going concern value*.

Run child support calculations yourself. You can find calculators on the Internet that will use your state's child support guidelines and give you an approximate amount of child support that you will receive or pay. Some websites even allow you to print out the child support forms you will need for court. Check the websites of your state's courts for possible examples.

Consider doing your own divorce without an attorney if you have a case with few complications (including children, alimony, and assets like real estate, pensions, or a family business). The more you can do yourself, the less you will pay in legal fees.

When you do have an attorney, try to have as many of your questions answered by his or her secretary as possible. These questions cannot include legal advice, but should include things like when the lawyer will finish your agreement or complaint. There is no charge for asking the attorney's secretary for such information.

Use your lawyer for legal and financial matters, and use your therapist for emotional issues. Know the difference between the two. Do not spend all your legal fees talking to your lawyer about emotional issues that he or she cannot do anything about.

Make your own copies. When you have to provide copies of documents in discovery, give your attorney two copies of everything—one for his or her file and one to give to the other side. Your attorney may charge the costs of staff, rent, and overhead for making copies for you. A copy center will usually charge a lot less.

Lawyers charge by the minute. When you call to ask a question, your lawyer has to retrieve your file, recall your case, answer the question, and make a memorandum of it. It is important to organize your interactions with your attorney. One woman called her attorney to complain that her husband was taking the garden hose from the garage. The attorney said that it would be worked out with the other attorney during settlement or with the judge at the divorce trial. The garden hose cost $12, but the brief telephone call to the attorney cost $50.

Let your spouse file the complaint for divorce first. That way, he or she pays the filing fee. You can usually file an answer and counterclaim in the same case without a filing fee. There is no advantage in filing first.

DIVORCE INFORMATION QUESTIONNAIRE
*(attach additional pages as needed
and bring to your first conference with lawyer)*

Date _____

1. CLIENT
Name _____
Address_____
_____
Home Phone Number _____
Work Phone Number _____
Cell Phone Number _____
Work Email_____
Personal Email _____
Date of Birth _____
Social Security Number _____
Occupation _____
Employer or Business _____
Year Started_____
Education Level _____
Annual Income _____
Number of this Marriage (1st, 2nd, etc.)_____
Religion _____
Health Issues, if any_____
Primary Care Physician _____
Therapist/Counselor_____

2. SPOUSE
Name _____
Address_____
_____
Home Phone Number _____
Work Phone Number _____
Cell Phone Number _____
Work Email_____
Personal Email _____
Date of Birth _____
Social Security Number _____
Occupation _____
Employer or Business _____
Year Started_____
Education Level _____

Annual Income _____

Number of this Marriage (1st, 2nd, etc.)_____

Religion _____

Health Issues, if any_____

Primary Care Physician _____

Therapist/Counselor_____

3. MARRIAGE

Date of Marriage _____

Place *(city, county, state, country)* _____
_____

Children
    Name(s) _____
    Date(s) of Birth_____
    Grade(s) _____
    School *(Include Preschool or Day Care)*_____
_____

    Extracurricular *(Sports, Music, Scouts, etc.)*_____
_____

    Health or Special Needs _____
_____

    Other _____
_____

Date of Separation _____

Last Marital Relations _____

Cause of Marital Stress _____
    Violence _____
    Drugs or Alcohol Problems _____
    Infidelity_____
    Client _____
    Spouse_____
Marital Counseling _____
    Dates _____
    Counselor _____

4. LITIGATION AND AGREEMENTS

Prior Proceedings
    Court _____
    Nature of Proceeding (Child Support, Divorce, etc.) _____
_____

    Case Number _____
    Date Closed _____

continued

Current Litigation
  Court _____
  Nature of Proceeding (Child Support, Divorce, etc.) _____
  Case Number _____
  Date You Were Served _____
  Date of Next Hearing_____
Prenuptial Agreement (Yes/No)_____
Postnuptial Agreement _____
Mediation _____
  Dates _____
  Mediator _____

5. CURRENT CUSTODY/VISITATION ARRANGEMENTS
(complete if you are now separated)
Children live with:
  Father_____
  Mother _____
  Both_____
  Split_____
  Time-sharing *(state when noncustodial parent has the children)*____
  _____

Agreement is:
  No agreement _____
  Oral_____
  Written _____
  Problems (Yes or No) _____

5.1 Current Financial Arrangement
Joint Accounts
  Bank _____
  Account Type _____
  Account Number_____
  Balance _____
  Account Manager (Husband, Wife, or Both) _____
  Client Currently Depositing Earnings _____
  Spouse Currently Depositing Earnings _____
  Client Currently Writing Checks_____
  Spouse Currently Writing Checks _____
Lines of Credit
  Bank _____
  Account Number_____
  Balance _____
  Limit _____

Credit Cards
   Issuer _____
   Account Number _____
   Balance _____
   Limit _____

   Issuer _____
   Account Number _____
   Balance _____
   Limit _____

5.2 Health Insurance
Client
   Carrier _____
   Plan Sponsor_____
   Plan or Account Number _____
Spouse
   Carrier _____
   Plan Sponsor_____
   Plan or Account Number _____
Children
   Carrier _____
   Plan Sponsor_____
   Plan or Account Number _____

6. PROPERTY

6.1 Marital Home
Titled To _____
Date Acquired _____
Cost _____
Source(s) of Down Payment _____
Original Amount Borrowed _____
Capital Improvements (description) _____
_____
Cost _____
Date Constructed _____
Current Mortgage and Liens
   Bank _____
   Loan Number _____
   Date of Loan_____
   Balance _____

continued

Second Mortgage or Equity Line
    Bank _____
    Loan Number _____
    Date of Loan_____
    Balance _____

6.2 Other Real Property
Titled To _____
Date Acquired _____
Cost _____
Source(s) of Down Payment _____
Original Amount Borrowed _____
Capital Improvements (description) _____

_____
Cost _____
Date Constructed _____
Current Mortgage and Liens
    Bank _____
    Loan Number _____
    Date of Loan_____
    Balance _____
Second Mortgage or Equity Line
    Bank _____
    Loan Number _____
    Date of Loan_____
    Balance _____

6.3 Retirement Plans and Other Deferred Compensation

6.3.1. Client
Pension
    Employer _____
    Dates of Service _____
    Date Eligible to Retire_____
    Projected Annuity
    Based on Service to Date _____
401(k) and Other Tax-Deferred Accounts
    Financial Institution _____
    Account Number_____
    Current Value _____
    Start Date of Contributions _____
    End Date of Contributions _____

IRAs
   Financial Institution _____
   Account Number_____
   Current Value _____
   Start Date of Contributions _____
   End Date of Contributions _____
Stock Options and Other Employee Benefits
   Employer _____
   Number of Shares _____
   Grant Dates _____
   Vesting Dates _____
   Exercise Price _____
   Current Stock Price _____
   Other Features _____
Other Deferred Compensation Plans
   Current Approximate Value of Deferral _____
   Type of Plan _____
   Start Date of Earning Period_____
   End Date of Earning Period _____
   Other Features _____

6.3.2. Spouse
Pension
   Employer _____
   Dates of Service _____
   Date Eligible to Retire_____
   Projected Annuity
   Based on Service to Date _____
401(k) and Other Tax-Deferred Accounts
   Financial Institution _____
   Account Number_____
   Current Value _____
   Start Date of Contributions _____
   End Date of Contributions _____
IRAs
   Financial Institution _____
   Account Number_____
   Current Value _____
   Start Date of Contributions _____
   End Date of Contributions _____
Stock Options and Other Employee Benefits
   Employer _____
   Number of Shares _____
   Grant Dates _____

continued

Vesting Dates _____
Exercise Price _____
Current Stock Price _____
Other Features _____
Other Deferred Compensation Plans
Current Approximate Value of Deferral _____
Type of Plan _____
Start Date of Earning Period_____
End Date of Earning Period _____
Other Features _____

6.4 Other Solely Owned Financial Assets

6.4.1 Client
Bank _____
Account Type _____
Account Number _____
Current Balance_____
Date of Marriage _____
Balance _____

Bank _____
Account Type _____
Account Number _____
Current Balance_____
Date of Marriage _____
Balance _____

Mutual Funds
Fund _____
Account Number _____
Current Value _____
Contributions During the Marriage *(All/None/Some)* _____
Fund _____
Fund _____
Account Number _____
Current Value _____
Contributions During the Marriage *(All/None/Some)* _____
Stocks
Issuer _____
Number of Shares _____
Current Price_____
Value _____
Purchased During the Marriage *(All/None/Some)* _____

Issuer _____

Number of Shares _____

Current Price_____

Value _____

Purchased During the Marriage *(All/None/Some)* _____

Other Investments

Description _____

Current Value _____

Acquired During the Marriage *(All/None/Some)* _____

6.4.2 Spouse

Bank _____

Account Type _____

Account Number _____

Current Balance_____

Date of Marriage _____

Balance _____

Bank _____

Account Type _____

Account Number _____

Current Balance_____

Date of Marriage _____

Balance _____

Mutual Funds

Fund _____

Account Number _____

Current Value _____

Contributions During the Marriage *(All/None/Some)* _____

Fund _____

Fund _____

Account Number _____

Current Value _____

Contributions During the Marriage *(All/None/Some)* _____

Stocks

Issuer _____

Number of Shares _____

Current Price_____

Value _____

Purchased During the Marriage *(All/None/Some)* _____

continued

Issuer _____
Number of Shares _____
Current Price_____
Value _____
Purchased During the Marriage *(All/None/Some)* _____
Other Investments
Description _____
Current Value _____
Acquired During the Marriage *(All/None/Some)* _____

6.5 Vehicles
Client Primarily Drives
Year _____
Make _____
Model _____
Titled To _____
Value _____
Date Purchased _____
Loan Balance _____
Payment_____
Lender_____
Borrower_____
Insurance Company _____
Policy Holder_____
Spouse Primarily Drives
Year _____
Make _____
Model _____
Titled To _____
Value _____
Date Purchased _____
Loan Balance _____
Payment_____
Lender_____
Borrower_____
Insurance Company _____
Policy Holder_____
Other Vehicles
Year _____
Make _____
Model _____
Titled To _____
Value _____

Date Purchased _____

Loan Balance _____

Payment_____

Lender_____

Borrower_____

Insurance Company _____

Policy Holder_____

6.6 Household Furnishings

Approximate Total Value _____

(Attach separate sheet listing any antiques, artwork,
or other high value items)

Already Divided by Agreement? *(Yes/No/Part)* _____

6.7 Clothing/Jewelry/Other Personal Items

Client _____

Approximate Total Value _____

(Attach separate sheet listing any high value items)

All in Your Possession? *(Yes/No/Part)* _____

Spouse _____

Approximate Total Value _____

(Attach separate sheet listing any high value items)

All in Spouse's Possession? *(Yes/No/Part)*_____

7. WILLS, ETC.

7.1 Wills

7.1.1 Client's will

Date _____

All to Spouse?_____

Other Beneficiary _____

No Will_____

Want Will Appointment _____

7.1.2 Spouse's will

Date _____

All to Client? _____

Other Beneficiary _____

No Will_____

Don't Know_____

continued

7.2 Life Insurance

7.2.1. Client
Company_____
Type of Policy_____
Policy Number _____
Date Issued _____
Amount of Insurance _____
Cash Value _____
Beneficiary _____
Owner _____

7.2.2 Spouse
Company_____
Type of Policy_____
Policy Number _____
Date Issued _____
Amount of Insurance _____
Cash Value _____
Beneficiary _____
Owner _____

8. GOALS
Custody
    Legal Custody _____
    Physical Custody _____
    Time-Sharing _____
    Other _____
Child Support_____
Property Distribution
    Marital Home *(Keep/Sell & Divide Proceeds/Sell Your Interest)*_____
_____
    Other Assets *(Equal Division or State Other Goals)*_____
_____
Alimony
    Amount _____
    Duration _____

9. QUESTIONS
Briefly state any questions you have or issues you would like to discuss
at the conference. _____
_____
_____
_____

Section Three:

Settlement
(The Third Ninety Days)

Chapter Nine

Child Custody
and Time-Sharing

As married parents, you and your spouse both start out with custody of your children under the law. However, a court has the power to change custody and determine access to children in a divorce. The court uses certain doctrines, presumptions, and considerations to decide custody.

Determining Custody

During the Industrial Revolution, the *tender-years doctrine* was created, giving mothers custody, particularly of young children. The idea was that mothers knew best how to care for young children and had a special bond with them. The only way that a father could defeat the tender-years doctrine was to prove the mother abused or neglected the child, or was an unfit parent in some manner.

As women began to enter the workforce, two-worker homes became more common, and men began to participate more in the parenting and caregiving of children. The legislatures and courts responded by eliminating the tender-years doctrine. Today (in theory), mothers do not have an advantage over fathers in a custody dispute.

Instead, *the best interests of the child* is now the test for determining custody. The court considers several factors in determining what is in the best interest of a child. Each state has similar factors, but with slightly different emphasis.

Some states have a presumption in favor of joint custody, except in cases where there is domestic violence. A *presumption in favor of joint custody* means that the court must find that joint custody is in the best interests of the child, unless one of the parties proves it is not. This is called *shifting the burden of proof.* It is not easy to overcome a presumption, but it can be done.

Although the legal standard is the best interests of the child, custody determinations are really the judges' educated guesses, and every judge sees it differently. Judges are not all-knowing and all-wise, and they run the cases through their own filters. To help standardize this, the legislatures and courts have set forth certain factors the judge must consider in determining custody.

◆ *Parental rights.* Parents almost always win custody of their own children before third parties such as grandparents or stepparents. The law presumes that parents are the children's best caretakers. The parents must be proven unfit to overcome this presumption.

◆ *Stability.* Children need routine and continuity. A court will not want to upset the status quo if children are doing well.

◆ *Preference of the children.* The court will take into account who the children want to live with. This is not binding on the court; however, the older the child, the more weight the preference will have with the court. The judge usually interviews the children privately in chambers.

◆ *Additional factors.* Other factors include health, age, income, resources, religious beliefs, and conduct of the parents. The court can also look at the type of home each parent has, psychological evaluations, where siblings live, school performance, and any other factors the court deems important.

Legal Custody

Custody means the care and control of a child. There are actually two types of custody—*legal custody* and *physical custody.* Legal custody involves making long-term parenting decisions regarding such things as education, medical treatments, discipline, and religious decisions. Legal custody can be joint custody or sole custody. *Joint custody* means that both parents will make decisions about the child together. *Sole custody* means only one parent makes the decisions.

In joint legal custody, neither parent has final decision-making authority without consulting the other parent. The parents share the responsibilities of raising their children, including decisions about education, religion, medical treatment, and where the children will live. Joint legal custody makes sense when the two parents can agree and can find a way of working together to take care of the children. Children benefit if the parents can raise them in harmony with each other, even though they are no longer married or living together. Parents have differing skills and personalities that can be combined for the benefit of the children in a joint custody situation. Each can participate in the real parenting effort and neither has all the burden of being solely responsible for the children.

If one parent has sole legal custody, then that parent makes all of the long-term parenting decisions. The sole legal custodian decides where the kids will go to school, what religion they will have, what doctors they will see, and where they will live. That parent can also give consent for a minor to marry or enter the armed services.

Physical Custody

Physical custody is also referred to as *residential custody*. It is simply where the children live most of the time. The parent with physical custody has the care and control of the children on a day-to-day basis, including the power to make short-term parenting decisions (rather than the long-term parenting decisions that come with legal custody). In other words, the parent with physical custody decides everyday issues like meals, bedtimes, and homework. Physical custody can be shared, sole, or split.

When the children spend equal or a substantial amount of time with each parent, it is called *shared physical custody*. Both parents have shared physical custody in law (*custody de jure*) until the court orders otherwise. This is true even if they are separated and the children are actually only living with one of them (*custody de facto*).

A shared physical custody arrangement can take several different forms, including the following.

- ◆ *Week on/Week off.* Alternating weeks at mom's house and dad's house is a schedule with few transfers and disruptions. The transfer can be done Friday after school, Monday mornings, or any other day of the week.
- ◆ *Nesting.* The children stay in the marital residence, while the parents move in and out on alternate weeks.
- ◆ *Three/Four.* One parent has the children for three days, then the other parent has them for four days. The schedule alternates.
- ◆ *School days/Summer vacations.* One parent has the children for the school week, while the other parent has them on the weekends. Holidays and summers are usually with the weekend parent, to make up for the school days.

When the children live primarily with one parent, it is called *sole physical custody.* That parent is the *custodial parent* and the other parent is the *noncustodial parent.* The noncustodial parent has access to the children, called *visitation* or *time-sharing.*

When siblings are split between parents, it is called *split physical custody.* However, the courts believe it is usually in the best interests of the children to keep siblings together.

Practical Considerations

It is possible to blur the lines between the different types of custody and visitation. For example, one party can be granted physical custody, but the other party can be awarded so much visitation that the children actually spend more time with the noncustodial parent. It is also possible to state that the parties have joint legal custody in one paragraph, and then take it away in the next by saying that only one parent will make decisions.

In real life, the party with primary physical custody often makes all the decisions, even when there is joint legal custody. For example, if the custodial parent takes the children to a doctor that the other parent does not like, the other parent has to hire a lawyer and go to court to try to reverse the situation.

The important thing is not to get hung up on words like *custody* and *visitation*. If you take the inflexible position that you want sole legal custody or equal physical custody, you may be headed for an expensive trial over the children. Then you will be sending your lawyer's children to college instead of your own. However, if you can focus on the important issues, such as how parenting decisions will be made and what quality time you will spend with the children, then you will be able to come up with a parenting plan that works.

Time-Sharing

The time that children spend with each parent is called *time-sharing* or *access*. When one parent has physical custody, most courts refer to time that the children spend with the noncustodial parent as *visitation*. However, since people do not like to be considered visitors with their own children, the modern approach is to refer to it as *time-sharing* or *access*. Because the children are in one parent's care and custody during time-sharing, it is really a form of abbreviated custody.

If you and your spouse can agree on a time-sharing schedule, you can include it in your parenting plan and the court will approve it. If you cannot agree, then you will have to ask the court to establish a schedule. Each party may present a proposed schedule to the court, and the judge will decide what is best for the children.

It should be noted that the amount of child support required of a parent frequently depends in part on the amount of time-sharing or physical custody each parent possesses. There is a direct correlation between time-sharing and child support. Therefore, disputes over custody and time-sharing may actually be disputes over child support. However, the court considers time-sharing and child support to be separate issues. Withholding access to the children when a parent does not pay child support is illegal. The court frowns on a parent for withholding access, and can hold that person in contempt of court or change custody to the other parent.

If you are on good terms with your spouse, at least as far as parenting is concerned, you may be able to handle time-sharing with no disputes. In these cases, the parties may provide for *reasonable* or *liberal* time-sharing and have no specific schedule. However, it is easy to set a detailed time-sharing schedule as a backup plan with flexibility to alter it when that becomes necessary.

A detailed time-sharing schedule includes provisions for the regular weekly routine, summers, and holidays. When creating your schedule, start with the regular weekly schedule. Cover transportation details and transfer times to avoid confusion and disagreements. It is also best to agree on who pays for travel expenses, like airplane tickets, if those are involved.

Different Types of Time-Sharing

Time-sharing usually involves overnight stays and is unsupervised. It usually stays the same until the children reach the age of majority. However, different types of time-sharing may be appropriate in some cases.

Overnights may not be appropriate in cases in which a parent has spent little or no time with a child, or is not interested in having overnights. Also, a parent might not have a living space that can accommodate overnights with the children.

Supervised time-sharing is sometimes ordered when the judge believes that a parent may cause some harm to the children. Supervised time-sharing means a third person is present, such as the other parent, a friend, or a relative.

Graduated time-sharing changes with time. This arrangement is sometimes used with very young children or when a parent needs to establish a relationship with children after a gap in time-sharing. To include a provision in your agreement for graduated time-sharing, use language similar to what follows.

> *For the first three months, the children will spend from 12:00 noon until 4:00 p.m. on Sunday with the Father each week.*

For the next three months, the children will spend from 8:00 a.m. until 4:00 p.m. on Sunday with the Father every other week.

For the next six months, the children will spend from 5:00 p.m. on Saturday until 4:00 p.m. on Sunday with the Father every other week.

Thereafter, the children will spend from 5:00 p.m. on Friday until 4:00 p.m. on Sunday with the Father every other week.

Age- and needs-appropriate time-sharing varies according to the age and developmental needs of the children. It recognizes that the needs of children change as they age. For example, infants require feeding, bathing, and changing on a regular schedule. Toddlers thrive best with consistent routines. When children enter school, they have school schedules and activities to consider. Preteens may become more involved in extracurricular activities. Teenagers want to spend time with their friends and they may have jobs. Structuring your agreement based on the ages and needs of your children simply makes sense.

Nesting is when the children will stay in one place, and the parents will move in and out, alternating time-sharing. A sample nesting arrangement may read something like the following.

Both parties acknowledge that it is in the children's best interests and future welfare that the parties have shared physical custody. The parties have decided and agreed that the Husband and the children will reside in the former family residence, and each party will have liberal time-sharing with the children. The Wife will have full and daily access to the former family home to feed the children, help them with their homework, put them to bed, and perform other related parental acts. The parties may agree between themselves from time to time that the Husband will vacate the former family residence so that the Wife may have overnight time-sharing with the children in the former family residence.

SAMPLE WEEKLY TIME-SHARING PROVISIONS

Each case and each child is unique. You are trying to arrange visitation to maximize the time spent with each parent, while at the same time minimize the transfers for the child from one residence to another. This calls for some creative thinking. The following are some sample provisions to consider.

Alternating Weekends

The Father will have time-sharing with the children every other weekend from Friday evening at 5:00 p.m. through Sunday evening at 7:00 p.m., and Wednesday evening of each week for dinner from 4:00 p.m. to 8:00 p.m.

Week On/Week Off

Each party will have time-sharing with minor children on alternating weeks from 6:00 p.m. Sunday until 6:00 p.m. Sunday. The noncustodial party, according to the foregoing schedule, will also have time-sharing with the minor children on Wednesday from after work or school until 7:30 p.m.

Another Equal Time Arrangement

The Father will have time-sharing with the children every other weekend beginning Friday after school and ending Monday when school resumes. The Mother will have time-sharing with the children every other weekend beginning Friday after school and ending Monday when school resumes. The children will be in the Father's care overnight on Monday and Tuesday. The children will be in the Mother's care overnight on Wednesday and Thursday.

School Year/Summer Break Arrangement

During the school year, the children will reside primarily with the Mother, and the Father will have time-sharing with the children (a) every other weekend from Friday morning through Monday evening and (b) Wednesday evening of each week.

During summer break, the children will reside primarily with the Father, and the Mother will have time-sharing with the children (a) every other weekend from Friday evening through Monday morning and (b) Wednesday evening of each week. In lieu of using a third-party day care provider during the summer, the Father will leave the children with the Mother for day care, if her schedule permits. Notwithstanding the summer schedule, each party will be permitted to spend at least two uninterrupted weeks of vacation time with the children each summer. The parties will coordinate their vacation schedules with each other.

The parties will discuss parenting issues and day care schedules each Monday night by telephone from 7:00 p.m. to 7:15 p.m.

Another Creative Time-Sharing Arrangement
Weekly Schedule. *The Father will have liberal time-sharing the last week of every month from 8:00 p.m. Friday until 2:00 p.m. the second Sunday following.*

Weekend Schedule. *In addition, the Father will have liberal time-sharing for the weekend that is between the week-long visitations from 8:00 p.m. Friday until 2:00 p.m. on Sunday.*

SAMPLE SUMMER TIME-SHARING PROVISIONS
The summer school vacation is about ten weeks. You can divide that in any way that makes sense based on your work and vacation schedule. An example of a summer schedule follows.

The Father shall have time with the children for up to four weeks during the summer months. During this four-week period, the Mother may have access to the children from time to time as agreed between the parties. In addition, by mutual agreement, either party may also take a vacation with one or more of the children. This particular summer time-sharing schedule shall supersede the regular time-sharing schedule and holiday schedule set forth in this agreement. The exact summer time-sharing schedule shall be established by the parties before March 1st of each year to avoid conflicts with summer camps. If the parties are

continued

not able to agree on the summer time-sharing schedule in any given year, then the Father shall have first choice in even-numbered years and the Mother shall have first choice in odd-numbered years.

SAMPLE HOLIDAY TIME-SHARING PROVISIONS
Most people prefer to alternate holidays and other events. Some examples of possible provisions read as follows. (The holidays can be changed to accommodate your family's celebrated dates.)

Alternating Holidays
In even-numbered years, the Mother has the children for Memorial Day, Labor Day, Halloween, Christmas Eve, and Christmas Day until noon. The Father has the children for President's Day, Easter, Fourth of July, Thanksgiving, and Christmas Day from noon through New Year's Day. The schedule is reversed in odd-numbered years.

Birthdays and Other Events
The children are with the Mother on her birthday and with the Father on his birthday. The children alternate spending their birthdays with each parent. The children are with the Mother on Mother's Day and the Father on Father's Day. The holiday schedule overrides the normal weekly schedule, which resumes after the holiday.

Disputes
There are various reasons that parents end up in disputes about time-sharing. Some of the most common reasons are discussed in this section.

Hurt Feelings
Parents will sometimes become involved in an argument about their children because they are upset about something else. A parent may feel angry at the other spouse for having an affair or for leaving. A spouse may feel that he or she has given up too much in the settlement of other issues. One parent may want to restrict the other's time-sharing or have no time-sharing at all. Sometimes one parent wants the other parent

to have time-sharing, and he or she refuses. The first thing to do is try to talk about these type of problems yourselves. If that does not work, try counseling or a mediator before you take your dispute to court.

Children's Preference

What if the children say they do not want to participate in time-sharing with a parent? The first rule is that adults determine time-sharing and not the children. If the parents support the children in making these decisions, they will negatively empower the children to refuse or resist time-sharing.

However, if you drag the children from the home or car kicking and screaming, they may dig in their heels even more and resent being forced to spend time with a parent. That can make the breakdown in the relationship with the children even worse, and the situation can spiral downward. One spouse might blame the other for brainwashing or alienating the children. The other spouse might make allegations of abuse.

Rather than concentrating on the dispute between the parents, try to focus on what is causing the children to act in this way. Counseling may help identify and solve the problem, but it will take time and patience.

The law favors *reunification* when there has been a breakdown between a parent and a child. Reunification is the restoration of a normal parent/child relationship. This is usually accomplished through therapy involving both parents and the child. This can be agreed to by the parents or ordered by the court.

Routine

Parents also sometimes become involved in a dispute about the school week. One parent may want equal time, while the other parent believes he or she is more disciplined in making sure the children do their homework each night and take the right books and supplies to school. Parents argue over the children's needs for the routine, including staying in the same house during the school week, or whether transitions are too disruptive for the children. Establishing a routine and sticking to it usually smooths out this dispute.

Third Parties

How and when new relationships will be introduced to the children can be a sensitive issue that sometimes causes disputes. While visitation is generally controlled by the parent having visitation, you can agree to certain restrictions, such as not involving third parties (like a new boyfriend or girlfriend) in the visitation time.

An example of how a provision for an agreement that a third party will not stay overnight when the children are present may read as follows.

> *The parties agree that neither will have overnights with members of the opposite sex, unless that party is remarried, when the children are present.*

A different provision for the gradual introduction of third parties may read as follows.

> *Although the Father and the Mother both understand that neither may dictate the way in which the other conducts his or her life, the Father and the Mother recognize that each of them will enjoy a social and dating life. It is important to both parents that the children are comfortable with the concept before another adult is introduced into their lives. Accordingly, the parties shall only introduce members of the opposite sex (not related by blood or marriage) to the children on a gradual basis.*

Parental Alienation

Parental alienation occurs when one parent undermines the children's relationship with the other parent. It can be intentional or unintentional, and it can be covert or overt. Even if nothing is said, children can pick up on hostility or fear between their parents. Judges disapprove of a parent interfering with time-sharing or actively encouraging the children not to see the other parent. If a judge finds one parent sabotaging the children's relationship with the other parent, the judge may take custody or time-sharing away from the alienating parent.

Reactive Attachment Disorder

Reactive attachment disorder happens when a child is so bonded with a parent that separation will cause psychological harm to the child. The argument from the other side is that some visitation with the other parent might cause the child to bond with that parent as well.

Litigation

Parents can either agree on time-sharing or ask the court to decide it for them. The court will establish a time-sharing schedule based on what is in the best interest of the children. As long as there is no danger or harm to the children, the court will encourage time-sharing and frequent contact with both parents.

The traditional legal approach—in which you fight until the other side loses or gives up—does not work very well in this situation. Judges are reluctant to put a parent in jail when the children are refusing to go with the other parent for time-sharing. You can win the battle by forcing time-sharing and lose the war by permanently destroying family relationships.

If a parent wrongfully withholds time-sharing in violation of a child custody order, the other parent can file a petition for contempt of court. There are criminal penalties for abducting the children unless it was necessary for the abducting parent to keep the children in order for the children to avoid harm from the other parent. However, it may take several trips to the courthouse before a judge will enforce visitation.

If you litigate your dispute over time-sharing, the end result will be a time-sharing schedule issued by the judge as an order of the court. It will not contain as much detail as you could do if you and your spouse could agree. If you can agree on time-sharing, the courts will usually approve your schedule.

Be Creative

There is no "usual" visitation schedule, such as every other weekend and Wednesday night. In truth, there is no typical schedule or default schedule in the law. Lots of other schedules will work. You can be as creative as you wish. If the parents are in agreement, the court typically will approve the schedule. No single plan suits every family. A good time-sharing arrangement will take into account work, school, social, and family schedules.

You should know that time-sharing disputes are frequently settled at the last minute before trial or on the courthouse steps. An agreement is made in the hallways outside the courtroom, notes are taken on legal pads, and the agreement is then read into the record before the judge. You are required to make instant decisions that will affect your future and the children's future. The transcript becomes a binding agreement and an order of the court. The following time-sharing checklist will help make sure that you do not overlook something important in the rush and pressure of court proceedings.

TIME-SHARING RIGHTS CHECKLIST

❑ Routine weekly schedule
❑ Holiday schedule
❑ Summer schedule
❑ Rules at each house
❑ Transportation
❑ Relocation
❑ Exposure to third parties
❑ Regular telephone conversations with the child
❑ Unopened and uncensored mail to the child
❑ Prompt notice of hospitalization, major illness, or death of the child
❑ Access to school records
❑ Access to medical records
❑ No derogatory remarks by either parent in the presence of the child
❑ Notice and participation in extracurricular events
❑ Itinerary and contact numbers if the other parent leaves the state with the child
❑ Access to school for lunch and other activities with the child

Modification

The time-sharing schedule ought to be followed as closely as possible. Children depend on seeing parents according to schedule.

Parents should be on time and not cancel at the last minute. However, work or other conflicts sometimes interfere, and you can change the schedule as long as both parents agree. It is wise to commemorate any changes in writing to avoid any disputes later.

If a change in circumstances occurs, such as a change in jobs or relocation, and the parents cannot agree to a change in time-sharing, you can petition the court for a *modification*. The court will be more impressed with an unexpected change of circumstances than a change you were aware of at the time the original schedule was created. Changes that every-body knew were coming may not convince the court to modify the time-sharing, because it should have been anticipated in the first place.

Relocation

Relocation is a change of circumstances, meaning either party can petition the court for a change in custody or visitation arrangements. Some states have a tendency to permit the chil-dren to relocate, some tend to prevent it, and others look at it on a case-by-case basis. The standard is whether the relocation is in the best interests of the children.

If the children's other parent is threatening to move, you can file a petition to stop the move. If he or she has already moved, you can ask the court to order him or her to bring the children back. The court will usually set a hearing. Be prepared to show the court that the children have strong attachments to their friends in the neighborhood, home, school, doctors, teachers, and coaches. You can also compare educational, social, economic, and cultural opportunities in your location to those in the new location to persuade the judge that it is in the best interest of the children to stay in their original location.

If you have custody and the other parent files to prevent your move, then you will have to marshal the evidence you need to show that the move is in the best interest of the chil-dren. You will need to prove to the court there is a good reason for the move, such as a better job, and not just to prevent visi-tation. Also, be prepared to show that the schools, doctors, and cultural opportunities are better where you plan to move.

It is always better for the parents to agree, preferably in advance, on relocation provisions. You will need to cover when each of you will spend time with the children, the methods of travel between homes, costs, communications, and holiday plans.

An example of a provision that permits relocation and sets up visitation arrangements in advance follows.

> *The parties have the right to move to any location in the United States. The moving party shall provide the other party with at least ninety days' written notice.*
>
> *In the event that one or both parties move, the parties will still share legal custody, and the Father shall still have primary physical custody. The time-sharing shall be the same as what is set forth, if the parties reside within one-hundred miles of each other.*
>
> *If the parties reside more than one-hundred miles from each other, time-sharing shall be changed to the following: The Mother shall have time-sharing for up to eight weeks of summer vacation, to be determined by the parties by May 1ˢᵗ of each year. The Mother shall also have visitation for either (a) the winter break or (b) the spring and Thanksgiving breaks, to be decided by the parties each year. If considered appropriate, the parties shall negotiate as to whether the children will be permitted to be kept out of school for one additional day at the end of a holiday, to permit additional time-sharing on the part of the Mother.*
>
> *The parties shall share equally in the cost of transporting the children back and forth for visitation.*

A provision that prevents relocation unless both parents consent—or if they cannot agree, until the court makes the decision—may read something like what follows.

> *A party planning to relocate away from the metropolitan area shall give not less than 120 days' written notice of such plans to the other party, setting forth the date of*

the intended move, the destination, and the reasons for making the move. In no event shall a child of the parties be removed from the metropolitan area until the parties have reached a revised agreement relative to custody and visitation, or failing such agreement, until a final determination of custody and visitation has been made by a court of competent jurisdiction.

Grandparent and Other Third-Party Time-Sharing

Third parties, such as stepparents and grandparents, may ask the court for time-sharing with children if it is denied by the parents. Children often have an important, special relationship with grandparents. The opportunities and extended roots that grandparents can offer children should not be disregarded. Many gifted children can point to a third-party caretaker in their lives who helped them with their homework, self-esteem, and emotional well-being.

Courts will grant reasonable time-sharing with grandparents, stepparents, and related third parties if it is in the best interest of the children. However, the United States Supreme Court has decided there is a presumption that the parent's time-sharing schedule is in the best interest of the child if it conflicts with the third party's schedule. The presumption may be rebutted in certain circumstances, and it may not apply when the parent is refusing all time-sharing with the third party.

Evaluations

The judge stays behind the bench in our legal system. Each side is expected to be proactive in presenting the evidence in his or her favor to the judge. The judge does not go to the children's homes or schools, or interview witnesses.

However, either party may ask for a *custody evaluation.* The court may rely on this evaluation to determine child custody and time-sharing. Because the evaluator is neutral, the court will usually give great weight to the evaluator's opinion. Custody cases may be won or lost depending on the findings of the evaluator.

The evaluator is usually a social worker or other mental health professional. The evaluator will visit each parent's home. The evaluator will investigate each parent's psychological makeup, parenting skills, and other factors to make a report to the court on the best custody and time-sharing arrangements.

The following are some tips to prepare for the evaluation.

◆ The evaluator will observe your house and living arrangements, and report about them to the court. You will want to make sure everything is clean, neat, and safe for children. Clean your house before the examiner gets there. The children should have suitable sleeping arrangements set up.

◆ Avoid coaching the kids in advance about what they need to say to the evaluator to stay at your house. This will come out in the interview and only make you look bad for trying to influence the children. You can tell the children that a person is coming to interview them and they should answer the questions truthfully and as best they can.

◆ If you are a smoker, now is a good time to give it up. Secondhand smoke is harmful to children, and the evaluator will count it against you.

◆ Keep your focus on the children and what is best for them. This is not the time to point out the flaws in their other parent, vent your anger, or say whatever is on your mind. Keep your emotions and ego in check and answer the evaluator's questions calmly. Showcase your own strengths as a parent. Show the other side's weaknesses indirectly by contrast. Instead of "she (or he) does not make the kids do their homework," you can say "I know the kids are missing homework assignments, so whenever they are here, I make sure their homework gets done."

◆ Put away any distractions. Turn off the television while the evaluator is there.

After interviewing both parents, the children, and possibly other witnesses, the evaluator will summarize the interviews and make a recommendation to the court about custody and visitation in written report. The evaluator will probably not tell you the results by telephone, and may not produce the report until a few days before trial. You can examine the evaluator at trial and try to correct any inaccuracies at that time. It is usually more constructive to question the evaluator about your positive points than about the other parent's negative points. You may also hire your own private custody evaluator to testify if you disagree with the first evaluator's recommendation. However, the court still makes the final decision.

There may be other people involved in your case besides a custody evaluator. A custody evaluator usually interviews the parents, the children, and collateral witnesses. Collateral witnesses include teachers, coaches, doctors, relatives, neighbors, and others.

The court may also appoint an attorney for the children called a *guardian ad litem* (GAL). The GAL is supposed to represent the children and be an advocate for them. The GAL can tell the court what the children want. The GAL can also tell the court what custody and time-sharing arrangement is in the best interest of the children, which may not be the same as what the children want.

Obviously, it is better to have the evaluator, assessor, and guardian ad litem on your side. Therefore, you do not want to make the mistake of treating the evaluator, the assessor, the GAL, the children's therapist, and the judge as your enemies. Do not treat these people with hostility or anger. Instead of seeing them as obstacles to visitation and custody, try seeing them as doors to which you must find the key. Your own private evaluator can give you advice on how to handle these people and make them your allies instead of your enemies.

Conclusion

You will want to think twice before you get involved in a custody fight. You will double your legal fees if you cannot agree on custody. Custody cases are expensive in both emotional and legal costs. A dispute over custody and time-sharing is almost guaranteed to put you right in the middle of a bitterly contested lawsuit. Custody cases are cruel and destructive. The damage caused by a custody case is great, whether you win or lose.

If you want to fight for custody, be certain that the children would be significantly better off with you rather than the other parent. While you and your spouse will not be living together, you will be in a long-term partnership to raise your children together. The end of a marriage does not end the family. Just because you are terminating the relationship between two adults, you are not terminating the parental relationships.

A sample *Parenting Plan* follows. It incorporates the matters of custody and time-sharing this chapter discusses. You can use it as a template for your own agreement, modifying it to best suit your needs and the needs of your children. In addition to the items in the sample agreement, make sure yours covers items in the checklist on page 98.

SAMPLE PARENTING PLAN

THIS PARENTING PLAN is made this _6th_ day of __March, 2007__, between __Mary Sims__ (hereinafter referred to as "Mother") and __Wayne Sims__ (hereinafter referred to as "Father").

WHEREAS, the parties hereto were married on __May 5, 1995__, in __Las Vegas__, __Nevada__; and

WHEREAS, one child was born of the marriage, namely __Alice Sims__, born __January 26, 1998__; and

WHEREAS, relations between the parties have been such that on __February 2, 2007__, they mutually and voluntarily separated; and they have mutually and voluntarily agreed to live separate and apart; and

WHEREAS, each party hereby declares that he or she has had independent legal advice by counsel of his or her own selection, or the opportunity to retain counsel; that each has made a full disclosure to the other of his or her financial assets and liabilities; that each fully understands the facts and all of his or her legal rights and obligations; and that after such advice, disclosure, and knowledge, each believes this Parenting Plan to be fair, just, and reasonable; and that each enters into same freely and voluntarily; and

WHEREAS, in view of the foregoing, the parties hereto believe it is in the best interests of their child to enter into this Parenting Plan with respect to the custody, time-sharing, and parenting of their minor child, thereby formalizing the details of their understanding regarding the care and custody of their child, and the time that each party spends with the child.

NOW, THEREFORE, in consideration of the premises and of the mutual promises and undertakings herein contained, and other good and valuable consideration, receipt of which is hereby acknowledged, the parties hereto mutually covenant and agree with each other as follows:

WITNESSETH:

1. Custody. The parties shall have joint legal custody of their minor child. The child's primary residence shall be with the Mother. The parties acknowledge that the welfare and best interest of their minor child are the paramount consideration of each of them. Toward this end, the parties shall confer with one another, and make decisions affecting their child's life, including but not limited to health, education, religious education, summer plans, disciplinary, and developmental matters as more specifically set forth in this Parenting Plan. It shall be, at all times, the objective of both parties to discuss all matters affecting the child so as to promote the child's welfare, happiness, growth, and well-being. Each party shall make every effort to promote the relationships between their child, the other parent, and his or her extended family. Neither party shall act or speak disparagingly of the other parent, or the other parent's family, to or in the presence or hearing of the child. The child will continue to have contact with all of the extended family members of each of his or her parents.

2. Regular Time-Sharing. The child will be with the Father from Friday evening until Monday morning every other weekend, and Tuesday and Thursday evenings during each week.

3. Holidays. The parties agree to the following holiday time-sharing schedule:

Federal Holidays. The child will spend New Year's Day, Labor Day, Memorial Day, Columbus Day, Veterans Day, Fourth of July, and the weekends appended to those holidays with the Father. The child will also spend Thanksgiving Day with the Father. These are superimposed on the regular schedule and take precedence over same. The holiday schedule will have precedence over the weekly schedule; and after the holiday visitation, the weekly schedule will resume at the point where it was interrupted.

Religious Holidays. The child will spend all religious holidays with the Mother. In the event a religious holiday falls on one of the Father's scheduled time-sharing days, the Father will still have time-sharing with the child unless it is a day of observance. In that case, the child will be with the Mother.

continued

Mother's Day and Father's Day. The child will spend Mother's Day with the Mother and Father's Day with the Father.

Child's Birthday. The parties will each spend time with the child on the child's birthday, specific times to be agreed.

School Breaks. The child will spend half of Winter Break with the Father and half of Winter Break with the Mother, specific times to be agreed, but Christmas Eve and Christmas Day will be with the Mother. The child will spend Spring Break and Summer Break with the Mother.

3. Vacation Time-Sharing. The parties may mutually agree upon extended vacation trips with the child from time to time. They will give the other parent as much prior notice of vacation plans as possible so that appropriate arrangements may be made. Each parent agrees to give the other parent all necessary contact information for the traveling parent. Schedules and arrangements will also be made in advance to speak with the child.

4. Telephone Contact. When the child is with one parent, she may call the other parent at any time. Both parents will expect a good night call from her unless otherwise arranged. Further, neither parent will open or otherwise censor any mail from the other parent to the child.

5. Education and Extracurricular Activities. The parents agree that the child will continue to be enrolled in private school. They will both make the decision on where the child goes to high school. The Father and the Mother shall jointly decide, with input from the child, the extracurricular activities in which the child shall participate. The child shall have the opportunity to have both parents present at any games or activities to which parents are invited. Neither party shall schedule activities for the child during those times when the child is scheduled to be with the other parent without that parent's consent. The child also shall have the opportunity to have both parents present at all secular and religious school activities, including back to school night, shows, and other events to which parents are invited, as well as all such events at summer camp.

6. Schedules. The parties agree to speak and exchange email regularly to discuss the child, and they will speak every Sunday night to go over the parenting schedule for the next week. Each party will keep a calendar, and the parties will keep each other informed of the child's schedule so that each parent can participate in scheduled activities whenever possible. Each parent shall provide the other with a copy of the child's school calendar, extracurricular activities schedule, and the like, as soon as he or she receives them. The parties shall notify each other as soon as possible of any illness, emergency, accident, etc., concerning the child;

provided, however, that the parent having responsibility for the child at the time of such illness, emergency, or accident may make medical decisions on behalf of the child.

7. Flexibility. The parties shall make every effort to work with each other concerning arrangements for the time that the child is to spend with the other party. The parties shall be flexible in scheduling their time with the child so as to coincide with the child's interests consistent with their schedules and notify the other party when time with the child is desired or is required. The parties acknowledge that either party may have work or other emergencies beyond their control. However, each party shall be respectful of the needs and schedule of the other by providing at least one day's notification of any request for a change in schedule. Each party may hire suitable day care providers for the child from time to time.

8. Routines. Both parties agree to establish the same household rules and responsibilities and discipline for the child in both their homes. They will have similar routines for the child, such as wake-up time, morning routine, allowance, bedtime, homework, television access, and so on. The parties will buy the child's major gifts together until one of them declines to do so, and they will discuss gifts prior to purchasing.

9. Religious Faith. The parents agree that the child will be raised in the ____ **Methodist** ____ faith and they will cooperate in enrolling her in the appropriate religious education classes.

10. School and Medical Records. Each of the parties shall be entitled to receive copies of all reports concerning the child, including, without limitation, school records and reports, medical reports, and psychological reports. If either party meets with a doctor, dentist, psychologist, therapist, teacher, or other professional, and a written report of such meeting is not created, then the party who met with such professional shall provide the other party with an oral report of the meeting. In the event that the school shall refuse to provide the Father or the Mother with school records or reports, then each parent shall be under a duty to inform the school that the other parent is entitled to and should be provided with such information. If the school should continue to refuse, each shall then be under a duty to notify the other of any and all teacher conferences or meetings involving the child, and both parents shall have the right to be in attendance at such meetings so that there may be unanimity with regard to a course of action designed to nurture the development and growth of the child.

11. Medical Care. Either parent may initiate emergency medical care for the child. The Mother and Father shall coordinate who will make the

continued

regularly scheduled medical and dental appointments for the child. Both the Mother and the Father shall make every effort to keep the other informed of any prescription and/or nonprescription medications that the child may be taking, or illnesses that the child may have. Ultimate responsibility rests with each party to maintain communication with the medical professional working with the child. When the child is sick or in case of emergency at school or elsewhere, the Mother will be the primary contact. If at any time the child should need to be taken to a hospital or come down with a major illness, or in the event of the child's death, the other parent will be promptly notified.

12. Relocation. Neither party shall change residence or relocate without the prior written agreement of the other. If a parent moves more than twenty-five minutes' driving time from the other parent, that parent will be primarily responsible for picking up and dropping off during time-sharing. That parent will also explain the move to the child. A relocation by either party outside the state of __Maryland__ shall be deemed a material and substantial change in circumstances with regard to the time spent by both parties with the child. To this end, both parties shall notify each other as soon as practicable of such intended relocation. In addition, so long as the child of the parties is under the age of 18 years, the parties shall be under a duty and obligation to notify the other of any change of their residence address and telephone number within three days of such change.

13. Parenting Discussions. The parties agree that when either parent wishes to discuss with the other important issues concerning the child's health, education, religion, recreation, and welfare, they will communicate out of the presence or hearing of the child and may communicate by letter or telephone with one another for this purpose. The parties agree that they will not discuss their marital or financial situation or parenting decisions yet to be reached in the presence of, or within the hearing of, the child. They agree not to have the child deliver messages, either written or verbal, to the other parent. They agree that neither of them will say, by word or gesture, anything that would diminish the child's love, respect, or affection for the other parent, nor will they allow their friends or relatives to do so.

14. Child's Self-Respect. The parties agree to nurture and assist in the proper development of the child's emotional state. They agree to support and encourage their child. The parties agree that neither of them will say, by word or gesture, anything that would diminish the child's self-respect.

15. Social Life. Although the Father and the Mother both understand that neither may dictate the way in which the other conducts his or her life, the parties agree that they will always have the child's best interest in mind in any of their actions. Father and the Mother recognize, however, that each of them will enjoy a social and dating life without interference from the other. Accordingly, the parties shall introduce members of the opposite sex (not related by blood or marriage) to the child only after they are divorced, and then after discussing it with the other parent and obtaining that parent's consent. The parties agree they will not cohabit unmarried with such person prior to the child reaching age 21. However, neither party shall make any derogatory remarks about such persons or attempt to undermine the child's relationship with any such person.

16. Death of a Parent. On the death or disability of either parent, the other parent shall have absolute and superior rights to the custody and guardianship of the parties' child, against all other persons, and both parties' rights are deemed to be paramount over all other persons, entities, or agencies. The parties unequivocally and mutually agree that this Parenting Plan is not to be deemed a surrender by the Father or the Mother in and to any parental right with respect to the child. Within ninety days of this Agreement, the parties agree to execute new wills or codicils naming **Ben and Jennifer Holland** as guardians of their child in the event of the death of both of the parties. The parties agree to give each other notice of any change in their wills thereafter. The parties further agree that in the event of the death of either parent, the grandparents, siblings, aunts, uncles, and cousins shall have the right to meaningful access to the child in order to preserve and foster any relationship they had with the child prior to the death of such parent.

LEGAL REPRESENTATION

17. The parties hereby declare and acknowledge that each fully understands the provisions of this Parenting Plan; that each has sought and obtained legal advise of counsel of his or her own selection and has been informed of all legal rights and liabilities with respect thereto or had sufficient opportunity to consult with counsel and has decided not to do so; and that each believes this Parenting Plan to be fair, just, and reasonable; and that each signs this Parenting Plan freely and voluntarily.

COUNSEL FEES/COURT COSTS

18. If either party breaches any provisions of this Parenting Plan, or is in default thereof, that party shall be responsible and pay for any reasonable legal fees and costs incurred by the other party in seeking to enforce this Parenting Plan. Each party hereby covenants and agrees without

continued

other or additional consideration, at any and all reasonable times, upon request of the other party to execute and deliver promptly in due form of law any documents, which may be required to accomplish the intention of this Parenting Plan and shall do all things necessary to this end. If it becomes necessary to enlist the help of a court of law or equity to enforce compliance, then the party against whom a court order is issued shall pay all court costs and reasonable attorney's fees incurred by the other in enforcing this Parenting Plan.

GENERAL PROVISIONS

19. This Parenting Plan contains the entire understanding of the parties as to custody, time-sharing, and parenting of their child. There are no representations, warranties, promises, covenants, or undertakings other than those expressly set forth herein.

20. This Parenting Plan shall be subject to and governed by the laws of the State of __Maryland__, irrespective of the fact that one or more of the parties may be or become a resident of a different state.

21. The parties recognize that the needs of their child will change with age and circumstances. Therefore, they agree to meet annually to review and revise this Parenting Plan as needed. In the event of a dispute concerning any matter in this Parenting Plan, the parties shall submit the dispute to at least three hours of mediation prior to petitioning the court to decide the outstanding issues. Any modification or waiver of any of the terms of the Parenting Plan shall not be effective unless in writing and signed by the parties hereto.

22. A waiver of any breach or default under this Parenting Plan shall not be deemed a waiver of any subsequent breach or default.

23. The provisions of this Parenting Plan shall be binding upon the respective heirs, next of kin, and personal representatives of the parties.

24. If any provision of this Parenting Plan is held to be invalid or unenforceable, all other provisions shall nevertheless continue in full force and effect.

25. No provision of this Parenting Plan shall be interpreted for or against any party hereto by any reason that said party or his or her legal representative drafted all or any part hereof.

IN WITNESS WHEREOF, the parties have subscribed their names to this Parenting Plan as of the day and year first above written, and do solemnly declare and affirm under penalties of perjury that the contents of the foregoing Parenting Plan are true and correct to the best of their knowledge and belief.

*Mary Sims*_____   *Wayne Sims*_____
MOTHER   **FATHER**

State of _**Maryland**___   )
) ss:
County of _**Montgomery**_   )

On this _**2ⁿᵈ day of March, 2007**_, before me a Notary Public in and for the aforesaid jurisdiction, personally came __**Mary Sims**__, personally known to or made known to me to be the __**Mother**__, who executed the foregoing instrument, and made oath under the penalties of perjury that the facts and statements contained in this document are true and that _**she**_ acknowledged to me that _**she**_ freely and voluntarily executed the same for purposes named herein.

*C. U. Sine*_____
Notary Public
My Commission Expires:

State of _**Maryland**___   )
) ss:
County of _**Montgomery**_   )

On this _**2ⁿᵈ day of March, 2007**_, before me a Notary Public in and for the aforesaid jurisdiction, personally came __**Wayne Sims**__, personally known to or made known to me to be the __**Father**__, who executed the foregoing instrument, and made oath under the penalties of perjury that the facts and statements contained in this document are true and that _**he**_ acknowledged to me that _**he**_ freely and voluntarily executed the same for purposes named herein.

*C. U. Sine*_____
Notary Public
My Commission Expires:

Chapter Ten

Child Support

When you have children, you have a legal obligation to care for them and protect them. You have to shelter, feed, and clothe them, and protect them from harm. You cannot neglect them. These legal obligations apply to both parents.

However, as far as the law is concerned, the custodial parent (the parent with whom the child lives most of the time) supports the child when he or she pays for rent or mortgage, car expenses, food, clothing, and such. These are direct payments for child expenses to third parties.

The noncustodial parent pays child support to the custodial parent. In this context, child support is a monthly amount paid directly by the noncustodial parent to the custodial parent. Child support is paid by both parents, one indirectly and one directly.

Child support is for food, housing, clothes, medical care, education, day care, summer camp, and other expenses for the child. Unless the children are being neglected by the custodial parent—not fed, clothed, sheltered, or protected—then the court will not require a parent to account for how child support is spent.

A parent can ask the court for child support, as can a third party who has custody of a child. The court can issue an *earnings withholding order* to have an employer deduct child support from your paycheck. Payment can be every month, twice a month, every week, or every two weeks, depending on how the payer is paid. Usually, the court sets a fixed monthly amount, but it has the power to order a parent to pay the mortgage, utilities, and other expenses each month instead of a fixed amount. In most cases, the court will not require future escrow payments, and will not withhold future child support payments from the sale of a house.

Monthly child support is calculated on an annual basis, taking into account the time that the child spends with each parent during the year. That means that child support will stay the same even though the children might be staying with the noncustodial parent for a longer length of time; for example, during summer vacation.

Marital misconduct, such as adultery, will not be a factor in determining child support. The court looks at the needs of the children and the financial resources available to the parents when determining child support. The court can also take into account:

♦ any special medical or educational needs of the children;
♦ any income or financial resources the children have; and,
♦ the lifestyle of the children during the marriage.

Calculating Child Support

Child support used to be, like alimony, left to the discretion of the judge. This meant different results in cases with similar facts. Now every state is required to adopt *child support guidelines.*

Child support guidelines are in the form of a chart, table, or formula in the laws of most states. They estimate the costs of raising children at respective incomes if the parents were still together. Most courts have worksheets to calculate guidelines that are presented to the judge at the divorce hearing. The judge will presume that the guidelines show the correct amount of child support unless there is a good reason for deviating from them.

It should be easy to determine child support, but sometimes it is not. The correct amount of income to use for the formula is often in dispute. A self-employed individual can manipulate expenses and income to make it seem like he or she earns less than the true amount. The court can use the income it thinks a person can actually earn if someone intentionally reduces income or refuses to work. Therefore, you may hire a vocational rehabilitation expert to determine about how much money an unemployed or underemployed spouse with certain skills can earn in the workforce. The unemployed party will want to show the court efforts made to find employment. The court will not be sympathetic to someone who simply does not wish to work.

The exact amount of child support you will pay depends on the guidelines, but you probably will not have to pay more than half of your take-home pay in family support (combined alimony and child support). Most states use the *income shares model*, a few use the *percentage of income model*, and the rest use the *Melson model*.

Income Shares Model

A majority of states use the *income shares model*. Under this formula, child support is calculated based on the relative and combined income of the parties, the number of children, and the time each parent spends with the children. The child support tables use an estimate of each parent's income used to support the child when the parents were living together. The theory of this model is that the children should not be harmed financially just because the parents are getting a divorce. The following is an example of how one state calculates child support under the income shares model.

Example:
*Step 1. Determine each parent's income. Depending on which state law applies, the tables use gross income, adjusted gross income, or net income. This includes every source of income, including wages, earnings from self-employment, interest, dividends, rents, gifts, capital gains, and inheritances. If you have what the IRS calls a **pass through entity**, your gross income is what the business earns, not what you have paid yourself in salary or draw. When a parent is unemployed or underemployed voluntarily, the court can impute income to that parent for purposes of determining child support. The court will usually not impute income for child support purposes to a parent who is caring for a very young child at home.*

Step 2. Deduct health insurance premiums, child support for previous children, and alimony from gross income of the party paying them. Add alimony paid in this case to the income of the party receiving it.

Step 3. Add the adjusted incomes of the father and mother calculated in Step 2 for their combined income.

Step 4. Look up the child support listed in the tables contained in the state law adopting child support guidelines, using the combined income determined in Step 3 and the number of children. (See the section "Finding the Law" in Chapter 2.)

Step 5. Calculate the relative percentage of each parent's income to the combined income calculated in Step 3. (For example, if the mother makes $55,000 per year, and the father makes $45,000 a year, their combined income is $100,000. The mother has 55% and the father has 45% of the combined income.)

Step 6. Multiply the percentages determined in Step 5 times the child support in Step 4 to determine the child support obligation of each parent.

Step 7. Various adjustments may be made for day care, extraordinary medical expenses, and other special circumstances, according to your state law.

Step 8. The resulting amount in the noncustodial parent's column is the monthly child support that parent will pay to the custodial parent. (The custodial parent is presumed to pay the amount in his or her column to third parties directly when paying for rent, utilities, and other child care expenses.)

Percentage of Income Method

The second most popular model is the percentage of income model. This is the model used by Alaska, Arkansas, District of Columbia, Illinois, Massachusetts, Minnesota, Mississippi, Nevada, North Dakota, Texas, and Wisconsin. Tennessee switched from the percentage of income model to the income shares model in 2005, and Georgia did so in 2006. Minnesota has adopted legislation to change to the income shares model in 2007.

The focus of this model is the income of the noncustodial parent. Child support is based on a percentage of that income. The custodial parent could be a billionaire and the noncustodial parent will still have to pay child support.

First, you calculate the total income of the paying parent. Some of the states then permit certain deductions to arrive at net income. Next, determine the percentage of child support from a table or formula contained in the statute, based on the total income or net income and number of children.

Example (for Texas):
Step 1 is determining the paying parent's gross income, which includes all pay, commissions, overtime, tips, bonuses, interest, dividends, rents, royalties, trust income, retirement income, and disability income.

Step 2. Deduct from total income social security taxes, federal income tax, state income tax, union dues, and health insurance premiums for the children.

Step 3. Look up the percentage of child support from the statute. For example, a father with two children from the same mother would pay 25% on net income as child support.

Step 4. The percentage is only applied to the first $6,000 per month of net income, unless the court finds that the children have additional or exceptional needs.

Melson Model
The third model is the Melson model, developed by a family court judge in Delaware. It is used by Delaware, Hawaii, and Montana. It was designed to ensure that each parent's basic needs are met in addition to the children's needs, and that any additional income is shared among the children and the parents.

First, each parent is allotted a subsistence level or minimum amount of income to keep for his or her basic needs. Then the children's basic needs are taken care of with a subsistence amount of child support that is assigned to the children before the parents can keep any more income.

If there is any income left over, after taking care of the parent's basic needs and the children's basic needs, then the children and the parents share the additional income.

Example (for Delaware):
Step 1. Determine total income.

Step 2. Determine net available income by subtracting taxes, health insurance, mandatory retirement contributions, union dues, other payroll deductions, and a self-support allowance of $850 per month.

Step 3. Make an adjustment for the support of other children not of this marriage according to the table in the statute.

Step 4. Calculate the primary child support allowance for the number of children in this marriage according to the table in the statute. For two children, it would be $650 a month.

Step 5. Add work related child care and certain other expenses related to the children.

Step 6. Determine the Primary Need and Primary Support Obligation for the children and allocate this between the parents based on their percentages of income.

Step 7. If there is income left over after the parents have met their own and their children's primary support needs, then an additional child support, called **standard of living adjustment***, is calculated based on the tables in the statute.*

Internet
An easy way to calculate child support is to use the Internet. There are several child support calculators online. For example, **www.alllaw.com** has calculators for every state. You just put in the income for each parent, the number of children, and the time with each parent. The program will calculate child support for you. Some sites will even print out the forms you need for court.

You can also experiment with different scenarios. Different alimony payments will yield different child support. You can try out different time-sharing arrangements. Ask yourself if it makes more sense for both parents to work and have day care expenses, or if one should stay home and take care of the children.

Income above the Guidelines

The guidelines only go up to a certain amount of income. When you are over that amount, you can extrapolate the guidelines or you can look at the needs of the children. The court recognizes that children of affluent parents should not be penalized because of a divorce. Therefore, when the guidelines do not apply or would not result in a fair amount of child support, the court has more discretion and can order child support above a straight-line extrapolation of the guidelines.

You do not have to litigate child support if you can agree on it. The court will approve an agreement that is consistent with the guidelines and meets the needs of the children. The court will even approve an agreement that is not consistent with the guidelines if there is a good reason for deviation.

SAMPLE CHILD SUPPORT PROVISIONS

Commencing and accounting from January 1, 2007, the Father shall pay to the Mother for the support and maintenance of the parties' children, the sum of $1,195 per month, in two equal installments on the first and fifteenth of each month by mail, directly to the Mother. Said child support payments shall continue until the first to occur of the following: a child dies, the Father dies, a child marries, a child enters the armed forces, a child no longer has principal residence with the Mother; a child obtains full-time employment (other than employment during school breaks), or when a child attains the age of 18; provided. If a child has not graduated high school by his or her 18th birthday, child support shall continue until graduation or the 19th birthday of that child, whichever first occurs.

The parties agree to recalculate child support every two years from January 1, 2007, based on a 10% extrapolation of the Child Support Guidelines for combined gross incomes in excess of $120,000. The parties agree to exchange tax returns every two years in September in order to recalculate child support.

The Mother agrees to continue the health insurance coverage for the children until age 22 or for so long as she is able to obtain

continued

gh her employment. The parties agree that
those physicians that participate in the
.n.

ee to share in proportion to income all unreim-
cal expenses incurred on behalf of each child until
, including orthodontia and psychotherapy if recom-
ended by a child's primary care physician. The Mother agrees
to provide full receipts for all such costs to the Father so they may
be submitted to the insurance company, whether covered or not.
Before either party may be liable for expenses that constitute
elective procedures, such as cosmetic surgery, both parties must
agree to the expense in writing.

Adjustments

Although all states have guidelines, they vary widely from
state to state. Adjustments can change your monthly child
support payment by hundreds of dollars a month. Various
states allow adjustments to the guidelines for second families
and new children, visitation, custody, health insurance,
medical expenses, day care, education, and extraordinary
expenses for the children.

Questions sometimes arise regarding whether child support
under previous obligations should be changed or if it should
stay the same when parents remarry and have children in a
new family. Some states say that it is your choice whether to
have additional children or not, and that should not affect the
child support for your previous children. Some states will permit
the judge to take subsequent children into account as a change
in circumstances for modifying child support. Also, when
establishing child support for children in a second marriage,
some states will allow the court to consider children of a previous
marriage and some will not.

The time a child spends with each parent during the year is
part of the guideline calculations in many states. Therefore, it
can sometimes make a big difference in child support whether
weekend visitation starts on Friday afternoon or Saturday
morning, and whether it ends on Sunday night or Monday

morning. That is one reason why there are fights over an extra night every other week, or extra time on holidays and during the summer.

In cases of split custody of siblings (when one parent has custody of one child and the other parent has custody of another child), calculate the guidelines for each parent individually with one child. Then, subtract one result from the other to find the net child support.

Example:
Mary has custody of Sally, and John has custody of Saul. The child support guidelines calculated for Sally alone say that John owes Mary $250 a month. The child support guidelines calculated for Saul alone say that Mary owes John $150 a month. The court will net one against the other and order John to pay Mary the difference, which is $100 a month.

Work-related child care expenses are a part of child support in some states. There may be a dispute over what portion of child care is work-related. Some states include child care as a part of child support, some add it to child support, some leave it to the discretion of the judge, and some do not count it in child support at all.

Health insurance premiums paid by the parents are included in child support by some states, some only include uncovered medical expenses, some include both, and others leave it up to the judge to decide. If your state includes health insurance premiums, only the cost of insurance for the children should be used, not the entire policy cost.

Deviations from Guidelines

The judge is required to follow the child support guidelines and award the amount of child support calculated by them unless there is a good reason to deviate from the guidelines. A judge will always permit someone to pay more child support than the guidelines show, but a judge must explain in the order why any award that is less than the guideline amount is made. A downward deviation from the child support guidelines might be allowed in the following circumstances.

- One parent takes on a higher amount of debt incurred during the marriage for the benefit of the children.
- One parent gets the child exemptions and child care deductions for taxes.
- One parent gets more than 50% of the marital property, the house, or a large capital gain from sale of stock.
- The children have their own financial resources, like trust funds from grandparents.
- The marital settlement agreement provides other resources for the support of the child, such as additional alimony or savings.
- There are prior or subsequent children to support from other marriages.

Education Costs

A parent may object to paying the extraordinary costs of private schooling for children when the paying parent believes they should be in public schools. The court will usually look at past history to determine the future, such as whether the children were in private school until the separation or divorce. The court may also consider whether the children have special needs that are best met by a private school or educational program.

College expenses are another area of controversy. Many states will not require a parent to put a child through college. However, you can agree that the parents will pay for college in a marital settlement agreement. The court will enforce such agreements even when they do not have the power to order it in the first place. However, the court cannot modify college support when it is by agreement and not by law.

You can agree to share college costs equally or *pro rata* to income. You can agree to be legally obligated to pay. You can put in an escape clause for financial hardship that states it is your present intention and desire to pay for college, and you will if you are financially able to do so when the time comes. You may want to limit the clause by time, such as to four years of college. You may want to put in a certain time by which your children must decide to go to college or not. Some parents cap the costs at in-state tuition.

SAMPLE COLLEGE SUPPORT PROVISIONS

A provision for an agreement in which the parties agree to provide support for college could read as follows.

It is the intent and desire of the parties that their children graduate from college. The parties agree that they will confer with each child, as he or she becomes eligible to attend college, in the selection of the school, taking into account the child's particular talents and abilities, the cost of the school that is under consideration, any financial aid that is available, and any factor deemed relevant to such decision. Upon selection of said school by all concerned, the parties hereto will each pay a pro rata portion for said education based upon the relative income of each party.

If you want to put a cap on college costs or include an escape clause if the costs would create a financial hardship, you can use a provision like the following.

The parties agree that they will pay, in proportion to their respective incomes, for up to four years of in-state college for each of their children, including tuition, room, board, books, fees, and reasonable transportation costs and allowance, unless such payment would work a financial hardship on either party; but said obligation shall not run beyond the school term in which the child has his or her 22nd birthday.

Modification

The court can modify child support in the event of a material change in circumstances. Some jurisdictions have a minimum period of time before you can petition for a modification. The following are generally considered a material change in circumstances.

◆ A child changes residence from one parent to the other.

◆ The visitation schedule changes.

◆ One parent or the other has a change in income either up or down.

◆ The children's needs increase.

◆ A child reaches the age of majority while there are still other minor children at home. Child support does not reduce by half when one of two children reaches majority. It is not a straight-line calculation, so you have to recompute child support for one child under the guidelines.

It is always a good idea to document in writing when a change occurs, such as emancipation. Many times, the legal system will not operate automatically to make these changes. It is best to try to obtain consent from both parents and the court for any modification of child support. The court will usually approve a *Consent Order to Modify Child Support*, which is signed by both parents and submitted jointly to the court.

A court may order that child support be paid retroactively. Some courts have the discretion to order child support back to the date of birth. Others will award it retroactively to the date of filing a petition. Therefore, it is important to file your petition early in the case. The court can also order the manner in which arrearages will be paid, and will usually give you time to pay if you ask.

While a court can establish retroactive child support, an existing child support order cannot be modified retroactively. Past child support cannot be modified. There is a federal law against this. Only child support going forward may be modified.

Termination

Inability to pay child support does not automatically terminate child support. If you become unable to pay child support—for example, through disability, involuntary unemployment, or incarceration—child support will still continue to accrue until you obtain a court order modifying support. Child support will terminate upon the emancipation of the child, death of the child, or the termination of parental rights.

Emancipation

Each state sets the age at which a minor becomes an adult, called the *age of emancipation*. It is usually 18, but some states are different. For example, it is 21 in the District of Columbia.

Child support may be continued past the age of majority for a child with a disability. In all but a handful of states, child support continues until the earliest of high school graduation or age 19, whichever is first, if a child is a full-time student in high school and living at home at age 18. Other ways for a child to become emancipated are by marrying, enlisting in the armed services, or becoming self-supporting.

Death

Child support terminates upon the death of a child. However, if the parent paying child support dies, his or her estate will be liable for any past-due child support, and a claim may also be made against the estate for future child support payments. If the parent receiving child support dies, the other parent will become guardian of the child, and pay the child's expenses directly to third-party providers.

Termination of Parental Rights

Child support terminates upon any order that terminates parental rights. Adoption by a stepparent terminates parental rights, and therefore terminates the obligation to pay child support by the parent giving up parental rights. However, you cannot give up parental rights voluntarily to stop child support. The courts will protect the interests of the child to receive child support.

Avoiding Payment

The *Office of Child Support Enforcement*, a part of the Department of Health and Human Services, was created to establish and enforce child support obligations. The law requires every state to have a child support enforcement agency that will attempt to collect child support for a nominal fee. You can also hire a private attorney to try to collect child support, but of course, that is more expensive.

The parent seeking enforcement of a child support order must file a petition with the court to hold the paying parent in *contempt*. The court that entered the original child support order is usually the court where the petition is filed. The court will hold a hearing to determine whether the parent intentionally failed to make his or her child support payments. The judge can issue a bench warrant to arrest a parent who fails to appear for the hearing.

If the court finds that the parent was not able to make the payments because that parent did not have the money, it will not find that parent in contempt. However, the parent will still owe the child support.

If the parent is found to be in contempt, the court can enforce its orders in several ways, such as:

- ◆ by taking away a driver's license;
- ◆ by taking away a professional license, such as a real estate license or license to practice law; or,
- ◆ by sending a delinquent payer to jail.

The court may give the payer a short time to pay the child support. If the payments are brought current, the court will purge the jail sentence.

A parent who is owed child support has other remedies as well, including:

- ◆ obtaining a *wage withholding order*, requiring child support to be deducted from the payer's paycheck and paid through the court;
- ◆ seizing the payer's assets, such as bank accounts, automobiles, furniture, and the like, with a *writ of attachment*;
- ◆ asking the state's attorney to prosecute the delinquent parent criminally for failing to pay child support (indictment and conviction can result in a criminal record, incarceration, or supervised probation); and,
- ◆ asking the court for attorney's fees, the other costs to enforce child support, and interest on child support arrears.

There is no way to get out of paying child support. Intentional impoverishment, hiding assets, or not paying can have dire legal consequences. You cannot discharge child support in bankruptcy.

Taxes

Your income tax is determined by applying the income tax rates to your taxable income. An item that qualifies as a *tax deduction* is deducted from your income in arriving at taxable income, thereby lowering your taxable income and your tax. If you are in the 25% federal tax bracket, a $100 tax deduction lowers your federal tax by $25. Home mortgage interest and alimony are examples of tax deductions.

An item that qualifies as a *tax credit* is deducted directly from your tax. Whatever your federal tax bracket, a $100 tax credit lowers your federal tax by $100. One example is the child tax credit.

You cannot deduct child support from income taxes. Likewise, child support is not taxable as income to the person receiving it. (Alimony payments are deductible for the person paying and must be included as income to the person receiving.)

The IRS has rules against disguising child support as alimony to make it deductible. For example, alimony that ends on a date tied to the age of majority of the children (such as six months after the youngest child turns 18) is not deductible. It is possible, however, to ask the judge to order lower child support or no child support because you are paying alimony that is equivalent to child support under the guidelines.

Generally, parents are entitled to the *dependency exemption* for the children who live with them and who they support. In divorce cases, one of the parents can take the dependency exemption if the parents together provide at least one-half of the child's support and if the child lives more than one-half of the year with the parents. If the child is primarily supported by or primarily lives with some other person, that person may be entitled to take the exemption and neither of the parents are entitled to it.

If the exemption is available to the parents under the foregoing requirements, and you are the custodial parent, under the IRS rules you are entitled to claim the dependency exemption. You are the custodial parent if you had physical custody of your child for more than one-half of the year.

However, the custodial parent cannot take the dependency exemption if, in the divorce case, he or she agreed or was ordered to release the exemption to the noncustodial parent, because only one parent can get the exemption for a child in any one year. The IRS does not care who takes the exemption as long as 1) a parent is entitled to the exemption, that is, the requirements listed above are met, and 2) only one parent takes the dependency exemption.

If you are the noncustodial parent, you are entitled to the dependency exemption if the requirements listed above are met *and* the custodial parent releases the dependency exemption to you. This is done by signing and delivering IRS Form 8332 to the IRS. The noncustodial parent must attach the release to his or her tax return. The custodial parent may release the dependency exemption one year at a time, or may execute a single release that covers all future years. Release of the exemption is often conditioned upon timely, full payment of child support. If the parents were never married, they cannot switch the exemption like this.

The parent entitled to the exemption subtracts this amount from income on the tax return. The exemption also entitles you to other valuable tax benefits, such as the *child tax credit,* the *dependent and child care credit,* and *educational credits.*

If you have a dependent who is under age 17, you are filing as single or head of household, and your annual income is less than $75,000, you are entitled to a *child tax credit* of up to $1,000 per child (this amount may adjust annually). Above that income level, the credit is phased out. The credit offsets your taxes, dollar for dollar, possibly down to zero. Some low-income taxpayers may qualify for an additional child tax credit, and receive a refund up to the maximum of $1,000 in combined child tax credits, even if they would not otherwise be receiving a refund check. This credit cannot be allocated to the other parent and cannot be detached from the child dependency exemption.

There is another credit to help offset baby-sitting and day care costs, after-school care, or recreation programs incurred to permit a custodial parent to work or look for work. It is called the *dependent and child care credit.* The amount is 20–35% of child care expenses between $3,000 and $6,000, which equals a tax credit of $600 to $1,050 for one child, or $1,200 to $2,100 for more than one child. This credit reduces your tax bill dollar for dollar, but it cannot reduce your taxes below zero like the child tax credit. The credit is also phased out at higher incomes. This credit can be detached from the dependency exemption and assigned to the other parent. If you have custody of the child for most of the year, but you have assigned the exemption to the noncustodial parent with IRS Form 8332, you can still claim this credit.

There is a *Hope Credit* of up to $1,500 per student for the first two years of education after high school. There is also a *Lifetime Learning Credit* of up to $2,000 per family after the first two years. This benefit is phased out at $50,000 income per year for a single person and $100,000 for a married couple filing jointly.

If the parents cannot reach an agreement on who gets the exemptions and credits, and file conflicting returns, the IRS may disallow both exemptions until the conflict is resolved. The dependency exemptions and the associated tax credits are usually more valuable to the tax payer in the higher tax bracket. The parties may save in the total taxes paid, and share in these tax savings, if they are able to agree on shifting the exemptions and credits to the higher income earner as long as that taxpayer can take advantage of them.

Uniform Laws

Approximately one-third of child support cases involve parties living in two different states. The *Uniform Reciprocal Enforcement of Support Act* (URESA) and *Revised Uniform Reciprocal Enforcement of Support Act* (RURESA) allow a parent to file for child support in the state where he or she lives (the initiating state). The order is sent to and enforced in the state where the payer lives (the responding state).

Every state has now adopted some form of URESA or RURESA. There are some problems with both acts, however, and they have been interpreted differently by different courts. This has led to conflicting orders from different states and lengthy child support proceedings.

The *Uniform Interstate Family Support Act* (UIFSA) was drafted to solve these problems. UIFSA replaces URESA and RURESA, and more than half the states have adopted it. UIFSA creates *continuing exclusive jurisdiction* in the first state that issues a child support. That state keeps continuing exclusive jurisdiction as long as one of the parties or the child resides there. The child support order cannot be modified by any other state unless the parties agree that jurisdiction may be transferred to another state.

UIFSA permits a payee to enforce an income withholding order in another UIFSA state by sending it directly to an employer without going through the court in the second state. UIFSA requires each state to establish a central registry to receive interstate documents. You can find the central registry under "child support" in your state government telephone directory, or call the Office of Child Support Enforcement of the Department of Health and Human Services in Washington, D.C.

Life Insurance

The court cannot require a parent to obtain life insurance. In some states, the court can order you to maintain the life insurance coverage you already have. The parties will sometimes agree to provide life insurance for the benefit of the children, especially if there is already a life insurance policy in place or an employer provides one. This can ensure that child support payments will continue in the event of the death of the payer. You may agree that the amount of life insurance decreases each year by the amount of child support payments.

Life insurance for the benefit of the children may also be appropriate on the life of the person receiving child support. In the event of that person's death, there may be expenses incurred for taking care of the children by the other parent.

Health Insurance

Congress amended the *Employee Retirement Income Security Act* (ERISA) provisions to guarantee the right of children to receive benefits under their parent's group health insurance plan. A parent may now ask the court for a *Qualified Medical Child Support Order* (QMCSO).

Under a QMCSO, the child becomes an *alternative recipient.* This means the child is a participant and beneficiary under the insured parent's health insurance plan with rights and remedies that are independent of the parent. The child, or the child's custodian, can communicate directly with the insurance company for benefits and payments, and does not have to go through the insured parent.

The child will be issued an insurance card, a list of providers, and an explanation of benefits and procedures by the plan provider. The child can select the options best suited to his or her needs. Any expenses paid for the child or custodian will be reimbursed by the insurance company.

Any order, judgment, or decree, including the approval of a settlement agreement, from a court of competent jurisdiction pursuant to state domestic relations law can be a QMCSO. The court order is sent to the plan administrator for qualification. To qualify, the order must contain:

◆ a specific provision for health coverage for the child of a participant enrolled in a group plan;

◆ the name and last known mailing address of the participant;

◆ the name and mailing address of each child covered by the order;

◆ a reasonable description of the coverage to be provided under the plan or the manner in which such coverage is to be determined;

◆ the period to which such order applies; and,

◆ each plan to which such order applies.

The plan cannot be required to provide any type or form of benefit or option not otherwise provided under the plan. It is advisable to include in any QMCSO who will pay the premiums for the insurance, increased costs due to options selected by the child, uninsured costs, deductibles, coinsurance, and costs for care outside the plan.

Military

The Soldiers' and Sailors' Civil Relief Act (50 U.S.C. Secs. 501-591) suspends civil actions against active duty members of the military. The suspension is not automatic, but rather provides that the military may request a stay or the court may stay the proceedings on its own.

If military service has no material effect on the service-member's ability to prosecute or defend the action, the court may deny the stay. The military member must present a reasonable timetable to the court for resolving the issue, taking into account the military obligation and family needs. The length of the stay is within the court's discretion.

Chapter Eleven

Alimony

Alimony is support paid by one former spouse to the other. It can be ordered in addition to, but not in place of, child support. The purpose of alimony is to permit an economically dependent spouse to become self-supporting. It is not meant to be an entitlement of marriage. Generally, alimony is based upon the needs and resources of the parties. Unlike child support, which is based on guidelines or a formula, alimony is very much up to the discretion of the judge.

Some states require the judge to consider certain factors in alimony awards. The factors differ from state to state, but in general they include income, education, length of the marriage, age, health, standard of living during the marriage, and fault for the divorce.

Theoretically, the law is applied to both sexes equally, so it is possible for either party to get alimony. In reality, it is probably harder for a man to get alimony than it is for a woman.

Types of Alimony

In most states, alimony can be *temporary* or *permanent*. Temporary alimony (sometimes called *rehabilitative alimony*) is for a set period for the purpose of restoring a party to an economic functioning level, which means earning a reasonable living. The public policy is to assist the former spouse to be self-supporting.

If rehabilitative alimony cannot bring about rehabilitation (for example, when a spouse has a disability), then the court can, in proper circumstances, order alimony on a permanent basis. Permanent alimony may also be granted when one spouse is disabled or the incomes of the spouses are far apart.

Permanent alimony (sometimes called *indefinite alimony*) is granted less often these days. It can be raised or lowered over time if there is a change of circumstances. *Permanent* usually means until you die, your spouse dies, or the spouse receiving alimony remarries (although alimony can continue even past remarriage).

Any type of alimony typically stops if you die, your spouse dies, or the person receiving alimony remarries, unless you agree otherwise in a marital settlement agreement. Living with someone after the divorce, called *cohabitation*, may cause permanent alimony at the time of the divorce, you waive your right to alimony and you cannot get it later.

You can also ask the court for *pendente lite alimony*, meaning temporary spousal support during the litigation. Depending on your state law, the test for pendente lite alimony may be different than the test for permanent alimony. It is supposed to cover the needs of the party seeking alimony—that is, necessities and lawsuit costs—until the time of trial. Of course, the other party must have the ability to pay alimony.

Tax Treatment of Alimony

You can deduct alimony from your income on your tax return if you are paying it. If you are receiving alimony, it is taxable income to you. (Since there is no withholding on alimony payments, you may have to file quarterly estimated payments with the IRS and state if you are receiving alimony.)

This is not the same tax treatment as for child support and property transfers. You do not receive a tax deduction for paying child support. Child support is not taxable income to you if you are receiving it. Payments for property—for example, the husband paying the wife for her share of the marital residence—are tax-free transactions and not tax deductible to the payer.

This presents an opportunity for tax planning during a divorce. Even if a judge would not order alimony in your case, you may agree to it because it may be an advantageous way to provide support to your family.

Example:
Jack and Wendy have two young children. Jack is a doctor making $195,000 a year, and Wendy is a nurse who makes $30,000 a year. When they run the numbers both ways, Jack will be able to pay Wendy more in the form of alimony than he would in the form of child support. Jack is in a higher tax bracket than Wendy, so the deduction for alimony is more valuable to him. In the lower tax bracket, Wendy will pay less tax on the alimony income than Jack would pay on his income without the alimony deduction. There is more money to go around because the government is paying part of the bill.

In order for payments to qualify as tax-deductible alimony, they must meet the requirements of the IRS Code, which defines alimony as follows.

> *Section 71(b) Alimony or separate maintenance payments defined*
>
> *For purposes of this section—*
>
> *(1) In general*
>
> *The term "alimony or separate maintenance payment" means any payment in cash if—*
>
> *(A) such payment is received by (or on behalf of) a spouse under a divorce or separation instrument,*
>
> *(B) the divorce or separation instrument does not designate such payment as a payment which is not includible in gross income under this section and not allowable as a deduction under section 215,*
>
> *(C) in the case of an individual legally separated from his spouse under a decree of divorce or of separate maintenance, the payee spouse and the payer spouse are not members of the same household at the time such payment is made, and*
>
> *(D) there is no liability to make any such payment for any period after the death of the payee spouse and there is no liability to make any payment (in cash or property) as a substitute for such payments after the death of the payee spouse.*

(2) Divorce or separation instrument
The term "divorce or separation instrument" means—

(A) *a decree of divorce or separate maintenance or a written instrument incident to such a decree,*

(B) *a written separation agreement, or*

(C) *a decree (not described in subparagraph (A)) requiring a spouse to make payments for the support or maintenance of the other spouse.*

IRS Code Section 71 goes on to say that you must file a separate return in order to deduct the payments.

In plain language, in order for payments to be deductible as alimony, they have to meet these tests.

◆ The payments must be in cash. A check or money order is the same as cash, but property or services is not. Payment of your spouse's obligation to third parties can qualify, but you should consult your lawyer or tax professional to ensure that any such arrangement will result in the payments being deductible.

◆ The payments must be paid under a decree of divorce or written separation agreement. Voluntary payments are not alimony. You cannot backdate a document to turn those past payments into alimony. If you are making payments to your spouse, you had better put it into an agreement if you want those alimony deductions.

◆ The payments cannot be designated in the agreement as nondeductible items such as child support or a property settlement. You can elect to reverse the tax treatment of alimony. You do this by saying in your agreement or divorce decree that alimony will not be deductible to the person paying it or income to the person receiving it. The IRS will honor such an election.

◆ You cannot live in the same house as your ex-spouse.

◆ Your liability to pay alimony must terminate upon the death of your former spouse.

◆ You must file a separate tax return.

Example:
Sean and Michelle have a provision in their agreement that Sean will pay Michelle $30,000 within thirty days to "adjust the equities of their marriage and divorce." Sean asks his lawyer if he can deduct that payment on his tax return as alimony. His lawyer tells him that it is probably not alimony because it fails the termination on death test. There is no provision that says Sean would not have to pay it if Michelle died.

What prevents a high-income taxpayer from trying to disguise tax-free property settlements or child support as alimony? While you can designate alimony payments as nondeductible in an agreement or divorce decree, the converse is not true. You cannot turn a nondeductible payment into a tax deduction by calling it alimony. If it fails one of the mentioned tests and does not meet the IRS definition of alimony, it is not alimony for tax purposes—no matter what the parties say in their agreement or divorce.

Example:
Mohadi and Yoko got divorced in 1982. Mohadi kept the marital residence and agreed to pay the mortgage for any house that Yoko bought. The parties said in their agreement that Mohadi's payments on Yoko's mortgage would be tax deductible as alimony payments by him. The agreement said it was binding on the heirs of the parties and that the husband would pay the mortgage entirely no matter what. Yoko did not report the mortgage payments as income for several years, and the IRS came after her for thousands of dollars in unpaid income taxes.

Even though Yoko said in her separation agreement that the payments were alimony (and therefore, taxable income to her), they did not meet the tests for alimony contained in the IRS code. They failed the test that alimony payments terminate on her death, because Mohadi would still have to pay the mortgage even if she died. Therefore, the IRS has to collect the tax from Mohadi if he deducted the payments as alimony—not from Yoko.

Excess Alimony Recapture

To prevent tax abuse, the IRS Code has set up a test to prevent taxpayers from claiming nondeductible property transfers as deductible alimony, called the *excess alimony recapture test* or *front-end loading test*. To prevent nondeductible child support from being deducted as alimony, Congress likewise established the *alimony fixed as child support test*.

Excess alimony means that too much of the payments are concentrated in the first two years of alimony. This is called *front-loading*. If your alimony payments are front-loaded, the IRS can recapture the excess alimony deductions by including them in the payer's income.

There can only be excess alimony in the first two years in which alimony is paid. The first calendar year in which alimony is paid is called the *first post-separation year*. The next two calendar years are called the *second and third post-separation years*. There is no such thing as excess alimony in the third post-separation year or later years. You are also safe if alimony does not decrease by more than $10,000 in any of the first three years.

The calculation of excess alimony recapture is as follows.

- ◆ *Step 1.* Start with the alimony paid in the third post-separation year. Add $15,000. Subtract the alimony paid in the second post-separation year.
- ◆ *Step 2.* Subtract the result in Step 1 from the alimony paid in the second post-separation year.
- ◆ *Step 3.* Add the result in Step 2 and the alimony paid in the third post-separation year, and divide by two.
- ◆ *Step 4.* Add $15,000 to the result in Step 3 and subtract that from the alimony paid in the first post-separation year.
- ◆ *Step 5.* Add the results of Step 1 and Step 4. This is the amount of excess alimony. It is added to the income of the payer and subtracted from the income of the payee in the third post-separation year.

Alimony that is Really Child Support

Sometimes in a divorce, a party will propose to pay deductible alimony until the children graduate from high school or until the children reach age 18. Congress has decided that this looks too much like nondeductible child support disguised as deductible alimony. Therefore, the IRS provides that the following payments to support children are not deductible as alimony.

Section 71(c) Payments to support children
(1) In general
Subsection (a) shall not apply to that part of any payment which the terms of the divorce or separation instrument fix (in terms of an amount of money or a part of the payment) as a sum which is payable for the support of children of the payer spouse.
(2) Treatment of certain reductions related to contingencies involving child
For purposes of paragraph (1), if any amount specified in the instrument will be reduced—
(A) on the happening of a contingency specified in the instrument relating to a child (such as attaining a specified age, marrying, dying, leaving school, or a similar contingency), or
(B) at a time which can clearly be associated with a contingency of a kind specified in subparagraph (A), an amount equal to the amount of such reduction will be treated as an amount fixed as payable for the support of children of the payer spouse.
(3) Special rule where payment is less than amount specified in instrument
For purposes of this subsection, if any payment is less than the amount specified in the instrument, then so much of such payment as does not exceed the sum payable for support shall be considered a payment for such support.

As you can see, the first rule is simple. You cannot deduct any payments that are called child support in your agreement or divorce decree.

The second rule is that payments are not deductible if they are conditioned on some event that happens to the children. You cannot deduct alimony that decreases or stops when a child turns 18 or graduates from high school. Other events relating to a child include the child marrying, dying, leaving home, leaving school, or reaching a certain income level.

The third rule is to prevent you from circumventing the second rule by referring to a time instead of an event. The reduction or termination of alimony cannot be related to a time that can be associated with one of the events relating to children in the second rule.

IRS regulations provide the following additional explanation of the third rule.

> You cannot deduct alimony that will decrease or terminate within six months of a child's 18th or 21st birthday (or whatever the age of majority is in your state).
>
> If you have two or more children, you cannot deduct alimony that will change two or more times within a year before they reach a certain age between 18 and 24.

Other Alimony-Related Issues

Alimony can be deducted from your paycheck by an *earnings withholding order* directed to your employer, much the same way as child support. Also like child support, alimony is not dischargeable in bankruptcy.

Life Insurance

Life insurance can be used to secure the payment of alimony and child support in a divorce if the payer dies. Generally, the court cannot order a payer spouse to obtain life insurance to protect the former spouse and children against the risk of an early death. However, settlement agreements often provide that the payer spouse will obtain life insurance in a specific amount and designate the former spouse, or in some circumstances, a trust in which the children are beneficiaries, as irrevocable beneficiaries. The amount of insurance required should be determined by the amount and duration of support obligations. Sometimes agreements provide for one or more decreases in the amount of requested insurance coverage as the number of future payments decreases.

Health Insurance

If one spouse has been providing health insurance for the whole family under an employer-sponsored health insurance plan, that will change in the event of a divorce. A former spouse will no longer qualify as a "spouse" under the health insurance policy after the divorce. A former spouse is entitled to continued coverage under that health insurance policy under the provisions of COBRA for three years, but at individual premium rates. However, the former spouse will now be responsible for the premiums unless you agree otherwise.

Conclusion

Alimony is one of the great unknowns in a divorce, because it is up to the discretion of the judge. Because there is no formula, lawyers cannot tell you how long it will be for or for how much. However, you can bring certainty to uncertainty by reaching an agreement on alimony with your spouse and putting that agreement in writing.

Chapter Twelve

The Marital Residence

The marital residence is usually one of the first assets that has to be dealt with in a divorce. If you are not able to reach an agreement, the law in some states might require the court to order a sale of the house. Division of the proceeds, after payment of mortgages and sales costs, depends on the law of your state. In some states, the proceeds will be divided equally and in others they might be divided *equitably* (which means fairly, but not necessarily equally).

Determining the Marital and Nonmarital Interests

In the state that recognizes it, most marital residences are held in *tenancy by the entireties*, which is the legal name for joint ownership by a husband and wife. If the house is put in only one name for some reason, it is still marital property if acquired during the marriage. However, if you contributed your own separate property to acquire the house, you may be entitled to some credit for that contribution.

There are several ways to account for that contribution, depending on your state law. You could return each party's separate down payment plus interest or a percentage based on the amount of appreciation. Another method adopted by several states is called the *Brandenburg formula*, named for a case by that name. In that calculation, you determine the proportion of your contribution to the equity in the house, and then you get that percentage of the net sales proceeds first, before the balance is divided.

Example:
If you paid $10,000, your spouse paid $5,000, and the marital contribution through reduction in the mortgage balance is $85,000, then 10% is your separate share, 5% is your spouse's separate share, and 85% is marital property to be divided equally. If the sales proceeds are $200,000, then you will get $20,000, your spouse will get $10,000, and you will split the remaining $170,000 (equally or equitably, depending on your state).

Sometimes, married couples move into houses that one spouse owned prior to marriage, and never changed the title to both names. If you are the one that is not on the title, you may still be able to claim a portion of repairs, principal payments on the mortgage, and appreciation during the marriage.

If the case goes to trial, the court may order the sale of the marital residence by a trustee. A trustee will charge a fee on top of the realtor's fee, so it is better to sell the house before the trustee is appointed if you can agree on a price and a real estate agent. The court will usually give you time to reach agreement if you ask for this at trial.

Keep It, Sell Your Share, or Sell the House

Maybe you want to keep the house. Sometimes one spouse will give the house to the other spouse—out of guilt, for a waiver of alimony, or in trade for a pension or family business. In this event, there is still the mortgage and other housing expenses to deal with. The spouse that gets the house must have sufficient income to pay these expenses after the divorce.

Another way to deal with the house is for one spouse to buy out the other. You can agree on a price or you can have the house valued by an appraiser. If you cannot agree on an appraiser, you can each hire one and average the two values, or have your lawyers or your appraisers select someone to value the property independently. Sometimes the parties will agree to subtract a percentage for costs of sale—a percentage that takes into account 5% for a real estate agent and 2% for transfer and recording taxes is reasonable. Of course, there is no real sale. The percentage recognizes that future sales costs are being transferred to the spouse who keeps the house. That spouse may or may not sell the house *and* gets the benefit of future appreciation, so the percentage is usually negotiated or not applied at all.

The spouse who keeps the house will also assume payments on the first mortgage and may assume other mortgages or home equity loans as well, depending on terms negotiated. However, the spouse that sells his or her interest in the house will still have a contingent liability as long as his or her name is on the mortgage, even though the other spouse has promised to pay it. This might prevent the selling spouse from getting a loan for a new house. The selling spouse may ask the buying spouse to refinance or sell the house within a certain period of time in order to remove the contingent liability.

Some states have laws that allow a custodial parent to live in the family home with the children for a certain period of time before the sale. Even if you are the other parent and do not want to live in the family home, you can still try to get something in negotiations for giving up a right to use and possession. If you are the other party and you agree to let your spouse stay in the house, you ought to agree on what happens to the rent if he or she takes in a tenant or a boarder during the period of use and possession. Be sure to put this agreement in writing.

Many people wonder if they should sell the house or try to keep it. Most financial advisors think it is usually a mistake to try to keep the house, because it is an illiquid and costly asset. You cannot eat the equity in your house, and divorce is expensive enough without a big mortgage, taxes, insurance, and other housing costs. However, it really depends on your entire financial picture. You probably should sit down with your accountant or other financial advisor and see if you have the resources available to keep the house.

If you decide to sell the house, you may wish to have a *right of first refusal* so that either party may buy the house on the same terms as any offer received. You will need both parties to agree to the sale if both names are on the deed. Usually, a real estate agent will not even list the house for sale if both husband and wife do not sign the listing agreement. One uncooperative spouse in the house can prevent real estate agents and prospective buyers from viewing the house inside. In a situation where one spouse is more eager to sell the house, the other spouse's cooperation in the sale of the house can be a bargaining chip for the uncooperative spouse.

Without the cooperation of both parties, you will have to wait for a court order to sell the house, and that might take up to a year or more. This can be expensive if only one party is paying the mortgage. You may be entitled to some contribution from the other party if you are paying the entire mortgage. However, you will have to wait for an agreement or court order to get the contribution—and the mortgage is due each month.

You can change the locks on a jointly owned marital residence, since you are one of the owners. Of course, your spouse can hire a locksmith or break into the house, since he or she is the other owner.

Tax Considerations

Selling the family home requires some careful tax planning. Since 1984, Section 1041 of the IRS Code has provided that there is no income tax on a transfer of property during a marriage or incident to a divorce. Therefore, transfer of the house from one spouse to another in a divorce agreement is a tax-free transaction. The buying spouse will take the selling spouse's *tax basis* after the transfer. Tax basis is essentially the cost of the house plus repairs and sales expenses.

There may be a tax when the house is sold. However, under current tax law, married couples can exclude up to $500,000 in gains on the sale of their home, provided they both lived in the house for at least two of the last five years (the *use test*) and one of them owned the house for at least two years (the *ownership test*). Single taxpayers or taxpayers filing a separate return can exempt $250,000 in gains.

Therefore, a spouse who moves out for three years before the house is sold may have to pay taxes on his or her half of the house, while the spouse who stays in the house may be able to exclude up to $250,000 of the gain on his or her share of the proceeds. If your spouse is granted use of the house by a court order or written agreement, you may tack his or her period of living in the house onto yours to meet the use test, even if you have not lived in the house for two of the last five years.

A transfer *incident to a divorce* is defined in the tax code. It means that the transfer occurs within one year after the date on which the marriage ceases or is related to the cessation of the marriage. The IRS takes the position that a transfer is related to a divorce if it takes place within six years from the date of divorce, and it is set forth in a separation agreement or the divorce decree.

If the transfer is not mentioned in your separation agreement or divorce decree, or is not within six years of your divorce, the IRS will presume that it is not related to your divorce unless you can demonstrate facts that convince the IRS otherwise.

Example:
Tom and Mary bought a house several years ago for $100,000. It is now worth $500,000. In their divorce, Tom agrees to transfer his one-half interest in the house to Mary. Tom's basis is one-half the cost, or $50,000. Mary will take Tom's basis in the transfer, so her total basis will now be $100,000. When Mary sells the house, her gain will be $400,000 (the sales price of $500,000 less the tax basis of $100,000). If Mary is divorced and files as a single taxpayer, she will be entitled to exclude $250,000 of the $400,000 gain, but she will pay capital gains tax on the balance of $150,000. At 15%, she will pay $22,500 in federal income taxes plus state taxes.

If Tom and Mary from the previous example make a different type of agreement, the tax consequences change.

Example:
Say Tom agrees to let Mary live in the house for the next five years, and then they sell it and split the proceeds. If the house is sold for the $500,000 exclusion amount—or even $600,000 ($600,000 - $100,000 basis amount = $500,000)—all of the capital gain can be excluded. Now Tom can tack Mary's use onto his, and he still owns the house when it is sold. Tom and Mary each have a $250,000 exclusion available, since they now both meet the use and ownership tests of the IRS code. The tax on the sale of the house will be zero.

Chapter Thirteen

Retirement Funds

Retirement funds are a hidden asset in a lot of marital estates. They are frequently overlooked or are decided at the last minute. Yet, retirement funds make up more than half of the assets transferred in divorces every year.

Retirement funds come in different forms. Your private employer might have set one up, or you can set up your own, called an *Individual Retirement Account* (IRA). Federal, state, and local governments have different pension plans for their employees.

Private Tax-Qualified Plans

Most private employer pension plans are *tax qualified*, meaning the plan meets the requirements of the *Employee Retirement Income Security Act* (ERISA) and Section 401(a) of the Internal Revenue Code. The plan cannot discriminate in favor of highly paid individuals, and benefits must be reasonably determinable. If a plan is tax qualified, the employer may deduct contributions when they are made, but the employee does not have to report them as income until he or she retires.

Under the anti-alienation provisions of ERISA, you cannot assign your pension plan benefits to someone else. There was some question in the past as to whether a plan could honor a court order dividing benefits in a divorce and assign some of the pension to a spouse who was not a participant in the plan, which would thus cause the plan to lose its tax qualification and tax benefits. Congress clarified this question by enacting a special exception to the anti-alienation provisions in the

Retirement Equity Act (REA) of 1984, which requires you to have a court order to divide pension plans. The provisions of ERISA provide that tax-qualified pension plans can be divided by a *Qualified Domestic Relations Order* (QDRO) issued by a state divorce court without jeopardy to the favorable tax treatment of the plan. Congress also required that tax-qualified plans adopt procedures for paying benefits in accordance with a QDRO.

The QDRO rules only apply to plans provided by private employers under ERISA. The plans include 401(k) plans, Keogh plans, money purchase pension plans, defined benefit plans, target benefit plans, and profit-sharing plans. They do not apply to government, military, international organization, IRA, or private nonqualified plans. These plans have their own rules for dividing pensions in a divorce.

A *defined contribution plan* is an account in which contributions are made by the employee, the employer, or a combination of both. The account is fully funded and the value can be obtained by looking at the latest statement. All company 401(k) plans are defined contribution plans.

A *defined benefit plan* is a promise by the employer to pay monthly benefits at retirement. It is funded on a statistical basis by trying to determine what funds will be needed in the future to pay the benefit. Monthly statements do not accurately reflect the value of this pension. You normally have to hire an actuary to value these plans, which will normally cost between $150 and $400. The actuary makes certain assumptions—based on life expectancy, retirement age, appreciation, and inflation—to determine the future value of this plan. Then it is discounted to present-day value.

Qualified Domestic Relations Orders

Qualified Domestic Relations Orders (QDROs) have specific requirements that are set forth in the law, and they must be approved by the court and the pension plan administrator. If a court order does not meet these requirements, then a plan administrator will reject it because it will jeopardize the tax treatment of the plan for the employer and other employees. You can divide a pension in your separation agreement, but you need to have the agreement incorporated in an order before the plan will divide the pension. A QDRO is a judgment, order, or decree that meets the following requirements.

◆ The order must relate to alimony, child support, or marital property rights of a spouse, former spouse, child, or dependent of the plan participant.

◆ The order must be made under a state domestic relations law.

◆ The order must assign a part of the pension to an *alternate payee*. The alternate payee is the person receiving the benefits who is not the participant in the plan.

◆ The order must contain the following specific information:

  • the name and address of the participant and the alternate payee;

  • the amount or percentage of payment to the alternative payee, or a formula to determine the amount or percentage;

  • the number of payments or period of payment; and,

  • the name of the plan or plans.

◆ The order will not qualify if it requires the plan to:

  • provide some option or payment that is not available under the plan;

  • provide more benefits than the actuarial value of the participant's benefits; or,

  • pay benefits that are already assigned by a prior QDRO.

Survivor Benefit

The most important (and sometimes overlooked) part of any defined benefit pension is the *survivor benefit*. This is basically a life insurance policy for the former spouse of the participant. It provides that if the spouse survives the employee, the spouse will continue to receive a monthly check, usually about one-half of the original payment, for his or her lifetime. The survivor benefit can be assigned by a QDRO. If you fail to assign it in your QDRO and the participant dies, the payments to the surviving former spouse will stop and the benefit is lost. There is a cost for this benefit, and it is usually subtracted from the pension payments each month. The QDRO can also establish who will pay for this benefit and how it will be apportioned.

There are usually three issues in regards to survivor benefits to bargain over in a divorce case.

1. Will there be a survivor annuity?
2. Will the former spouse get all or just a portion?
3. Who will pay for it?

Nonemployee spouses bargain hard for survivor annuity, and it is easy to see why. When planning for retirement, you want to be receiving a monthly pension for the duration of *your* life, not your ex-spouse's life. If the employee spouse will not agree or the plan does not permit a former spouse to receive a survivor annuity, the nonemployee spouse can obtain a life insurance policy on the life of the employee spouse. Most employee spouses are not receptive to this solution.

Sometimes, the alternate payee is awarded the entire survivor annuity. This is inappropriate and a bad idea. It usually happens because the parties or counsel are not focusing on this issue, and the person whose rights are being traded—the future spouse of the plan participant—is not at the table. The alternate payee's survivor annuity should be limited to a percentage of the marital portion of the annuity.

Usually the survivor annuity is paid for by selecting the payment option *joint and survivor annuity,* rather than *single life annuity.* The joint and survivor annuity election results in a lower monthly annuity than the single life annuity option. This lower annuity is then divided between the plan participant and the alternate payee. The parties share the cost of the survivor annuity, but the survivor annuity only benefits the alternate payee, so he or she should pay the entire cost. This can be accomplished by lowering the percentage of the monthly annuity paid to the alternate payee from the percentage that would be paid before taking into account the cost of the survivor annuity. Of course, this can be a very complicated calculation.

Many times, a separation agreement will call for the division of retirement plans without giving many of the details. That leaves room to argue when it is time to draft the QDRO. It is better to resolve the details at the time of the separation, including whose lawyer will be responsible for drafting the QDRO and who will pay for it, and perhaps even attaching a copy of the QDRO to the agreement. Most plan administrators will review a QDRO in advance and tell you whether it will be accepted or not. Some have QDRO instructions and forms.

It is advisable to include a provision in the QDRO that the court will keep jurisdiction over your case if you need to make any changes in the QDRO required by the plan administrator. You can also include an alternative provision for compensation out of other assets if the plan administrator does not approve the QDRO.

Individual Retirement Accounts

Individual Retirement Accounts (IRAs) are relatively easy to value and divide. While the court can order the division of an IRA, it is not required. IRAs are not subject to the anti-alienation provisions of ERISA or the QDRO rules. Therefore, the parties can divide them by agreement. Your financial institution may only require a letter or a form to transfer the funds. In order for the transfer to be tax-free, however, it must be made under a divorce or separation instrument incident to a divorce.

Federal Government Plans

If you work for the U.S. Government, the Post Office, or Congress, or if you are a civilian employee of the military, then you have a defined benefit retirement plan (either Civil Service Retirement System or Federal Employee Retirement System, both discussed in the following sections). You also have a *Thrift Savings Plan* (TSP), which is a defined contribution plan.

The *Office of Personnel Management* (OPM) has issued regulations for dividing pension and health benefits for former spouses of federal employees. Government plans are not ERISA plans, and OPM will not recognize any order that is titled a Qualified Domestic Relations Order, unless the court specifically states that there are FERS or CSRS benefits involved and includes proper citations to the OPM regulations. Therefore, these orders are usually given a different name, such as *qualifying court order.*

Civil Service Retirement System

The *Civil Service Retirement System* (CSRS) plan covers federal government employees who entered the civil service before January 1, 1984. Benefits are based on your average annual earnings in your three highest salary years. You get 1.5% of this average for each of the first five years of service, 1.75% for each of the next five years of service, and 2% for all other years of service. Members of Congress, congressional employees, law enforcement officers, air traffic controllers, and certain other government employees are entitled to an enriched benefit computation. The survivor benefit can be any amount up to 55% of the retiree's annuity.

By applying this formula, you can estimate the monthly benefit of a federal CSRS pension if you know the three highest years of earning and the number of years an employee has worked for the civil service. An actuary can calculate the present value. The employee can obtain information about his or her benefits, or can authorize someone else to do so in writing. If you have to, you can obtain the information with a subpoena from the court.

Civil Service Retirement System employees can also elect to contribute up to 5% of their earnings to the federal Thrift Savings Plan (TSP). Contributions are tax deferred, and the government does not contribute to this plan. You will need a separate Qualifying Court Order to divide the TSP, which is administered by the Federal Retirement Thrift Investment Board. You can obtain information about an employee's interest in a TSP from:

Federal Retirement Thrift Investment Board
1250 H Street NW
Washington, DC 20005
202-942-1600
www.frtib.gov

Under CSRS, a federal employee does not make Social Security contributions or qualify for Social Security as a result of his or her federal employment. Sometimes, one spouse works for the federal government and the other spouse works for private industry. Federal law prevents states from treating the right to receive Social Security as an asset to be divided in a divorce in the same way a federal pension can be divided. Some states say that Social Security is not to be taken into account in dividing pensions. Other states give the courts discretion to make some equitable adjustment to the pension division in consideration of this factor.

Federal Employees Retirement System

The *Federal Employees Retirement System* (FERS) plan covers federal employees who were hired after January 1, 1984. The FERS benefit consists of the basic benefit plan, which pays 1% of the high three earnings average for each year of service; Social Security; and, a Thrift Savings Plan contribution by the government of 1% of the employee's pay, plus matching the first 3% and half of the next 2% the employee contributes.

International Organizations

International organizations and local governments have their own pension plans and their own regulations. For example, the World Bank and the International Monetary Fund have defined benefit plans with special rules for distribution. Contact these organizations for their required documents and any specific requirements.

Chapter Fourteen

Business

You may have a business—in the form of a sole proprietorship, general partnership, limited partnership, limited liability company, or corporation—that has been the source of income for the family. The family business may be in joint names.

For example, if it is a corporation, you and your spouse may *each* own fifty shares of stock, or you may own one-hundred shares of stock *jointly*. This ought to be sorted out in your agreement or by the divorce court.

When the business is not in joint names, the business owner is frequently surprised to learn that his or her spouse has a marital interest in the venture. When he or she receives discovery papers from his or her spouse's counsel asking for the books and records of the business, the owners ask, "They can't do that, can they?" Yes, they can.

The law provides that any assets acquired during a marriage other than by a gift or inheritance are marital or community property, regardless of who owns them. This applies to any business started during the marriage. Unless you have a prenuptial agreement, marriage creates a contract, which makes your spouse a silent partner in your business. This means you have to pay your spouse something to buy him or her out.

Valuing a Business

How much you need to pay depends on the value of the business. There are experts who will value a business based on the income of your business. They also make assumptions based on other similar businesses. Each party can hire experts, and experts can disagree widely on value, depending on the assumptions they use. If you cannot agree on a price, then the judge will listen to the experts for each party and make a decision.

When experts value a business, they look at more than sales and revenue. They include intangible aspects of a business and apply discounts based on each business's circumstances. Experts apply a discount for *lack of control* of a business. If you own less than 50% of a business, you may not have control of that business. This makes your interest less valuable. Another important discount is *lack of marketability*. The value of your business is reduced if it would be difficult to sell. This can sometimes reduce the value of a small business by half.

There may also be a large discount for *personal good will*. Personal good will is that portion of the value of a business attributed to the individual owner and not the business itself. In some states, that part of the business's value is not considered marital property, because it is based on the owner's continuing work at the business postdivorce. The rest of the value is *business goodwill*. If you have several retail stores in malls with a lot of employees, the personal aspect of your business may not be that great. However, if you are a one-person operation and all of your customers come to you because of your personal reputation, then personal goodwill may be most of the value of your business.

If you sell your business to someone else, you will pay capital gains tax on the sale. Sometimes these future taxes are subtracted in valuing the business for a divorce, even though there is no taxable sale in a divorce.

Double-Dipping

Divorcing spouses who own businesses often complain that their spouses and the divorce courts engage in "double-dipping" when both equitable distribution of material property and alimony are issues.

The argument is that the plaintiff's business valuation expert determines and testifies to the expected future earnings of the business, and the business's value is determined by a multiple of those earnings (capitalizing the earnings). The judge then awards a non-owning spouse a monetary award to adjust the equity, because the business owner keeps the business. Next, the plaintiff testifies about his or her future needs, additional education requirements, and other alimony facts, and the judge awards alimony. The business owner will have to pay alimony from the future earnings of the business, but the judge just awarded the spouse one-half of the value of the business based on those same earnings. Business owners feel like the judge awarded one-half of the business twice, so the owner is left with nothing.

Whether the business owner's double-dipping objection is a winner, a loser, or still in doubt depends on the law of the state. Equitable distribution deals with the past and present—it is the division of accumulated property between the spouses. Alimony awards are based on the future needs of the payee spouse and the future ability of the payer spouse to pay.

The analysis is tricky because both issues are decided at the same time on the same evidence. In general, there is no prohibition against the court dividing an asset and considering the income flow from that asset in the alimony award. The payer spouse's burden is to present evidence to the court, or in negotiations with the other party, of the impact of the equitable distribution (usually the business owner's cash payment to the other spouse) on the alimony issue. That payment reduces the business owner's ability to pay alimony and it reduces the payee's need for alimony.

Conclusion

The treatment of a business or business interest owned by one or both spouses in a divorce is extremely important to the overall outcome. It is important because the business interest is often a very valuable asset that is not sold, and therefore, must be valued, and that valuation can be the subject of expensive and controversial negotiations or litigation. Also, the business is often the primary source of income for the higher or sole income earning spouse, from which he or she will pay alimony and the monetary award granted in equitable distribution or the agreed buyout. Consequently, the business owner must present his or her case skillfully to avoid a result that amounts to "double-dipping" for the other spouse.

Chapter Fifteen

Bank Accounts, Stocks, and Other Assets

Distributing the assets of a marriage in a divorce can be complicated. It involves the intersection of domestic relations law and property law, and at times tax, business, and bankruptcy law as well. The court can distribute the marital property no matter who owns it, but not the separate property of the parties. In general, *marital property* involves property acquired during the marriage and *separate property* is property owned before the marriage, or obtained by gift or inheritance. Depending on your state law, marital property is divided equally or equitably (which means fairly but not necessarily equally), and you are free to divide property by agreement in any way you wish, whether it would be the same as the outcome of a trial or not.

Bank Accounts

Bank accounts are easy to divide equally—you just go to the bank and close the account. If you have been living apart for a time and keeping your own checking and savings accounts, you may wish to just let each party keep those individual accounts, provided they are roughly equivalent. You can adjust the difference in the division of other assets.

You can usually withdraw funds from a joint account with only one signature. Sometimes, a spouse will withdraw half or all of a joint account without the knowledge of the other spouse. That can be an unpleasant surprise if it happens to you. If you are in the early stages of a divorce, it may be wise to split your joint accounts into two separate accounts. You can do this by going to the bank and withdrawing half of a joint account and putting it in an account with only your name on it. Your spouse can do the same with the other half.

If you do not divide the accounts until later in your divorce, you can close your joint accounts and divide the proceeds once you have signed an agreement.

Stock and Stock Options

If you agree to divide a brokerage account, remember that appreciated stock has a hidden tax burden attached to it. Getting $20,000 in cash may not be the same as getting $20,000 in stock, because you might have to pay taxes when you sell the stock if it has gone up in price since you bought it.

The date you value the stock is important, because its price changes daily. One way to do it is to use the value on the date of division. That way, the spouses have the risks and benefits of ownership until the stock is divided.

There is no tax on the transfer of stock incident to a divorce. You take the same basis in the stock you receive incident to a divorce as your spouse had. However, there is no tax exemption for stock like there is for a personal residence. You need to be sure that you take into account the tax basis for the stock as well as the current price.

Example:
Your spouse paid $5,000 for the stock when it was purchased. That is your tax basis. You receive $20,000 in stock from your spouse as part of your divorce settlement. You sell the stock for $20,000. You have a capital gain of $15,000, which is the sales price minus your tax basis. Depending on your income (and other potential tax status issues), in most cases you will pay 15% long-term capital gains tax on the $15,000 capital gains, which is $2,250. Instead of $20,000, you really only got $17,750 after taxes. There may be state taxes to factor in as well.

You can see that all assets are not equal. If your spouse offers to give you $20,000 cash (or $20,000 worth of real estate) for $20,000 worth of your appreciated stock, it would be a good deal because the stock carries a hidden tax burden.

Many companies grant employees *stock options* as part of their compensation. A stock option is the right to buy the stock at a stated price. Usually, it is the employer's stock and the employee cannot exercise the option until some time in the future. These stock options are sometimes referred to as *golden handcuffs*, because the employee has to keep working for the company in order to cash in the stock option at some date in the future.

Stock options have a value, whether they are vested or unvested. They also have a value even if the stock is less than the option price. Stock can go up and down, and your future opportunities to sell a stock are factored into the formula for computing present-day value. Generally, stock options are entirely marital property if they were granted and became exercisable (vested) during the marriage. If they were granted before or became exercisable after, in most states the options are part marital and part nonmarital. It will take an expert to properly value stock options, but you can shortcut the process by one of two ways. You can simply agree on a value between the two of you, or you can agree that the proceeds will be divided equally, or in some other agreed portion, such as when the options are exercised.

Automobiles

You can sell your automobiles and divide the proceeds, but most people want to keep the automobile they are driving and adjust for the difference in values with a payment or with other assets. You can look up the *blue book* value on the Internet. Do not forget to subtract any automobile loans when determining the automobile's actual value. The parties can agree to execute automobile titles transferring ownership to the person who is keeping the car. You may also have to execute additional documents from the department of motor vehicles to make the transfer free from local automobile taxes. There is no income tax on the transaction. Each person will usually be responsible for his or her own automobile expenses after the transfer, including loan payments, insurance, repairs, gasoline, and traffic tickets.

Furnishings

In some states, if you try your case, the court will probably order you to sell your jointly owned personal property and split the proceeds. It will be easier if you can agree on how to divide the furniture, furnishings, clothing, jewelry, and other miscellaneous household items.

One method for doing this is to inventory everything. Then, flip a coin to see who will have the first choice. The winner picks the first item he or she wants on the list, then the other person selects. You alternate until everything is divided.

A lot of people get stuck on dividing the household items. It is good to keep it in perspective. Compared to the house and pension plan, this usually represents only a small portion of the marital estate, and it is not worth anything near what you paid for it.

Other Assets

There may be various other assets to distribute or dispose of, such as cash value of life insurance policies, frequent flyer miles, credit card award points, and country club memberships.

One of the areas that can become hotly contested concerns who will take ownership of family pets. People grow very attached to their pets and sometimes view them almost as though they were children. Therefore, you may agree to custody and visitation of a pet in a marital settlement agreement. If you have to try your case, however, the law views pets as personal property—like a table or a lamp. The judge will try to determine who owns the pet from all the facts and circumstances, and will give it to that person.

Chapter Sixteen

Debts

People who have a lot of property can afford to fight over who gets what. However, a lot of people do not have much in the way of assets. Mostly, they have a lot of debt. Their divorce is not only about dividing property, it is also about deciding who will pay what debt.

Identify Your Debt

The first thing to do is determine what debts you and your spouse have. You can order your credit report for free at **www.annualcreditreport.com**. Debts include credit cards, mortgages, home equity lines, car loans, student loans, tax liabilities, personal guarantees, or other loans. They can be in your name, your spouse's name, or both of your names.

Individual Debt

Ordinarily, you are not responsible for paying off the *individual debt* of another person. A credit card company cannot sue you for the individual debt of your spouse. Likewise, your spouse's late payments do not affect your credit report. However, there is an exception for community property states, where you may be held responsible for debts accrued during the marriage, even if they are the individual debts of your spouse. The individual debts of your spouse may also appear on your credit report in those states. Community property states are Arizona, California, Idaho, Louisiana, Nevada, New Mexico, Texas, Washington, and Wisconsin.

Joint Debt

Both spouses are responsible for paying off *joint debts*, such as credit card accounts, mortgages, other loans, and taxes. Credit card companies will report late payments or failure to pay under both names. A creditor can sue both of you or either one of you for the entire amount. This is called *joint and several liability.* A creditor can only collect the debt once. If you pay the entire amount, your spouse is off the hook to the creditor.

Authorized User

You can also be an authorized person on your spouse's credit account. This is usually done for convenience, so you can use your spouse's credit. It does not mean that you are responsible for payment of the entire account, but you may be responsible to a creditor for debts you charge as an authorized user. A creditor can report late payments in an authorized user's account.

Controlling Debt

You want to stop your debt from increasing. The best way to do this is to call the credit card company and divide any joint accounts into two separate accounts, one for you and one for your spouse. By law, a creditor cannot close a joint account because of a change in marital status, but can do so at the request of either spouse. You will still be responsible for the balance up until the call, but not for any charges your spouse makes after the account is divided. You will want to tell your spouse you are doing this before he or she is embarrassed by a declined card at the checkout counter.

If you are getting a divorce and you have joint credit cards, you can ask the creditor to close the accounts or convert them to individual accounts. It is a good idea to do this with accounts if one spouse is an authorized user as well. A lender does not have to convert the account to separate accounts, and you may have to apply for a new line of credit based on your income and assets alone. In the case of a mortgage or home equity line, the lender will usually require refinancing to remove a spouse's name from the mortgage.

However, the creditor is not a party to the divorce or marital settlement agreement. The original agreement between you and the creditor is still enforceable, even if you agree to something different in your divorce.

Example:
In their marital settlement agreement, Alex agreed to pay the joint credit card account of $5,000, because he used it to buy furniture for his new apartment after he left the marital residence. Months later, the credit card company called Anne, because no payments have been received from Alex. Anne sent copies of the marital settlement agreement to the credit card company, but the credit card company said it is not a party to the agreement and is not bound by it, and sues Anne. It also placed an adverse report in her credit record. Anne has no recourse except to sue Alex.

Allocating Debt

In a divorce, the court can take into account the debts that each person has in dividing the marital assets. You will provide the court with the latest statement for each debt, and ask the court to allocate property and debts in a fair and reasonable fashion. You can also agree which debts each person will be responsible for in a marital settlement agreement. The following are several ways to handle debt in a settlement agreement with your spouse.

◆ If there is cash available in a bank account or through the sale of the marital home, you can agree to use it to pay off the debt.

◆ You can allocate the debt by individual liability, indicating which party will pay which debt.

◆ You can divide debt by percentages, either equally or otherwise.

◆ One person can agree to pay the debt in exchange for getting more property.

It is easier to deal with debt if you can pay it off entirely, or assign responsibility for each debt to one person or the other. That is simpler than trying to keep track of each other's percentages in the future.

Indemnity

Typically, you will ask the other person to *indemnify* you and *hold you harmless* if he or she does not pay the debt. An *indemnity* means he or she will pay you back if you have to pay the debt. To *hold you harmless* means he or she will pay any costs you incur, such as attorney's fees, in such event.

Sometimes debt becomes overwhelming, and in those cases, bankruptcy can provide relief. Bankruptcy is discussed in some detail in Chapter 23.

Chapter Seventeen
Taxes

Every divorce causes tax consequences to the divorcing spouses. In your divorce, you may sell property and divide the proceeds with your spouse, divide marital property between you and your spouse, transfer property to your spouse, pay or receive alimony or child support, and determine which spouse shall be entitled to tax benefits related to the children. Your divorce will also result in a change in your federal tax filing status.

Because of all this, it is important to take tax consequences into account when going through a divorce. As you have seen in other chapters in this book (for example, in the discussions about alimony, child support, and the marital residence), tax considerations can be very complex. There are certain basic principles that provide ready answers to many divorce tax questions. This chapter will explain these basic tax principles as they may apply to your divorce.

Deductions and Credits
Your income tax is determined by applying the income tax rates to your taxable income. An item that qualifies as a *tax deduction* is deducted from your income when determining taxable income, thereby lowering your taxable income and your tax. If you are in the 25% federal tax bracket, a $100 tax deduction lowers your federal tax by $25. Home mortgage interest and alimony are examples of tax deductions.

An item that qualifies as a *tax credit* is deducted directly from your tax. Whatever your federal tax bracket, a $100 tax credit lowers your federal tax by $100. The child tax credit is an example of a tax credit.

Support

In determining your income taxes each year, you are entitled to deduct the amount you pay to your spouse or former spouse as alimony, and he or she is required to include it as income. You cannot deduct the money you pay as child support, and your spouse or former spouse is not required to include this amount in income.

You financial and family situation may indicate that you will pay (or be paid) both child support and alimony. In negotiating, it is always best to be clear about this distinction. If your income is substantially higher than your spouse's, you can save money (or pay more to your spouse at the same after-tax cost to you) by paying more alimony and less child support, or by some other transfers.

If you are the payee spouse, in evaluating an offer, be certain to take into account the fact that the alimony is taxable to you, and all the ramifications of that fact will fall to you. For example, your receipt of taxable alimony may result in a decrease or loss of the earned income credit you would be entitled to otherwise.

Once you reach an agreement, be sure that the agreement carries out your intentions regarding the tax character of support payments. In order to qualify as alimony, your payment must meet all of the following requirements.

- ◆ It must be to or on behalf of a spouse or former spouse.
- ◆ The payment must be in cash.
- ◆ Payment must be under a written divorce agreement or order.
- ◆ The agreement or order must not designate the payment as something other than alimony.
- ◆ Parties are not in same household.
- ◆ There cannot be a payment requirement after the death of the payee.
- ◆ Payment is not made in a year for which the parties file a joint return.

- The payment is not child support.
- Payment is not disqualified under the tax code's front-end loading rules.
- Payment is not disqualified under the tax code's rules regarding alimony payments that are really child support. (see Chapter 11.)

If your agreement or order lacks one or more of these requirements, your alimony payments may turn out to be nondeductible.

You may pay support after separation and before there is any written agreement or order. These payments cannot qualify as alimony. Usually, you will be eligible to file a joint income tax return for the year during which you make these early payments. If you do, the issue of whether a payment is alimony or not is of no importance. However, filing a joint return is voluntary. Your spouse could choose not to after you have made substantial payments. Always obtain a written agreement that payments are alimony, or if appropriate, that you will file joint returns, before making substantial support payments that are intended as alimony.

Deductions Related to the Family Home

You can deduct home mortgage interest and real property taxes of the marital home even if you no longer live there, if a dependent of yours lives in the home. If your divorce agreement or order provides that your spouse has use and possession of the jointly owned home, and that you must pay all of the mortgage payment and property taxes, you can deduct and your spouse must include one-half of your total payments as alimony. You can also deduct one-half of the home mortgage interest and real property taxes. If you solely own the home, you cannot claim any of the payments as alimony because it is your mortgage debt and your property tax obligation, but you can deduct all of the interest and taxes.

Transfers of Property

When you sell an asset, your *tax basis* in the asset is deducted from the sale price and the difference is capital gain (or loss). *Tax basis* means cost (sometimes adjusted as required by the tax rules for depreciation and other deductions).

Your separation agreement or divorce decree may provide that you transfer property to your spouse. For example, you may jointly own a stock brokerage account and agree that you will transfer your interest in the account to your spouse. The tax laws provide that such a transfer between spouses, or former spouses if pursuant to divorce, is not a taxable event. You do not report any gain or loss, and the tax basis you had in the property is transferred along with the property to your spouse. When you transfer an asset to your spouse or former spouse in a divorce settlement, the nontaxable treatment is automatic and cannot be avoided by the parties.

Example:

George and Mary jointly own stock they purchased for $20,000 that is now worth $200,000. They agree that it is fair and equitable that Mary pays George $100,000. Pursuant to an agreement, Mary transfers her interest in the stock to George. Has she paid the $100,000? She certainly has not paid $100,000 in after-tax dollars. Assuming a 20% combined federal and state capital gains tax, the transfer is only worth $82,000 in after-tax dollars (($100,000-$10,000 (Mary's basis)) x 20% = $18,000 built-in capital gains tax).

If you or your spouse own traditional IRAs, 401(k) accounts, or other such retirement assets, there are similar considerations. The funds in the accounts are not taxed when they are earned and deposited to the accounts. Therefore, when you withdraw these funds, you have to pay income taxes on the withdrawals. Watch for and take account of built-in tax gains and untaxed income in property to be transferred in divorce agreements.

When you sell your principle residence, you can exclude up to $250,000 ($500,000 on a joint return) of your gain from capital gains taxation.

Retirement Funds

A *Qualified Domestic Relations Order* (QDRO) is a court order that provides for payment of benefits from a qualified plan to someone other than the plan participant, generally the participant's former spouse. The benefits are taxable to the former spouse under the same tax principles that apply to payment to the plan participant.

The transfer of all or part of your traditional *Individual Retirement Account* (IRA) to your spouse is not a taxable event. From the date of the transfer the account is treated as your spouse's traditional IRA, and your spouse will incur the tax consequences of withdrawing funds from the IRA.

Filing Status

Your federal income tax is computed by applying the appropriate tax rates to your income. The tax rates depend upon your *filing status*, which in turn depends on, among other things, your marital status at the close of the taxable year. You are married until the judge signs the judgment or decree of divorce.

While married, you and your spouse can report your combined income on a joint tax return and calculate your tax using the *married, filing jointly* tax schedule, or you can file separate tax returns. In that case, you calculate your tax using the *married, filing separately* tax schedule. For years when you are unmarried, your tax filing status is either *single* or, if certain conditions are met, *head of household*.

Note that even if you are still married at the end of the year, you may be able to file as single if you qualify under a special rule that permits a married person to file as single. You may qualify if you meet the following guidelines:

♦ you file a separate return;
♦ you maintain as your home a household where a child for whom you may claim a dependency deduction lives for more than half the year;
♦ you provide more than half the cost of maintaining the household during the year; and,
♦ during the last six months of the year, your spouse did not live in the same house.

Each filing status has its own schedule of tax rates at various income levels. The married, filing separate schedule has the highest tax rates at any given income level below the maximum. The married, filing jointly schedule has the lowest tax rates. The rates on the tax schedule for the head of household or single filing status are the second and third lowest, respectively.

Married taxpayers generally will pay a lower total tax by filing a joint return. Sometimes divorcing spouses do not even check whether money can be saved by filing a joint return because they cannot work cooperatively. This is a mistake. For one thing, little cooperation is required. Generally, to file a joint tax return with your spouse (or maybe former spouse by the time the tax return has to be filed), you simply deliver your tax return paperwork to the same preparer.

In some cases, you (or your spouse) might pay a lower tax by filing separately, but that savings would be more than offset by the much higher tax that the other spouse would have to pay by filing separately. Unless there is an existing agreement to file jointly, the latter spouse may have to buy the other's cooperation in filing jointly. This can be done to mutual benefit. The spouse who saves by filing jointly pays the spouse whose tax increases by filing jointly an amount less than his or her savings and more than the other spouse's tax increase. By doing this, you have divided the tax savings from filing jointly. Of course, there may be a possible increase in tax preparation costs.

Head of Household

The tax rate schedule for head of household has lower rates than the single schedule. In order to qualify for filing as head of household, you must meet all of the following requirements.

- ◆ You must be unmarried on the last day of the year.
- ◆ You must maintain a household that is the home of a qualified dependent for more than one-half of the year.
- ◆ You must pay more than half of the cost of the household for a qualified dependent.

◆ Your former spouse cannot be a member of your household.

◆ You may not file a joint return.

Note the requirement of furnishing more than one-half of the support of the household for a qualified dependent. If you only have one child, you and your former spouse cannot both qualify as head of household, even if physical custody is divided equally.

Pitfalls and opportunities related to filing status often arise during the course of the divorce. For example, you may be able to have the divorce entered by December 31st or delayed to the next year. If you both have significant income, it is usually better to be divorced before the end of the year. Generally, if you or your spouse has little or no income, and you can and will file jointly, it is better to delay the divorce until next year.

If you have two or more children, another opportunity for tax planning around filing status is presented. If you and your spouse are each entitled to the dependency exemption for a child, then you can both qualify for head of household status.

Children

There are several tax benefits associated with children that can be allocated between the spouses by agreement or order, including:

◆ exemption for dependents;

◆ child tax credit;

◆ child care credit;

◆ Hope Credit;

◆ Lifetime Learning Credit; and,

◆ head of household status based on furnishing cost of a household for a qualified dependent.

Exemption for Dependents

You can deduct an amount from gross income for each dependent you are entitled to claim (including yourself). The dependency exemption is subject to phase out above a certain income, depending on filing status. In 2005, the phaseout began and ended at the following *adjusted gross incomes* (AGI).

Filing status	Phaseout begins at AGI	Phaseout complete at AGI
single	$149,950	$268,450
joint	$218,950	$341,450
married, filing separately	$109,475	$170,725
head of household	$182,450	$304,950

For divorced or separated parents, the requirements for claiming the dependency exemption include the following.

◆ *Qualified relationship.* Your children and stepchildren qualify, and certain other relationships may qualify as set forth in the Internal Revenue Code.

◆ *Support.* The parents together provided more than one-half of the child's support.

◆ *Custody.* The child was in the custody of one or both parents for a total of more than one-half of the year.

◆ *Marital status.* The parents are divorced or legally separated by court decree, separated under a separation agreement, or have lived apart the entire last six months of the year.

◆ *Age.* The child must be under age 19 at the close of the taxable year, or under age 24 at the close of the taxable year and a full-time student for at least five months.

If these requirements are met and you are the custodial parent, you are entitled to claim the dependency exemption. You are the custodial parent if you had physical custody of your child for more than one-half of the year.

If you are the noncustodial parent, you are entitled to the dependency exemption if the requirements are met and the custodial parent releases the dependency exemption to you. This is done by signing and delivering IRS Form 8332. The non-custodial parent must attach the release to his or her tax return. The custodial parent may release the dependency exemption one year at a time, or may execute a single release that recovers all future years. Release of the exemption is often conditioned upon timely, full payment of child support.

All other things being equal, your agreement should allocate the dependency exemption to the spouse who will obtain the most tax benefit from the exemption. This will generally be the spouse in the higher tax bracket, unless that spouse is well into the phaseout income range.

If you have two or more children, and both spouses have significant taxable income, your agreement should generally allocate at least one dependency exemption to each parent so that you both can qualify for head of household filing status (if you meet the other requirements).

Child Tax Credit

You are entitled to a child tax credit against tax for each child under age 17 for whom you can claim the dependency exemption. The credit is subject to a phaseout at incomes beginning at an AGI of $110,000 on a joint return, $75,000 for a single or head of household return, and $55,000 for a married, filing separately return. If you are divorced or separated, and you are the custodial parent, you are entitled to claim the credit unless you release it to the noncustodial parent.

Dependent Care Credit

You may be able to claim the dependent care credit in connection with day care or similar expenses. If you are the custodial parent, or the noncustodial parent and the custodial parent has released the dependency exemption to you by executing Form 8332, this credit is available for your expenses for child care services you incur to enable you to work. In order to qualify, your child must be 13 years or under at the close of the tax year. In 2005, the credit was 35% of the allowable expense, up to a maximum of $3,000 credit per child and subject to a phased reduction to 20%, which begins at an AGI of $15,000 and is complete at an AGI of $43,000.

Cafeteria Plans

Many employers offer so-called *cafeteria plans* that permit employees to elect to receive part of their salary as reimbursement of certain tax-favored expenses, such as day care expenses on an income tax-free basis. Depending on your circumstances, it may be more advantageous to elect tax-free reimbursement, if it is available to you, rather than claiming the dependent care credit.

There is a Hope Credit of up to $1,500 per student for the first two years of education after high school. There is also a Lifetime Learning Credit of up to $2,000 per family after the first two years. This benefit is phased out at $50,000 income per year for a single person and $100,000 for a married couple filing jointly.

Chapter Eighteen

The Marital Settlement Agreement

The marital settlement agreement is the essence of your divorce. It resolves every issue of your marriage and divorce, and it will eventually become incorporated by the court into your divorce decree. Therefore, you need to take great care in what you put in it.

If you have a marital settlement agreement, when the time for divorce comes, you can tell the judge that everything has been resolved and there is nothing left for the court to do but give you a divorce. In the meantime, you can live as though you were single and unmarried.

Once the agreement is signed, you can even date other people without risk to your legal case. You are still technically married until the court grants your divorce, and adultery is still adultery. However, adultery cannot affect property division and alimony, because they have already been decided by your agreement.

Only the court can grant a divorce, but an agreement is a contract between the two of you. You do not need to file it with the court until the divorce. It is valid and enforceable by the court from the day it is signed. It is like a private divorce.

While the court has legal requirements for a divorce, such as residency, jurisdiction, and grounds, there are no such requirements for a marital settlement agreement. You might have to live apart for a period of time before you can file for divorce, but you can sign a marital settlement agreement today, whether you are living apart or not.

A divorce court judge is limited by the legislature in what he or she may order in a divorce. You do not have these limitations in a marital settlement agreement. For example, if the court in your state cannot order title to real estate changed, then the judge could only order your home sold if you go to trial. However, you are free to work out a different arrangement by agreement, and one spouse can agree to buy the house from the other.

An agreement can be more specific and go into greater detail than a court decree. A judge may order custody and visitation in one paragraph. You can include a parenting plan in your agreement that specifies the details of custody, a visitation schedule, homework and television routines for the children at each house, and much more.

Many states do not make provisions in the law for a judge to order support for college costs for children. However, if the parties agree on this, they can put it in their marital settlement agreement.

Even when the court cannot order certain provisions in a divorce trial, the court does have the power to enforce such provisions if they are included in a marital separation agreement. In other words, the parties can make an agreement with provisions that the court could not order in the first place, and these provisions will become a valid and enforceable order of the court when the agreement is incorporated into the final order of divorce.

What to Include

The marital settlement agreement needs to cover everything about your divorce, including children, support, property, and legal fees. The marital settlement agreement begins with the effective date and the parties. The agreement will set forth the facts of your marriage, which are called *recitals* or *whereas clauses*. This will include the date and place of your marriage, your children and their birth dates, and the date of your separation (if you are separated).

Every agreement requires *consideration,* or an exchange of something of value, in order to make it valid. This is a formality required by law, and it can be one dollar, ten dollars, or anything else of value. The consideration in marital settlement agreements is usually the *mutual promises* you are making to each other in the agreement.

Your agreement will set forth the terms of your separation and state that you can live separate and apart as though you were single and unmarried without interference from your spouse. It will also state that from the date of the agreement forward, you will no longer have a marital interest in the income, property, or estate of the other, except as set forth in the agreement. You will each waive your right to inherit from the other.

The agreement will address all issues related to your children. You will need to decide who will make long-term parenting decisions, such as education, medical care, and religion.

Issues to Be Negotiated

You can use the questions on the following pages as a way to organize what you want in a settlement.

POINTS OF NEGOTIATION CHECKLIST

Children

❏ Where will the children go to school?
❏ Who will decide if they go to public or private school?
❏ What about tutors and extracurricular activities?
❏ Who will decide about the need for the children's medical and dental care?
❏ What doctors and dentists will they see?
❏ What medications will they take?
❏ Who will decide if they need braces, cosmetic treatment, or therapy?
❏ What religion will the children be raised in?
❏ What will be their last names?
❏ Who will give consent if they want to get married or join the armed services before age 18?
❏ Who will select a lawyer if the children have a lawsuit?
❏ Where will the children live most of the time?

continued

❑ What will be their routines at each house for homework, television, and going to bed?

❑ What will the schedule be for time-sharing or visitation?

❑ What will the schedule be for each week, holidays, vacations, and summer?

❑ What will happen to these arrangements if one parent relocates?

Child Support

❑ How will the financial needs of the children be supported?

❑ Who will pay child support and how much?

❑ Will it be paid directly to the other party by personal check or through the court?

❑ Will it be paid once a month, twice a month, or every two weeks?

❑ Will it be adjusted each year for inflation or not?

❑ When will child support stop?

❑ Who will pay for health insurance?

❑ What about uncovered medical expenses?

❑ Who will pay for day care and summer camps?

❑ What about expenses for extracurricular activities like piano, soccer, ballet, or karate?

❑ Who will pay for religious celebrations, weddings, or automobiles?

❑ How will college expenses be handled?

Note: The court always has the final say on child custody, visitation, and child support. It cannot delegate this authority to the parties, a third party mediator, or an arbitrator. The court can consider the opinion of the parties and third parties, and often follows these recommendations. However, the court must make its own decision based on the best interest of the child. The court can always modify custody, visitation, and child support if circumstances change and modification would be in the best interest of the child.

Alimony

❏ Is any type of spousal support needed?
❏ How much and for how long?
❏ Should there be a cost of living escalation?
❏ When does spousal support terminate?
❏ Is it modifiable or non-modifiable in the future?
❏ Who will pay the legal fees for the divorce?
❏ Is there life insurance to secure child support and spousal support?
❏ What about health insurance for each spouse?

Property

❏ What will happen to the marital home?
❏ If it is to be sold, when will it be listed for sale and at what price?
❏ How will the sales proceeds be divided?
❏ If one spouse buys the other one out, what is the price and what are the terms for payment?
❏ How will you deal with the mortgage if it is in both names?
❏ Who will draft the deeds and pay the costs for transfer?
❏ What happens to the automobiles, household furniture, furnishings, jewelry, clothing, and other personal items?
❏ How will bank accounts and stock be divided?
❏ What happens if there is a family business?
❏ How will retirement funds be divided? Will there be a survivor annuity, and if so, who will pay for it?
❏ Whose lawyer will draft the court order for dividing retirement funds and who will pay for it?

Taxes

❏ Will you file joint or separate returns?
❏ Who will prepare the returns or pay for their preparation?
❏ Who will get the exemption for the children?
❏ Who will pay if there are taxes due?
❏ How will a refund be divided?
❏ What happens if there is an audit for past years?
❏ Who will pay any taxes due on sale of the house, stock, or distribution of pensions?

Negotiating the Marital Settlement Agreement

The easiest and most inexpensive way to reach an agreement with your spouse is to sit down at the kitchen table and talk about it. This will be difficult and it will not always work, because after all, if you were able to discuss your differences and resolve them, you might not be getting a divorce. However, some couples are able to work out their own agreement. This section discusses some tips for doing it yourself.

Start Talking Early

Most divorces can be settled in a couple of hours with a sharp pencil and a calculator—if everyone approaches it rationally. Stick to the finances and do not get caught up in the emotional part of it. Remember, this is a business deal—not a time to extract revenge. You can settle your divorce now, or after a lot of litigation and legal fees when everyone is worn down. Guilt, which frequently can be used as a negotiating tool, loses its power with the passage of time.

Set Aside the Time

Pick a quiet time when you can concentrate. You may be making progress, but if you stop to take a telephone call, you may return to find that things have unraveled.

Reschedule if Necessary

If things do not go well, someone gets angry, or you feel that you are losing the negotiation, reschedule for another time. It is important that both sides feel good about the agreement. Try not to leave a meeting open, even if the only decision left is when to schedule the next meeting. Take it two or three hours at a time, even if you have to schedule several sessions. Set a deadline for the end of each meeting so that the meeting does not just drag on and on without anything being accomplished.

Set an Agenda

Agree ahead of time on what to cover. For example, this week focus on the children and next week on the house. You can use the questions on pages 181–183 as an agenda.

Stay Focused

Try to stay on track and do not get distracted by arguments. After you have been married for even a short time, you both know what buttons to push to irritate each other. Try not to push any buttons or let any of your buttons be pushed.

Do Not Get Bogged Down

Try to discuss the issues you can resolve easily first. No matter how bad things are, you will be able to find something you can agree on. If you come to trouble or an impasse, mark that issue down as "not agreed" and come back to it later, after addressing some of the other items on your agenda.

Select a Neutral Place

The kitchen table is usually a good place to meet. Your office or your spouse's office may not be a good place. Find a place where you both feel comfortable.

Keep the Children Out of It

This is a matter for adults. Assure the children that no matter what happens, they will still have a mother and a father who love them very much. Do not involve them in the dispute. Do not even have them around. They will interrupt and distract you, and it will upset them and you. Assure them that they will be provided for, even if you are worried about it.

Listen Carefully

Many people think that if they just talk and talk, the other person will finally see that they are right and agree with them—but it does not happen that way in real life. In negotiations, it is usually more productive to listen. Do not presume you know what is or is not important to your spouse. Asking questions is better than trying to read minds.

Listen for Verbal Clues

People frequently telegraph their thoughts unknowingly. "I don't think I can go much higher" is different than "I cannot go any higher." It means that person can go a little higher. A good question to keep asking is, "Is that the best you can do?" Then, see if you get any verbal clues.

Set Goals and Objectives

Knowing what you want is a powerful negotiating tool. One of the questions good lawyers ask in the initial conference is "What do you want from your divorce?" Most people do not know what they want from the divorce. Before you begin to negotiate, write down your best, middle, and last position for each issue. Then, number them according to your priorities. That way, you will know what is more important to you; for example, the marital home or the retirement funds. A *negotiation worksheet* on page 189 is included for this purpose. This, of course, is for your use only. You do not want to show it to the other side.

Ask for What You Want

You not only need to know what you want, but you need to say what you want. It is not enough to just think about something. You also have to say it out loud. Salespeople call this *asking for the order*. It is surprising how many people forget to ask for what they want or just feel uncomfortable about asking.

Be Flexible

If you have an item with weak priority, and you find by asking questions and listening that your spouse feels strongly about it, you may want to be flexible on that issue. A good agreement requires some compromise on both sides. You cannot have it all your way and you cannot let your spouse steamroll you either. You need to strike a balance between knowing what you want and being flexible with the other side.

Know Your Best Alternative to a Negotiated Agreement

Professional negotiators say it is good to know your *best alternative to a negotiated agreement* (BATNA). In this case, your BATNA is always going to be to let the judge decide. With a little research, you can determine what a judge will likely rule, or at least get some parameters.

Gather Information

Having information at your fingertips can sometimes be key to controlling and winning a negotiation. If you complete the financial information forms in this book before your negotiation and prepare the financial notebook as discussed in Chapter 3, you will have every detail at your fingertips.

Be Polite but Firm
People want to give more in negotiations to others who are nice to them. When people are not nice, it causes others to dig in their heels and be defensive in negotiations. If your spouse is rude or controlling, simply postpone the discussions to another day. Remember, studies have shown that negotiators who are bullies are usually far less effective than negotiators who are polite but firm.

Have High Expectations
Negotiators who start out expecting more usually do better than negotiators who have lower expectations, even if they do not get everything they want.

Let Your Spouse Make the First Offer
You can make sure you are not aiming too low by letting your spouse say what he or she wants first. Sometimes, a spouse really does not know what he or she wants, or cannot make a decision. In those cases, you will have no choice but to make the first offer, but always try to ascertain what the other side wants first.

Repetition Sometimes Works Better than Persuasion
Children are the best persuaders, because they will ask for something ten times and if you say no ten times, they will ask an eleventh time in hopes that you will change your answer to yes. Sometimes a spouse will finally just give in to a repeated request the same way parents sometimes do.

Slow Down
If everything is going your way, you want to slow things down. Someone who agrees in haste will likely repent in leisure. In order to make this agreement stick and be something that everyone can live with, you will want to take your time and not just steamroll over your spouse.

Stay Positive

Instead of using negative threats, reframe your positions as positive affirmations. Rather than saying "If we do not settle, I will have to sue you and we will both spend a lot of this money on lawyers," you can rephrase and say the same thing as a benefit—"I am pleased that we are able to discuss a settlement, because we can save a lot of money on lawyers if we can reach an agreement."

Beware the Nibbler

After you have reached an agreement and shake hands, the nibbler will ask for "just one more thing." At that point, there may be goodwill and you might be inclined to make concessions to keep the deal, but keep in mind that most concessions are made in the last 10% of negotiations—so keep your guard up. The appropriate response is "If I do that, what will you do?" That will usually be enough to send the nibbler back to the original deal. On the other hand, if nibbling is a technique you can use to your advantage, then by all means, nibble away.

Notes

If you do work out an agreement and you make notes, signing those notes might be considered an agreement. If it is not in the proper legal language, you may be signing something other than what you intended or thought you agreed to. This might be a good time to have a lawyer review your agreement before you sign it.

NEGOTIATION WORKSHEET

Issue	Best	Middle	Worst
1. Child Custody			
2. Child Support			
3. Alimony			
4. Property			
5. Legal Fees			

SAMPLE VOLUNTARY SEPARATION AGREEMENT

THIS AGREEMENT, the original of which being executed in triplicate, is made this **15**[th] day of **April, 2007**, by and between **Mary Jo Johnson**, hereinafter referred to as "Wife" and **William T. Johnson**, hereinafter referred to as "Husband."

WITNESSETH:

WHEREAS, the parties hereto were married on the **9**[th] day of **June**, **1993**, in **Augusta, Georgia**; and

WHEREAS, no children were born to the parties as a result of said marriage; and

WHEREAS, relations between the parties have been such that they have separated as of the **2**[nd] day of **January, 2007**; and they have mutually and voluntarily determined to live separate and apart; and

WHEREAS, in view of the foregoing, the parties desire to settle and determine their obligations to each other, including the maintenance and support of the parties, and their children, and all rights, claims, relationships, or obligations between them arising out of their marriage or otherwise; and

WHEREAS, each party hereby declares that he or she has had independent legal advise by counsel of his or her own selection, the Wife being represented by **Nicholas Johns**, Esquire, and the Husband being represented by **Jacob James** Esquire; that each has made a full disclosure to the other of his or her financial assets and liabilities; that each fully understands the facts and all of his or her legal rights and obligations; and that after such advice, disclosure, and knowledge, each believes this Agreement to be fair, just, and reasonable and that each enters into same freely and voluntarily;

NOW, THEREFORE, in consideration of the premises, and in the mutual covenants and agreements hereinafter contained, and in further consideration of the sum of **One Dollar ($1.00)**, to each of the parties in hand paid by the other, the receipt whereof is hereby acknowledged, the parties hereto covenant and agree as follows:

SEPARATION

1. The parties separated mutually and voluntarily on **January 2, 2007**, with the intent of ending their marriage, and said separation has continued to the present time. It shall be lawful for each party at all times hereafter to live separate and apart from the other party at such place or places as he

or she may from time to time choose or deem fit. Each party shall be free from interference, authority, and control, direct or indirect, by the other, as fully as if he or she were single and unmarried. Neither party shall endeavor to compel the other to cohabit or dwell with him or her, nor in any manner or form whatsoever molest or trouble the other party. Nothing herein contained shall be construed to bar or prevent either party from suing for divorce in any competent jurisdiction because of any past fault on the other party's part. Henceforth, except as set forth herein, each of the parties shall own, have, and enjoy, independent of any claim or right of the other party, all items of property of every kind, nature, and description, wheresoever situated, which are now owned or held by him or her with full power to him or her to dispose of the same as fully, effectively, and effectually in all respects and for all purposes as if he of she were unmarried. Both parties agree to execute all necessary documents to carry out the terms of this Agreement.

WAIVER OF ALIMONY

2. In consideration of the mutual agreement of the parties to voluntarily live separate and apart and the provisions contained herein for the respective benefit of the parties, each party releases and waives to the other any claim or right to temporary or permanent alimony, support, or maintenance, whether past, present, or future.

HEALTH INSURANCE

3. Each party has his or her own health insurance coverage.

PERSONAL PROPERTY

4. Furnishings and Miscellaneous Items. It is agreed that the parties will be able to separate all their household furnishings, clothing, jewelry, and similar items of tangible personal property to their mutual satisfaction, and all of such property shall be and become the sole and separate property of the individual who has possession and control thereof following a dissolution of the marriage, except that the parties may, by separate mutual, written agreement signed by both, agree that specific items in the possession of one shall be the sole and separate property of the other, to be distributed to the rightful owner at such time as the rightful owner may request.

5. Vehicles. The parties agree that the Wife shall keep the ___**2003**___ ___**Toyota**___ automobile, which is in her name, and has no lien. The Husband shall keep the ___**2002 Ford**___ automobile, which is in his name, and has no lien. Each party shall assume all financial responsibility for his

continued

or her vehicle. The parties agree to do any and all acts necessary to assign their interests and financial responsibilities in said vehicles accordingly. Each party will insure his or her own vehicle.

6. Bank and Brokerage Accounts. Each party will keep the individual bank and brokerage accounts that are in his or her own name. The parties have a joint bank account at the __Main Street Bank__, which they agree to close and divide equally.

7. Retirement Funds and Other Employment Benefits. The Husband has a pension plan and other benefits through his employer. The Wife has a pension plan and other benefits through her employer. In consideration of the other property transfers in this Agreement, the parties agree that each shall keep the retirement funds and other employment benefits that are in his or her own name.

8. Frequent Flyer Miles. The parties agree that each will keep the frequent flier miles in his or her own name.

OUTSTANDING DEBTS

9. The parties have closed all joint credit cards, and each party will obtain credit in his or her own name. The parties agree to assume all responsibility for the payment of his or her own individual debts described in this paragraph, and each agrees to indemnify and hold harmless the other party from any obligation or liability for the aforementioned credit card debt.

10. Except as otherwise proved herein above, neither party has incurred any debts or obligations heretofore for which the other may be held liable. The parties agree that neither will incur hereafter any liability or obligation whatsoever upon the credit of the other, or for which the other might be held liable, except that the parties may refinance the marital residence by mutual agreement, which shall not be unreasonably withheld. Each party agrees to indemnify and hold harmless the other from any obligation, liability, or expense incurred by the other by virtue of any breach of this paragraph, including attorney's fees he or she may necessarily incur in connection therewith.

TAX MATTERS

11. It is understood and agreed by the parties that the parties may file separate or joint tax returns as allowed by law.

REAL PROPERTY

12. Marital Residence. The parties are the joint owners of the real property located at __123 Bond Avenue, St. Louis, Missouri 63401__, valued at approximately __$500,000__ (the "marital residence"). The marital residence is encumbered by a first mortgage of approximately __$250,000__. Promptly upon the signing of this Agreement, the parties will list the marital residence for sale at an agreed-upon listing price. The __Wife__ will have exclusive use and possession until the sale. The parties will split equally the costs associated with the marital residence until the sale. The net proceeds of sale will be divided equally between the parties.

13. **Rental Condominium.** The __Husband__ owns a condominium at __456 Jackson Avenue, St. Louis, Missouri 63401__, which the parties agree is his premarital property. The __Wife__ waives any interest in said rental condominium.

LEGAL FEES

14. Each party agrees to be responsible for his or her own legal fees in connection with the negotiation of this Agreement and any action that either of the parties may undertake for either a limited or absolute divorce in whichever jurisdiction said action is ultimately filed. The reasonable cost of any legal services required in the Court enforcement of this Agreement will become the obligation of the person whose breach required the enforcement of the Agreement, provided the movant prevails and provided that the Court feels a legal fee should be awarded.

MUTUAL RELEASES

Except as otherwise provided in this Agreement:

15. Each party shall be fully released by the other from any obligation for alimony, support, and maintenance, except as hereinabove set forth, each accepts the provisions hereof in full satisfaction of all obligations for support, or otherwise arising out of the marital relation of the parties, and relinquishes any right or claim to the earnings, accumulation, money, or property of the other.

16. All property and money received and retained by the parties pursuant hereto shall be the separate property of the respective parties, free and clear of any right, interest, or claim of the other party, and each party shall have the right to deal with and dispose of his or her separate property, both real and personal, as fully and as effectively as if the parties had never been married.

17. Provided all obligations hereunder have been performed, each party hereby releases and forever discharges the other, his or her heirs, executors, administrators, assigns, property, and estate from any and all rights, claims, demands, or obligations arising out of or by virtue of the marital relation of

continued

the parties, including loss of consortium, dower rights, curtesy, homestead rights, right of election regarding the estate of the other, or to take against the Will of the other, right of inheritance or distribution in the event of intestacy, right to act as administrator of the estate of the other, similar or related rights under the laws of any state or territory of the United States or of any foreign country, as such laws exist or may hereafter be enacted or amended. Nothing herein, however, shall constitute a waiver of either party to take a voluntary bequest or bequests under the Will of the other.

18. Except for any cause of action for divorce which either party may have or claim to have, and except for the enforcement of the provisions of this Agreement, each party does hereby release and forever discharge the other of and for all causes of action, claims, rights, or demands whatsoever, in law or in equity, which either of the parties ever had or now has against the other.

INCORPORATION IN ANY DECREE OF DIVORCE

19. The parties hereto agree that any action for Divorce between them shall be subject to and governed by the terms of this Agreement, and that this Agreement shall be presented to the appropriate court for affirmation, ratification, and incorporation in any Decree of Divorce, Limited or Final, which may be entered in any action between the parties, and shall merge in the Decree.

FULL DISCLOSURE

20. The parties represent that each has made full disclosure to the other of his or her financial assets and liabilities, and that all such assets and liabilities have been addressed in this Agreement. The parties are relying on this disclosure, and the knowledge gained through their marriage, and not upon the representations of any other person. Their rights to discovery and valuation of assets, including real estate and pension plans, have been explained to them, and they have knowingly waived such rights. If assets of either party are discovered after the signing of this agreement, such assets shall be divided between the parties in the following manner: forty percent (40%) of the value of each previously undisclosed asset shall be the property of the party failing to disclose the asset, and sixty percent (60%) of the value of each previously undisclosed asset shall become the property of the party to whom disclosure was not made. If liabilities of either party are discovered after the signing of this agreement, such liabilities shall become the sole responsibility of the party failing to disclose the liabilities. The parties shall do any and all acts necessary to assign their interests and financial responsibilities in said assets and/or liabilities accordingly.

GENERAL PROVISIONS

21. The parties agree that no provision of this Agreement, except as otherwise set forth herein, shall be modifiable by any court except by agreement of the parties. Any modification or waiver of any of the provisions of this Agreement shall be effective only if made in writing and executed with the same formality as this Agreement. The failure of either party to insist upon strict performance of any of the provisions of this Agreement shall not be construed as a waiver of any subsequent default of the same or different nature.

22. Each of the parties hereto shall, from time to time, at the request of the other, execute, acknowledge, and deliver to the other party any and all further instruments that may be reasonably required to give full force and effect to the provisions of this Agreement.

23. If any provision of this Agreement is held to be invalid or unenforceable, all of the other provisions shall, nevertheless, continue in full force and effect.

24. Failure to perform any of the obligations contained herein shall create a lien on the estate of the obligor.

25. This Agreement contains the entire understanding of the parties, and there are no representations, warranties, covenants, or undertakings of, by, or between the parties other than those expressly set forth herein.

26. This Agreement shall be construed in accordance with the laws of the state of __Missouri__ .

IN WITNESS WHEREOF, the parties being fully advised as to the matters herein set forth, have set their hands and affixed their seals on the date set forth below.

WITNESSES:

*Mary Jo Johnson*_____(SEAL)
 __Mary Jo Johnson__, WIFE

*William T. Johnson*_____(SEAL)
 __William T. Johnson__ , HUSBAND

continued

STATE OF __Missouri__   )
COUNTY OF __Boone__   ) to wit:

I HEREBY CERTIFY that before me the undersigned Notary Public, person-ally appeared __Mary Jo Johnson__ known to me to be the person whose name is subscribed to the within instrument, who, after being sworn, made oath in due form of law under the penalties of perjury that the mat-ters and facts set forth in the foregoing Agreement with respect to the voluntary separation of the parties are true and correct as therein stated and acknowledged said Agreement to be her act.

WITNESS my hand and official seal this __15ᵗʰ__ day of __April, 2007__.

C. U. Sine
Notary Public
My commission expires:

STATE OF __Missouri__   )
COUNTY OF __Boone__   ) to wit:

I HEREBY CERTIFY that before me the undersigned Notary Public, person-ally appeared __William T. Johnson__, known to me to be the person whose name is subscribed to the within instrument, who, after being sworn, made oath in due form of law under the penalties of perjury that the mat-ters and facts set forth in the foregoing Agreement with respect to the voluntary separation of the parties are true and correct as therein stated and acknowledged said Agreement to be his act.

WITNESS my hand and official seal this __15ᵗʰ__ day of __April, 2007__.

C. U. Sine
Notary Public
My commission expires:

Ways to Reach an Agreement

There are other ways to reach an agreement if you and your spouse are not able to work it out yourselves. Some are more cooperative in nature, like mediation and collaborative law, while others are more traditionally adversarial, like arbitration, negotiation by attorneys, or trial.

Mediation

A *mediator*, who is a neutral third party trained in special mediation techniques, can sometimes bring the parties together and try to resolve their disputes. A mediator does not represent either party. The mediator will guide the discussions, explore and offer options, explain the law, and facilitate an agreement.

Both parties must agree to mediation, or a court may require mediation. Mediation is less costly than a trial, and the parties can control the outcome rather than a judge. It is also faster than litigation.

You may hire your own private mediator. Lawyers, psychologists, accountants, ministers, or anyone else with proper training can be a mediator. Fees range from $100 to $300 an hour, split between the two parties.

Mediation sessions are usually two or three hours long in the mediator's office or conference room. The first meeting may be an orientation and the second meeting might be an exchange of financial information.

Once you have reached an agreement, it will not be final or binding until it is in writing and signed by both parties. In mediation, you are not required to sign the agreement if you do not like it. The mediator will probably recommend that you have a lawyer review the agreement before you sign. Once you do sign, the agreement will be binding and can be enforced by the court.

Collaborative Law

Collaborative law allows everyone to concentrate on settling the case instead of focusing on litigation. Each party hires a lawyer trained in collaborative law, and everyone signs a participation agreement that requires both lawyers to withdraw if the case does not settle and goes to litigation.

To reach a resolution and settle your matter, there are a series of four-way meetings among the parties and the lawyers. Everyone participates in the meetings. Instead of communicating through lawyers, everyone can talk face-to-face to all the participants at the meetings.

Another feature of collaborative law that differs from a traditional trial is that both sides make full and early disclosures of all financial issues. Also, instead of hiring competing experts to value assets or make custody assessments, the parties agree on one expert, thus saving the double expenses (sometimes triple, if a tiebreaker is needed), and setting an environment of cooperation and agreement.

Collaborative lawyers are allowed to consider long-term issues as opposed to just resolving the financial issues. This helps to preserve the relationship for the future.

You each have to hire and pay a lawyer, but you will probably save money compared to litigation. The collaborative law process is faster than litigation. It differs from mediation in that each party has a lawyer representing his or her individual interests in the four-way meetings.

Negotiation by Attorneys

In the traditional approach, the parties each hire a lawyer who can try their case to a judge unless an agreement is reached. Some attorneys are skilled negotiators, while others are not.

Negotiation may proceed side by side with litigation. One attorney makes a settlement offer and the other responds. The attorneys go back and forth with offers and counteroffers. Concessions and compromises are made on each side until an agreement is struck (or not, as the case may be).

Negotiation may be by telephone, correspondence, or face-to-face meetings. All of these are costly.

Arbitration

If you reach an impasse but do not want to litigate, another way to resolve a dispute is to submit it to an arbitrator for a binding or nonbinding decision. Lawyers, retired judges, or any other agreed-upon party can be an arbitrator. Each party presents their case to the *arbitrator*, and the arbitrator makes a decision.

You can agree on the rules for the arbitration. You can present testimony, have the lawyers argue, or just submit documents. You can limit the issues the arbitrator needs to decide if you can agree on other issues, or you can give the arbitrator brackets for a decision (such as, "alimony has to be between three and five years").

Arbitration is faster and less costly than a trial. Since you (and your spouse) can direct the proceedings to a certain extent, they may provide a better resolution than a court. However, both parties must agree to arbitration as a way to settle issues.

Section Four:

Litigation as the Last Resort

(The Fourth Ninety Days and After)

Chapter Nineteen

Advantages of an Uncontested Divorce

The purpose of a divorce is to end a marriage, divide property and debts, provide for future support, and resolve custody issues. Sometimes these issues are hotly contested, and other times the parties can reach an agreement on some, if not all, of the issues. Many cases that begin as contested eventually settle and become uncontested divorces.

Settlements and Evaluating Offers

If you and your spouse are able to reach an agreement, you will want a written and signed document that sets forth the agreement. These documents go by names such as *marital settlement agreement, voluntary separation, custody, support and property settlement agreement*, and variations on that theme. If you at least agree on some things, you can sign a written agreement that documents what you have agreed upon and keep working on the outstanding issues.

If you and your spouse are negotiating money issues, you should analyze matters much the same as you would any other financial decision. If your spouse makes an offer, use all the information you have to evaluate it. If you are already represented by counsel, you will want your counsel's judgment on your chances of improving the offer either though further negotiation or by rejecting it and going to court.

One of the most important parts of evaluating the offer is determining the stakes. For example, say you and your spouse are negotiating an out-of-court equitable distribution of marital property. You agree that you will divide the property equally, you will have certain items, he or she will have certain items, you will value all of the property, and the spouse who receives more property by value will write a check to the other spouse for one-half of the difference. It is agreed that your spouse will have the family home. He or she proposes to value it at $800,000, but you think it is worth $900,000. All other values are agreed. In this situation, the stakes are $50,000, because you will receive $50,000 more or will have to pay $50,000 less if your value prevails instead of your spouse's.

In deciding whether to accept the offer, you should obtain and consider certain information. Ideally, you will want to confirm your opinion of value by obtaining an appraisal from a reputable appraiser whose opinion will carry significant weight with your spouse, your spouse's lawyer, and the judge. You will want to know from your lawyer how much it is likely to cost to get from where you are to the end of the trial, and how long that process will take. You will want your lawyer to give you some idea of your prospects for prevailing on the issue of the value of the house.

Whether to reject an offer and take the matter to court includes examining more than just the potential gain or loss of money. The uncertainty and stress of litigation, concluding with a contested divorce trial, should be factored into your decision, as should the opportunity costs of delaying the division of marital property and moving on with your postdivorce financial life. If you have children, you should also consider the damage a divorce trial will do to the relationship with your spouse—who you will still have to work with in raising your children.

The offers you will make and receive in working to move your divorce from contested to uncontested are not likely to have just one contested issue with a dollar value that can be precisely determined. You have lots of assets with unknown values—assets consisting of untaxed funds like traditional IRAs, and assets with built-in tax gains, some spendable cash, and some illiquid assets. Monthly support claims and demands will also be in the mix.

It will be important to carefully review settlement proposals to be sure you understand them and can compare them to your last proposal. Do not be rushed by your spouse or your lawyer. However, you will have to live by the court's deadlines, and they may make you feel rushed. In any case, do not needlessly delay negotiations. You cannot settle the case if you do not tell your adversary what you want.

Divorce litigation is a long process, and cases settle early, in the middle, on the courthouse steps, and sometimes not at all. The process requires lots of communication between the adversaries, and those communications create lots of opportunity for settlement.

In addition to or instead of informal negotiations, you can use mediation, other alternative dispute resolution methods, or the collaborative law process to help you reach an agreement out of court. These methods are explained in detail in Chapter 18.

Disputes about Grounds for Divorce

Disputes regarding the grounds for divorce are usually resolved before trial for several reasons. If you are proceeding to court on fault grounds, such as adultery or desertion, you are leaving open the possibility that the judge will find that neither party has proven grounds for divorce. This will mean none of the financial issues will be resolved and it will all have to be done over.

Furthermore, even when cases begin as adultery or desertion cases, it may be a year or more before the case goes to trial. By that time, the parties may have no-fault grounds for divorce, such as separation for a period of time. The case may proceed faster on those grounds, because they are easier to prove and corroborate.

Also, after spending so much time and money battling over the division of the marital estate, alimony, and other issues, once an agreement is reached, litigants generally do not want to go to trial with grounds in dispute.

Sometimes adultery or other fault grounds remain an issue if the resolution of that issue will affect the distribution of marital property, or the amount and duration (or denial) of alimony.

This depends mostly on the law of your state. Make sure you also have uncontested grounds if you are going forward on fault grounds. In most states, you can prove adultery using a helpful friend instead of a private investigator to do the stakeout and testify as a witness. Ask your attorney how to go about this. If you use a private investigator, it is best to wait until you know when the investigator should go to your spouse's (or the paramour's) house. You should have pictures or physical descriptions of your spouse, as well as vehicle make, model, and plate numbers to give the private investigator.

Custody and Visitation

Custody and visitation issues require special attention for several reasons. As you would expect, the separation of the parents and the divorce process has been shown to deeply affect children. However, the effect is both more negative and more lasting in high-conflict divorces. You may not be able to choose whether you have a high-conflict divorce. After all, it takes two to reach an agreement.

In dealing with the custody and access issues, keep in mind that children grow and change, and are affected by the process and whatever interim arrangement you have while you litigate or settle custody. The litigation process is both expensive and intrusive. The court may require the appointment of a guardian ad litem or an attorney to represent the interest of the children. The court may order a custody evaluation by a social worker or other mental health professional. These usually involve interviews with the parents, the children, and third parties, as well as home visits.

A typical contested custody case costs tens of thousands of dollars. The cost of a high-end, hotly contested case can reach six figures. All of this has to be paid for from assets that would otherwise be distributed between the parties. Sometimes the marital estate is completely depleted, yet the battle wages on with borrowed funds or extended family funds. Many judges and lawyers say that in custody cases, the stress, damage to relationships, and uncertainty of the process are far worse than the financial costs.

Secondly, as long as the children are minors, custody and access are never settled. In most states, if there has been a material change in circumstances, the court can review an existing custody and access order, make a new determination, and enter a new order in the best interests of the children under the new circumstances. This is because children (and parents) grow and change. The law recognizes that what is in the children's best interest today may not be tomorrow. The money you spend on winning the custody battle may turn out to be a short-term investment.

The financial wisdom in custody disputes is easier to state than apply. The general principles to keep in mind are:

◆ almost all settlements are better than a trial;

◆ mediation is better than litigation;

◆ one court-appointed expert is better than two hired guns; and,

◆ set aside all emotions except love of your children and a sincere level-headed determination to do what is best for them—even if it ends in a loss for you or a win for your spouse.

Always keep in mind that the custody war in which you are engaged may really only be the first battle—budget and spend accordingly.

Attorney's Fees

Most lawyers charge by the hour for their time, and for associates' and paralegals' time. In metropolitan areas, you can expect to pay $250 per hour and up for an experienced divorce lawyer. Hourly rates can be as high as $500 per hour for top divorce lawyers. Obviously, you want to be sure the stakes and the issues involved warrant it before you engage a $500 per hour lawyer.

Rates for lawyers who are junior associates can be significantly less than $200 per hour. Paralegals who can do much of the routine work in divorce case cost much less—experienced paralegals may cost around $100 per hour. Depending on your case, it may be important to hire counsel who can properly staff it so that you are not paying your experienced, talented, high-priced lawyer for work that can be done at a more junior level.

The costs incurred in your case come from completing the tasks required, such as:

◆ client counseling;

◆ document review;

◆ miscellaneous problem-solving;

◆ preparing pleadings;

◆ preparing and arguing motions;

◆ legal research;

◆ negotiations;

◆ documenting agreements;

◆ discovery;

◆ trial preparations; and,

◆ trial.

This list is very approximately in chronological order, although negotiations and documenting agreements can often precede the litigation and eliminate most of that work. There is a great deal of overlap. It has been reported that in large, urban areas, the average fee is $18,000 per spouse in divorce cases when lawyers are used. You want effective representation in your divorce, but you also want to be on the low end of costs if you can.

If your case settles before contested litigation begins or early in that process, you will spend far less than you would on a contested trial. The general rule is that a case that goes to trial will cost about ten times as much as the same case would cost if it settled before the divorce case was filed in court. Also, in most states, if both financial and custody issues are in dispute, there will be two separate trials.

Allocation of Divorce Costs

In most states, if you are the income earner, you can expect to pay a disproportionate share of the divorce costs. You can expect the court to order you to contribute to payment of your spouse's attorney's fees and other costs. Also, the costs of court-appointed experts and children's counsel are often allocated in proportion to income. Viewed one way, this is requiring one litigant to pay for his or her defense and pay for the adversary's attack on him or her. Viewed another way, it is perfectly fair, as all of the money is coming out of the marital estate that will be divided if not spent on divorce costs. Perspective aside, you want to make sure that, if you are in this position, you plan and act to make sure that your costs come out of marital property that would be divided, and not out of your end or out of your postdivorce earnings.

Some of the things you can do to protect your assets that will work in most states include the following.

◆ Divide sufficient joint funds to pay divorce costs at the beginning of the case.

◆ Pay all of your costs from marital assets before trial so the court only divides what is left.

◆ If you have to borrow to pay divorce costs, document the loan and prove it at trial.

◆ Include payment of fees in your offers and negotiations. Properly structured, it can be treated fully or partially as deductible alimony. It can be a powerful inducement to settlement.

If you are the financially dependent spouse, in most states you can expect that the court will order your spouse to contribute to your fees. This is not undiluted good news. The courts almost never order one spouse to pay all of the other spouse's fees, so you cannot safely litigate expecting it will all come out of your spouse's funds. Your agreement with your attorney will undoubtedly provide that you are responsible for payment of the balance of your attorney's fees, no matter what the court orders or what your lawyer collects from your spouse.

Perhaps more importantly, you may have a liquidity problem. Most experienced divorce lawyers require an advance payment commensurate with the complexities and stakes involved in the case. If you have no access to sufficient funds, you may have a problem retaining effective representation. If you have to borrow funds to pay your counsel, make sure you properly document the loan and prove it at trial. The court may order your spouse to contribute to your fees at a hearing on *pendente lite* issues. The likelihood of an order for payment of fees at an early hearing may affect your ability to retain counsel without a substantial advance payment. If there are substantial marital assets, you may be able to use those assets to assure your counsel of payment, even if they are jointly owned and you cannot actually grant a mortgage or other security interest in the property. If this becomes necessary, be certain you fully understand the arrangement by discussing it with your lawyer and your financial adviser.

The primary cost that you will incur will almost certainly be the hourly charges for the time your lawyer spends on your case. You may also incur costs for:

◆ associate attorneys and paralegals;
◆ financial expert witnesses, such as:
  • appraisers;
  • accountants; and,
  • pension evaluators;
◆ custody expert witnesses, such as:
  • court-appointed custody evaluators and
  • privately retained psychiatrists, psychologists, or other mental health professionals; and,
◆ private investigators, court reporters, and process servers.

You will have a far less costly divorce if you can move it from the contested to the uncontested category early in the process, consistent with accomplishing your reasonable goals. It is easy to state and sometimes difficult to apply the principles to follow in accomplishing this. You must make informed and sensible decisions. Know the stakes, know the options, know the transaction costs, and keep your emotions out of the decision-making process. The following chart serves as a summary between contested and uncontested divorces.

CONTESTED VERSUS UNCONTESTED

Item	Contested Divorce	Uncontested Divorce
Residency	One Year	None
Grounds	Statutory	None
Separation	Possibly One or Two Years	None
Cost	$20,000 and up	$5,000 or less
Time	One Year or More	One Day
Trial	One Day to Two Weeks	Ten to Twenty Minutes
Appeal	Possible	None
Restrictions	Statutory Limits on Judge	Public Policy
Detail	One or Two Pages	Unlimited
Control	Judge	Parties
Privacy	Public	Private Until Filed with Court
Remarriage	After-Divorce Order	After-Divorce Order

Chapter Twenty

The Court Proceeding

If you cannot agree with your spouse on all issues, then a judge or judicial officer (such as a magistrate or master) will hold a trial and listen to both of you and your witnesses, and then make a decision. The divorce case is started by filing a lawsuit at the courthouse. Filing a lawsuit does not necessarily stop settlement discussions—settlement and litigation can proceed in parallel. Sometimes cases settle during the litigation process. Sometimes you have to file to get the other side's attention. If you are able to settle before trial, you have changed a contested divorce into an uncontested one.

This chapter explains the litigation process so you will know what to expect as you go through it. It is intended to guide you through the case if you are representing yourself. The next chapter gives you tips on working with your divorce lawyer. Deciding whether or not you should retain a lawyer to represent you in the divorce case is one of the most important financial decisions you will make in your divorce. If you are in doubt, refer back to Chapter 8 for a discussion regarding the factors you may need to consider in making this decision.

Preliminary Requirements

Certain requirements have to be met before a court can hear your case. The court must have jurisdiction, venue must be proper (you have to be in the right county), and you have to be able to claim grounds for divorce.

There are two kinds of jurisdiction. *Subject-matter jurisdiction* means you are in a court that has the power to decide the controversies you have brought to it. For example, you cannot file your divorce case in the United States Tax Court. *Personal jurisdiction* means that the court has the power to bind the parties to its decision. If you and your spouse have always lived in Florida, you cannot sue for divorce in Alaska.

Most state laws provide that the state's courts have jurisdiction to decide the issues in a divorce case (*subject-matter jurisdiction*) if one of the parties has been a resident of the state for some required period of time, such as six months or a year. In some states, if the grounds for divorce occurred in a different state, that state's court will also have jurisdiction.

You have to meet the residency test when you file your lawsuit. It does not matter if you move away later; you can still maintain your lawsuit. Even if nobody objects, if the court decides it does not have subject-matter jurisdiction, it will dismiss the case. If challenged, residency can be established by testimony and documents like a lease, utility bills, driver's license, or voter registration card.

There are various kinds of courts in your state. You have to file your case in the right one. It is usually the trial court of general jurisdiction, often called the *circuit court*, or it is a special family court.

Generally, a court can acquire personal jurisdiction over people living in the state, or people who have some connection with the state and are properly served with suit papers. You can sue your spouse for divorce in the state where he or she lives. In most states, you can sue your spouse for divorce in the state where you last lived together, if one of you meets the residency requirements. If your spouse sues you in a state other than the state of your residence, and you want to object on the ground that the court lacks personal jurisdiction over you, you may be able to make a special appearance to contest jurisdiction without submitting to jurisdiction.

Venue means the location in which you file your suit. Venue rules require that your case have some connection to that county. In most cases, you will file your divorce in the county where you live or where your spouse lives. If the case is filed in the wrong county, the other spouse can object and require transfer, but if nobody objects, that court will hear it.

You cannot file your divorce case until you have *grounds* for divorce. Most state laws include fault grounds and no-fault grounds. Fault grounds usually include such things as adultery, cruelty, desertion, insanity, and felony. No-fault grounds include separation for a required statutory period of time, such as six months or one year. Some states have a shorter period if the separation is mutual and voluntary, or if the parties have no children. A few states allow divorce for *irreconcilable differences* without a waiting period.

You must plead grounds in your complaint, and you cannot file until you have them. If your state requires a one-year separation for a no-fault divorce, you cannot file the case until you have been separated for one year. Then, you have to prove grounds at the trial.

There are certain defenses to the various grounds for divorce that may be raised by the defendant in a divorce. For example, renewing sexual relations starts the separation period over again in a no-fault case based on separation. It may also be raised by the defendant as the defense of *condonation* to a claim of adultery. In states where condonation is not allowed as a defense, it may still be considered by the court as a mitigating factor to an adultery claim.

Fault matters in contested divorces. Most states' divorce laws provide that the court is to consider fault, if applicable, in determining the equitable distribution of marital property, in determining whether to award alimony, and in setting the amount and duration of alimony. Marital fault is not a required consideration in determining custody of children. In court, a bad spouse does not equal a bad parent.

Beginning the Lawsuit

Once you meet the preliminary requirements, you begin a case by filing a *complaint* in the clerk's office of the proper court. Your filing might also be called a *petition, bill of complaint,* or some other name, depending upon the custom of your jurisdiction and the type of case you are filing. Call ahead or check the court's website to find out how many copies the clerk requires, the amount of the filing fee, and any other requirements. You should go to the courthouse in person and file your case—do not mail it. Clerks are prohibited from giving legal advice, but they can tell you what forms you need and answer similar questions. There is usually a process to apply for a waiver of the filing fee if you are impoverished.

Service of Process

Once the complaint has been filed, the court issues a *summons.* You give the other side notice of the case by serving him or her with a summons and a copy of the complaint. This is called *service of process.* Formal service of process upon the defendant is a necessary step to the court acquiring jurisdiction to decide the case and bind the defendant by its decision. State laws vary on how service of process can be accomplished and who can serve, so check the rules. Keep in mind that if the defendant files an *answer,* all objections regarding service of process are waived.

The first method is personal service. You probably cannot serve the summons and complaint yourself. You have to have another adult serve it for you. This can be a deputy sheriff, a commercial process server, or a friend. The average cost of a process server is about $40. Whoever it is will try to personally deliver the papers to your spouse and put them in your spouse's hand. If successful, the server will file a return of service or affidavit of service with the court. If you think your spouse might be a tough serve, give the process server home and work addresses and telephone numbers, a picture, description of car and plate number, and any other information that might be useful.

Some states authorize service by certified mail, which will be effective if the defendant signs for the delivery, but not otherwise. If your spouse avoids service or you do not know where your spouse lives, you will have to proceed by alternative service of process. The process varies from state to state. The first step is showing that you cannot hand-deliver the papers despite diligent efforts. This would include service attempts at various hours of the day. If you do not know your spouse's address, it would include a reasonable search—phone book, Internet, inquiry to last known employer, friends and relatives, and so on. You generally have to file a motion requesting alternative service and an affidavit describing your diligent efforts or search.

The second step is *alternative service*—mailing to or posting at the last-known address, posting at the courthouse, publishing notice in a local paper, or often some combination of these means. You may also be able to leave the summons with a person of suitable age at your spouse's residence. If you need to follow alternate service of process procedures, follow the rules carefully and do not by shy about asking questions at the clerk's office. Judges do not like to enter judgments by default, so they are very strict about requiring compliance with the rules about alternative service.

Once the defendant has been served, notice of all subsequent filings are made by mailing a copy to the other party's address of record. Add a *certificate of service* at the end of each paper you file, stating that you mailed a copy to the other party at his or address and the date you mailed it. Accordingly, if you move during the case, you have to notify the court and the other party.

Contents of the Complaint

A divorce suit starts with a *complaint*. The purpose of the complaint is to tell the court what you want and why you are entitled to it. It sets out what is going to happen in the case and why—if everything goes your way. Many states have forms that you can fill in and file as your complaint, so you do not have to write the entire complaint. Check the court's website or ask at the clerk's office. The complaint contains:

◆ the name of the court;
◆ the names and (usually) the addresses of each of the parties;
◆ space for the case number the clerks office will assign;
◆ a title, such as *Complaint for Absolute Divorce*;
◆ allegations, including:
  • the parties' ages, residency, and military status;
  • the date and place of the marriage;

- the names and dates of birth of the children;
- a statement regarding whose care and custody the children are in;
- an allegation that plaintiff is a fit and proper person to have custody of the children;
- allegations stating the grounds for divorce;
- allegations regarding income, property, and debt; and,
- an allegation of financial need;

◆ prayers for relief, including:

- that the court enter a judgment or decree of divorce;
- that the court grant the plaintiff custody of the children;
- that the court determine the amount of child support, order the defendant to pay it, and enter an earnings withholding order;
- that the court award the plaintiff alimony, order the defendant to pay, and enter an earnings withholding order;
- that the court identify and value marital property, determine an equitable distribution of marital property, enter appropriate orders for division, transfer, and sale of marital property, and order defendant to pay plaintiff a monetary award;
- that the defendant be ordered to pay or contribute to the plaintiff's attorney's fees;
- that the plaintiff be granted any other appropriate relief; and,

◆ signature and name, address, and telephone number of the plaintiff or attorney filing the complaint. (Sometimes a *verification* under penalties of perjury or notarized signature of the plaintiff is required.)

The court may require attachments to the complaint, such as an information cover sheet, affidavit, financial statement, and a child support guidelines worksheet. If your case is uncontested when you file your complaint, you may attach a copy of the marital settlement agreement to the complaint.

You can certainly prepare your own complaint with the documents the courts in your area provide. If you have an attorney, he or she will do this for you. If your area does not provide sample forms, there are many additional resources available for finding this form. Check online or at your local bookstore for a resource that is right for you.

Answer

Once properly served, the defendant has to file a response to the complaint within the time set by the rules, or he or she may be put in default. Usually, the defendant responds with an answer, but in some circumstances the defendant may file a *motion to dismiss* that challenges jurisdiction or raises some other legal issue.

The answer is formatted the same as the complaint, in that it contains the name of the court and identifies the parties, the case number, and title (such as *Answer to Complaint for Absolute Divorce*). All the papers you file with the court should follow this format. The answer should respond to each allegation with a statement that it is admitted, denied, or that the defendant lacks sufficient information to admit or deny it. You can admit part of an allegation and deny the remainder, or state that you lack sufficient information to admit or deny the remainder. Make sure that it is clear what you admit and what you deny. The answer can also allege additional facts. For example, if your spouse alleges that he or she is a fit and proper person to have custody of the children and you agree, you can admit that and state in further answer to that allegation that defendant is also a fit and proper person to have custody.

Close your answer with your prayers for relief and your signature, name, address, and telephone number. If you are going to file a countercomplaint, your prayer for relief may be simply that the court deny the relief the plaintiff requested in the complaint and grant the relief requested in your countercomplaint. Sign the answer and attach a certificate of service. The answer may also be accompanied by an *information cover sheet*, as well as a *financial statement* and *child support guidelines worksheet* if there are financial issues in dispute.

When an answer has been filed denying all or some of the allegations of the complaint, the case is said to be *at issue*, unless a countercomplaint is also filed. In that event, the case is not at issue until an answer to the countercomplaint has been filed.

Your state's courts may have forms to fill in and file as your answer. If not, your lawyer will prepare one for you.

Countercomplaint

The defendant may file a *countercomplaint* with the answer, or within some required period of time after filing the answer. The countercomplaint (which may be called a counterclaim, cross-bill, or other such name) serves the same purpose as the complaint and the same principles apply. If your case is not settled and your spouse files the complaint for divorce, you should generally file a countercomplaint rather than just filing an answer that denies any allegation you disagree with (although, of course, you always have to file an answer). First, if you do not file a countercomplaint, the case is limited to the facts your spouse alleged and the relief your spouse requested. You may not be able to ask the judge later for relief not raised in the pleadings, even if you are otherwise entitled to it. Second, your spouse may decide for some reason to dismiss his or her complaint. In most states, this can happen over your objection. If you do not have a countercomplaint pending, the case is over and you have to go back to square one.

Default

If the defendant fails to file an answer or other pleading within the required time (twenty to thirty days in most states) after service of process, you may seek to proceed upon default. This is also true when you cannot find your spouse and are proceeding by alternative service, such as publication in a newspaper or posting on the courthouse bulletin board, or by whatever method has been authorized by the court.

Divorce by default typically requires a motion for default, proof of service, a nonmilitary affidavit, and some sort of last-chance notice by the court clerk's office. Once the judge enters a default, the defendant cannot participate by filing an answer or counterclaim without obtaining another order voiding the default.

However, you cannot really win a divorce by default like you can other lawsuits. You still have to go to a hearing and prove that you are entitled to the divorce and any other relief you are requesting. You will have the advantage of no opponent, and it is likely the judge will grant your requested relief as far as the law allows. For example, if you want child support, you must have some proof of the defendant's income. Even if the defendant appears for the hearing, he or she cannot present any witnesses or other evidence while in default, but the defendant can question your witnesses.

Pretrial Proceedings

Most cases that are filed as contested cases settle before the trial, and in other cases, one or more issues settle and are not tried. One reason pretrial proceedings are important is that what happens in those proceedings can influence whether your case settles and the terms on which it settles.

Scheduling Conference

Once the case is at issue, most courts hold at least a scheduling conference to set the date of the trial or the pretrial conference, set the discovery deadlines, schedule any needed *pendente lite* hearings, and order and schedule mediation sessions and parent education classes.

If your spouse is interfering with your custody of or access to the children, and you cannot resolve it, ask for a pendente lite hearing on custody or visitation. The lawyers and judge may refer to this as a *P.L. hearing*. If you need immediate financial support from your spouse and you are unable to reach an agreement, ask the court for a hearing on pendente lite financial issues.

In cases involving custody disputes, most courts in effect divide the case into two—a custody trial, and a grounds, property, and alimony trial. Each side of the case has its own mediation sessions, discovery deadlines, and pretrial conferences.

In a fully contested case with property and children, you will get lots of dates at the scheduling conference. At the end of the scheduling conference, read the scheduling order before you leave the courtroom to make sure that everything you asked for is listed.

The court does not technically decide anything at the scheduling conference and it often will not be before the judge who will conduct the trial, but it is a good idea to dress and behave appropriately at all conferences and hearings. Remember that your adversary is also part of your audience at conferences and hearings. It is generally true that all meetings between the parties to litigation move the case closer to or away from settlement.

In most jurisdictions, the court clerk controls the calendar, and there is a scheduling conference or something similar during which dates are set. In other jurisdictions, the parties have to take action to get hearings and trials by calling the clerk's office or the judge's secretary. Make sure you always know what the next step is and whether you have to do anything to make it happen.

Mediation

In most states, the court can order the parties to custody mediation. If the court cannot order it, it can encourage the parties to try mediation. Custody mediators are usually mental health professionals, and they have a high rate of success in settling custody cases. The court may also require you to participate in mediation or *alternative dispute resolution* (ADR) on the other issues in your case. ADR facilitators are experienced family lawyers who will attempt to help you settle the financial issues in your case, such as child support. Mediation is described in more detail in Chapter 18.

Pretrial Conference

The *pretrial conference* is where the judge makes sure that everyone is ready for trial and sets the trial date. The parties may be required to present pretrial statements, which inform the court about such matters as mediation, discovery, pending motions, disputes, agreements, trial exhibits, and trial witnesses. The judge will also usually ask about the possibility of settlement.

Discovery

Discovery is the process by which parties to a lawsuit find out the facts about the case. Formal discovery uses the court's rules and processes to accomplish this work. The scope of discovery in divorce cases is wide. Usually, if a question has something to do with the marriage, children, property, debt, income, or expenses, you can ask it and it will have to be answered.

Requests for production of documents are written requests describing the categories and types of documents you want your adversary to produce. These are good for obtaining tax returns, pay statements, bank statements, credit card statements, loan applications, résumés, and other financial documents. You can also ask for telephone bills, calendars, report cards, and other documents that might be relevant to grounds or custody.

Interrogatories are written questions that must be answered in writing and signed under oath and penalty of perjury. Interrogatories are a good way to find out your adversary's positions on the issues. Examples include "List all property you contend is nonmarital and state all the reasons for your contention" or "State whether you contend you are unable to work outside the home, and if so, why." You can ask for detailed explanations of the conclusory allegations of the complaint or for explanations of denials in the answer.

You can also send your adversary a request for *admissions*, which are statements of fact that you want the other side to admit to help you prove your case. If the other side does not serve an answer denying the statements within the required time, they are deemed admitted. This is a good tactic with an unresponsive or passive-aggressive defendant, who will not cooperate in discovery, but always manages to avoid outright default.

You can also depose your adversary and other witnesses. At a *deposition*, the witness is sworn and answers oral questions on the spot in front of a court reporter, who records the testimony. The purposes of a deposition are to find out what a witness knows and to pin the witness down to what he or she said at deposition, so that the witness cannot change his or her story at trial. A deposition is more expensive than the paper discovery methods discussed above. You have to pay a court reporter to attend the deposition to swear in the witnesses and record testimony. In metropolitan areas, court reporters charge a minimum of about $175 for a reporter's presence at a deposition. You also have to pay to have the testimony transcribed if you want to use it in court to impeach the witness's testimony or put the transcript itself in evidence. Court reporters charge about $3.50 per page for routine service, and much more for expedited service. If you do not order a transcript, most court reporters charge an hourly rate for the reporter's time.

Of course, your adversary can also make use of the discovery rules, sending you interrogatories and requests for production of documents, and taking your deposition. You also have to follow the rules and respond truthfully, fully, and on time to your adversary's discovery requests.

Discovery generally takes place between the parties and out of court. You go to court when there is a discovery dispute that the parties cannot resolve. Judges hate discovery disputes. Try to be reasonably sure that you are right and that it is important before you go to court over a discovery dispute.

Preparing for Trial

At trial, you want to prove that the *contested* facts are what you say they are and argue that they support the outcome you want. One useful tactic is to reach agreements on what facts are uncontested and write a *stipulation* of those uncontested facts, sign it and get your spouse to sign it, and present it to the judge at or before trial. Then you will not have to prove those uncontested facts. In some states, the parties in divorce cases are required to submit joint statements of marital property, and set out their agreements and disagreements regarding property.

Prepare a trial notebook. Your trial notebook should have at least the following:

- ◆ outline of your opening statement;
- ◆ outline of your testimony;
- ◆ outline of the examination of your corroborating witness;
- ◆ outline of your examination of your other witnesses, if any;

- outline of your examination of opposing party, if applicable;
- exhibits you will use at a hearing; and,
- any pleadings you have filed and orders you want signed.

Exhibits may include:
- marriage certificate;
- pay statements;
- tax returns;
- financial statements;
- marital property statement;
- discovery responses; and,
- deposition transcripts.

Before the trial, you will want to review your trial notebook and read your discovery responses, and if there were depositions, read a transcript of your deposition and your adversary's deposition. Review any documents you will identify or refer to during your testimony. Review any statement you made.

If you have never observed a trial, it may be a good idea to go to court before your court date and watch a trial. It will help you feel more comfortable at your trial.

All of the testimony and exhibits at trials are technically matters of public record and open to public inspection. Unless you are famous, you can rest assured that it is extremely unlikely that anybody will look into your divorce.

Try not to discuss your case with mutual friends before trial. Sometimes "friends" become witnesses for the other side and contradict your testimony. On the other hand, at this time in your life, you will no doubt feel the need to discuss things with a trusted friend or two.

It is a good idea to call the court clerk a couple of days before your trial to make sure your case will be heard. Cases are sometimes continued and court notices can get lost. You do not want to do your final trial preparation and make the trip to court if your trial has been rescheduled.

The Rules

Your divorce case will be governed by the applicable *rules of procedure*. The rules of procedure are designed to give each side a chance to present its case fully and fairly. The rules govern the filing of pleadings, discovery, pretrial proceedings, and other matters.

The court uses the *rules of evidence* at trial. These rules govern how you prove your case at trial. There are rules on how you question witnesses, as well as identify and introduce documents. There are rules that limit evidence to things that are relevant to the controversy and rules for determining what is relevant.

There are a lot of rules of evidence, but try to remember these two. First, witnesses can only testify from their own personal knowledge. They cannot testify about what someone else said—that is *hearsay*, and it is inadmissible. An important exception to this rule is that a witness generally can testify to what an opposing party said. If your spouse admitted to adultery and now denies it, you can testify to what he or she told you. Second, documents must have a proper foundation to be admissible. Generally, a witness has to identify the document, tell the judge what it is, and explain its significance to the case.

The Trial

The purpose of a trial is to prove facts. You want to prove the important facts that are necessary or helpful to your case. You want to present those facts in an organized, persuasive way. You want to leave facts that are not helpful and facts that are not important out of your case. Judges appreciate it when you stick to the point and do not give them a lot of unnecessary information. If possible, you want to keep facts that are not helpful to you out of your adversary's case.

Courtroom Dress and Conduct

You should wear neat business clothing when going to court. Do not wear blue jeans or causal clothing. Address the judge as "Your Honor," and witnesses as "Mr." or "Ms.," and use their surnames. Be polite and respectful to all of the participants, especially your adversary and his or her witnesses.

Look at the judge when you are speaking to the him or her. Be prepared, and speak directly and forcefully. Avoid mumbling or stalling. Plan your case and follow the script.

Overview of the Trial

Listen to the judge and follow all of the judge's directions. You may find that the judge will ask you questions when you are testifying or ask your witnesses questions. Do not worry about this. If you are the witness, listen to and answer the judge's questions. If he or she asks another witness questions, wait until the judge is finished and then return to your trial outline. Lawyers say Rule #1 in the courtroom is *the judge is the boss*. Do not forget that rule or it may cost you.

When the clerk calls your case, come to the front of the courtroom and identify yourself. Usually, there is a counsel table for each party and a podium. The judge may ask whether there are any preliminary matters. These are usually motions about the conduct of the trial. One thing you may want to ask for is a rule on witnesses. If you ask, the judge will exclude all witnesses, other than the parties, from the courtroom when they are not testifying. This prevents witnesses from hearing other testimony and adjusting their own. You can use the blank witness form on page 230 to keep track of witnesses.

Once preliminary matters have been taken care of, the judge will ask for *opening statements*. Use your opening statement to give the judge a preview of the evidence you will introduce in the trial. Your statement should be organized and straightforward. Do not be argumentative. If you are the defendant, you may have a choice of making your opening statement now or reserving it until after plaintiff's case. It is best to make it now. Let the judge hear from you before he or she hears all of the plaintiff's evidence.

After opening statements, the presentation of evidence begins. First the plaintiff puts on his or her case. Then the defendant puts on his or her case. Next the plaintiff will be given an opportunity to respond to the defendant's case by putting on additional evidence in *rebuttal.*

The plaintiff begins by calling his or her first witness and asking the witness a series of questions (*direct examination*). These questions could include asking the witness questions about documents to lay a foundation for the documents to be admitted into evidence as *exhibits*. You cannot ask your own witness questions in a way that lets the witness know how to answer, such as "Haven't you observed that I am the better parent?" These are called *leading questions*, and they are not permissible on direct examination.

At the conclusion of direct examination of a witness, the other side can ask that witness questions (*cross-examination*). You can only ask questions about what the witness testified to on direct examination. If you want to question the other side's witness about other matters, you have to call that witness to the stand in your case, even if the witness is your spouse. You can call your spouse as a witness in your case.

You can ask leading questions on cross-examination. In fact, in cross-examination, all of your questions should be leading. It is another chance for you to tell your story to the judge. It is almost as though you are testifying, while the witness merely punctuates your testimony with yeses and nos. The chief rule of cross-examination is *do not ask a question if you do not know the answer.* For some witnesses, the best cross-examination is no cross-examination at all.

After cross-examination, the plaintiff can ask additional questions to clarify anything that came up on cross-examination (*redirect*). You cannot go into new areas on redirect.

During the examination of witnesses, the other party can raise *objections* to questions and to the admission of documents, or ask the judge to *strike* a witness's answer to a question. The basis for this sort of request is that the answer or document is not admissible under the rules of evidence.

After all of the plaintiff's witnesses have testified and all of the plaintiff's exhibits have been offered into evidence, the plaintiff *rests*. This is legally significant. The plaintiff cannot safely keep required evidence in reserve to spring on the defendant later in rebuttal, because the defendant is not necessarily required to put on any evidence. If the defendant says "Your Honor, I have no evidence," the introduction of evidence is over. If some necessary element has not been proven, the plaintiff loses. It is possible, if you represent yourself, that these technical rules will not be harshly applied to dismiss your case, but it is best not to rely on getting special breaks. Be organized and make sure you prove all the necessary points in your case. If you are the plaintiff, put all your evidence on before you rest.

After the plaintiff rests, the defendant puts on his or her case in the same fashion as plaintiff. If you are the defendant, this is your opportunity to tell your side of the story. Follow your trial outline in presenting witnesses and exhibits the same as you would if you were the plaintiff.

When the defendant rests, the plaintiff puts on the plaintiff's rebuttal evidence, if any. Remember, rebuttal can only respond to the defendant's case; it cannot include new, unrelated evidence. If appropriate under the circumstances, the defendant may request and be granted an opportunity to respond to the plaintiff's rebuttal evidence in *surrebuttal.*

When all the evidence is in and both sides have rested, the parties make their *closing arguments.* A good closing argument summarizes the evidence and makes a persuasive argument to the judge as to why that evidence supports the result for which you are asking.

WITNESS LIST

Name	Address	Phone Number	Subjects

The Evidence in a Divorce Case

In a divorce case, the two spouses are the most important witnesses. You may want to call yourself as your first witness. You would use your own testimony to establish some or all of the following facts.

◆ Date and place of marriage (identify the marriage license and certificate).

◆ Names and dates of birth of the children of the marriage.

◆ Grounds for divorce (typically).

◆ The date of separation.

◆ The parties' intention that the separation be permanent, and if necessary, that the separation was the voluntary act of both parties.

◆ That the separation continues uninterrupted and there have been no marital relations between the parties.

◆ That there is no reasonable prospect of reconciliation.

◆ The property you and your spouse, or either of you separately, own. In testifying about property, you will probably identify and explain your financial statement, and perhaps other documents, such as bank statements, brokerage statements, deeds, closing papers, titles or registration for vehicles, and so on. This is a part of the case where stipulations between the parties regarding property can be helpful.

◆ That property is marital or is nonmarital. Usually, this will be evidence regarding when and how the property was acquired.

◆ The debts owed by you and your spouse, or either of you separately. This is another area where documents will be required and pretrial stipulations would be useful.

◆ Your income and perhaps your spouse's income. Most likely, you would testify about your spouse's income if he or she has already testified. You would identify and discuss income tax returns and pay statements in this part of your testimony.

◆ Your household and personal expenses, and perhaps your spouse's personal and household expenses. You would identify and discuss your financial statement. If your spouse's financial statement is in evidence and you can attack it based on your personal knowledge of the expenses claimed, this would be the place to do it.

◆ Your contributions to the family, to the acquisition of property, to your spouse's career, and all the other factors that are relevant to marital property distribution in your state. Documentary proof is often more persuasive than self-serving testimony, as is true in other areas.

You will probably need other witnesses. Many states require a *corroborating witness* for the facts, establishing the grounds for divorce. You may need additional witnesses as well. Long-term mutual friends can be good witnesses regarding the contribution to the well-being of the family and fault for the breakup of the marriage.

Prepare your witnesses by discussing the case with them ahead of time and finding out what they know and do not know, and what they think. Then, write out your questions and ask the witness all your questions ahead of time. That way, they will know the questions and you will not surprise them, and at the same time, you will know the answers. If you do not like the answers, you can look for another witness.

You must have each exhibit marked with a number by the clerk and must show it to the other side before you question a witness about it. After your witness has identified the document and explained its connection to the case, you ask the judge to admit into evidence. There is a sample exhibit list on page 233.

Our legal system also allows for *expert witnesses.* Unlike *fact witnesses,* expert witnesses can give their opinions on matters for which they are qualified. They have to be approved by the court as an expert witness first. In marital property cases in which there is a contest regarding the value of real property, you might use a real estate appraiser as an expert witness. You would qualify the appraiser as an expert by asking him or her questions regarding education and experience, and offering the appraiser's *curriculum vitae.*

After these questions, you offer the witness as an expert in his or field. The other side can object, and if it does, the other side can cross-examine the witness on the issue of qualifications. When and if the witness is qualified as an expert, you ask the witness questions about the investigation in this case; for example, about his or her visit to the marital residence, his or her observations there, and his or her research into the market. Then you ask the expert for his or her bottom-line opinion of the property's value.

EXHIBIT LIST

Exhibit No.	Description	Date	Witness

Evidence in a Custody Case

In custody litigation, you want to put on evidence regarding custody, visitation, and access to the children that supports your request. First, you have to establish the current custody situation by testimony or documents, such as custody agreements, report cards, or a calendar showing time spent in each home. Pictures of the children having a good time with you never hurt. Neighbors and teachers are good witnesses regarding your care for the children. Then, you put on evidence of your proposal, probably through your testimony.

If there has been a court-ordered custody evaluation or assessment, that report and probably the evaluator's testimony will be important evidence in the custody trial. If the report or testimony is favorable to you, refer to it every chance you get. If it is unfavorable, you have to try to minimize or undermine the evaluator's testimony. Possible areas to explore in cross-examination or to mention later in argument are:

- ◆ the evaluator's observations were too limited or not typical;
- ◆ the evaluator lacks experience or experience with families like yours;
- ◆ the evaluator did not talk to the right people (the teachers and neighbors who like you);
- ◆ the evaluator's report contradicts other evidence (the report says your child is doing well in school and the report card says he or she is doing badly);
- ◆ the evaluator did not know and therefore did not consider some crucial fact; or,
- ◆ the evaluator is biased against you (if you do not have much else).

Usually, the children do not testify. The judge hears the children's wishes indirectly through a guardian ad litem, the evaluator, or the parties themselves. A recent study found that most children, when given the choice, prefer joint custody.

In most states, children do not testify in open court in custody trials unless they are at least teenagers. Judges will sometimes hear from younger children in their chambers without the parties present. In most states, if a child is about 10 or older and at least one of the parties wants the judge to hear from the child, the judge will. The judge will record these sessions or take notes to provide a record for appeal, and the judge will usually provide the parties with some indication of what the children told the judge. Of course, all of this puts the children right in the middle of the parents' dispute, and from their point of view, forces them to choose between their parents. You can hardly imagine something more stressful to the child. It should be avoided at almost all costs.

If you are the defender of the status quo, you have to persuade the judge that the children are fine where they are, and the current visitation and access schedule is in their best interest. If you are the proponent of change, your evidence has to show that the children are not doing well or not well enough. In both situations, your evidence must focus on the children. The judge usually does not want to hear how all of this is affecting you. Even if you think what is bad for you is bad for the children, and even if that is true, do not frame your testimony or your closing argument that way.

Your Testimony
The following are a few tips for your own testimony.

- ◆ Stay calm and make all your remarks to the judge, not to your spouse or your spouse's attorney, no matter how provoked you may be by the other side.
- ◆ Do not be a smart aleck or appear nervous, scared, argumentative, or angry. If your adversary baits you into becoming angry, he or she is probably trying to set you up for a trap, so keep your cool.
- ◆ Tell the truth. It is going to come out eventually anyway, and it is better coming from you than from the other side. If the other side catches you in a lie, you may lose your case.
- ◆ Listen carefully to all questions. Pause, make sure you understand the question, then take your time and answer that question. You cannot give a truthful and accurate answer if you do not understand the question. If you ask, the attorney will repeat the question.

◆ Do not guess when you do not know the answer, and do not sound like you are guessing when you are not. If you are asked a question to which you do not know the answer, say, "I don't know." If you know the answer, say it in a direct, straightforward way. If the question calls for an amount as an answer and you know the approximate answer, give the answer and say that it is approximate.

Closing

After the plaintiff's case, the defendant's case, the plaintiff's rebuttal evidence, and maybe the defendant's surrebuttal evidence, the court will hear *closing arguments*. The parties use this opportunity to summarize the evidence in a manner that is favorable to them and supports the result they are asking for. The plaintiff goes first, the defendant follows, and then the plaintiff can respond to the defendant's argument. If you did a good job planning and presenting your evidence, you will be talking about the evidence and how it means the judge should rule in your favor. If you left a lot of things out and think you really ought to win because of all the bad things your spouse did in the marriage that did not make it into evidence, resist the temptation to talk about those things. The judge cannot consider them and it can only hurt you at this point.

The judge may announce a decision right away—called *ruling from the bench*—with a written order to follow. In more complex cases, the judge may take the case under advisement and give a decision later. The court's decision is sometimes called an order, judgment, or decree. You may be required to prepare a proposed order before or after the trial.

You may not like the judge's decision. The judge may not always believe everything you said, may not understand part of your case, or may just plain disagree with you. Judges are not always right, but they are paid to make the decisions. There is a court of appeals looking over their shoulder if they do make a mistake. You also can ask the judge to change his or her mind, called a *motion to alter or amend judgment* or a *motion for reconsideration*. You can decide to accept the decision or you can appeal it.

SAMPLE LITIGATION TIMELINE FOR A DIVORCE

It takes a considerable amount of time—about a year or more—to litigate a case to completion, plus another six months if there is an appeal. The following is a sample trial timeline.

Date	Event
January 1, 2007	Plaintiff's Motion for Temporary Protective Order
January 10, 2007	Defendant's Opposition to Motion
January 11, 2007	Hearing on Motion, and Order
February 11, 2007	Plaintiff's Complaint for Divorce
February 28, 2007	Affidavit of Plaintiff's Process Server
March 28, 2007	Defendant's Answer
April 18, 2007	Scheduling Conference and Scheduling Order
April 18, 2007	ADR Facilitation
May 15, 2007	Custody Mediation
May 18 and 25, 2007	Parenting Classes
May 30, 2007	Temporary Support Hearing and Order
June 30, 2007	Plaintiff's Discovery
July 15, 2007	Defendant's Discovery
July 31, 2007	Plaintiff's Responses to Discovery
August 15, 2007	Defendant's Responses to Discovery
September 15, 2007	Defendant's Deposition
September 15, 2007	Plaintiff's Deposition
September 30, 2007	Witness Depositions
October 1, 2007	Plaintiff's Motion to Compel Discovery
October 18, 2007	Defendant's Opposition
October 19, 2007	Defendant's Motion to Compel Discovery
November 10, 2007	Plaintiff's Opposition
November 30, 2007	Hearing on Discovery Motions and Order
December 1, 2007	Pretrial Conference
December 31, 2007	Trial and Order
January 5, 2008	Plaintiff's Exceptions
February 5, 2008	Hearing on Exceptions and Order
February 27, 2008	Plaintiff's Notice of Appeal
March 25, 2008	Plaintiff's Brief
April 24, 2008	Defendant's Brief
May 5, 2008	Plaintiff's Reply Brief
July 30, 2008	Hearing on Appeal
November 1, 2008	Appeals Court Decision

Chapter Twenty-One

Working with Your Lawyer During the Divorce Court Case

This chapter assumes that you are represented by counsel in your divorce case and focuses on how to work effectively with your counsel. It covers the process from filing the complaint for divorce up to and including trial. However, most cases that are filed as contested cases end up settling before trial.

Your Lawyer's Role

During litigation, your lawyer's role is all-important. He or she has been down this road before. Tell your lawyer everything he or she asks and everything he or she needs to know. Follow your lawyer's advice.

On the other hand, it is *your* family, *your* life, and *your* money. Only you know what is essential, what is important, and what is unimportant to you. Your lawyer does not know the facts of the case the way you do.

You set the agenda and the goals, and your lawyer decides on strategy and tactics to achieve those goals (or tells you if he or she believes they are not achievable). If your divorce litigation is viewed as a business enterprise, you are both the CEO and the clerical staff, while your lawyer is middle management.

At the Start of Litigation

You and your lawyer should have a discussion regarding the goals of the litigation, the approximate schedule your lawyer expects the court to set, and the litigation budget. This is an important meeting that you should be prepared for. Do not ask for the meeting on Tuesday and expect to have it on Wednesday.

Objectives

Be clear about what your goals are and what outcomes are acceptable to you. You should have objectives for property and debt distribution; spousal support; child custody, visitation, and support; and, your contribution to fees and costs. All of these issues are interrelated, but this does not mean that you cannot settle one or more issues and leave one or more for trial. Settling one or more issues reduces the risk and expense of the trial. This is especially the case if you are able to settle all custody issues or all financial issues, because in most states, that will eliminate one of the two trials you will have to participate in and pay for (if both custody and financial issues are tried in your state).

Budget

Ask your lawyer for a litigation budget. Many lawyers are uncomfortable setting litigation budgets. It can be difficult to predict the course that litigation will take. Unexpected problems often come up and require a great deal of effort, time (the lawyer's), and money (yours) to solve. Nonetheless, it is very reasonable for you to insist on some kind of budget. It can have predicted ranges of expense rather than predicted amounts. Also, you should expect that the budget will have a couple of broad categories rather than many detailed categories. A sufficient budget for most cases would give an expected range of the expenses for pleadings and pendente lite issues; discovery; negotiations and alternative dispute resolution; and, trial preparation and trial. As a general rule, if you live in a large, metropolitan area and your divorce is contested through trial, you can expect to spend more than $20,000 on litigation costs. A sample litigation budget for a divorce is on pages 241–242.

SAMPLE LITIGATION BUDGET FOR A DIVORCE

Assuming your lawyer charges $200 an hour for his or her time and $80 for paralegal time, the following is a sample budget for a contested divorce case.

Legal Services	Hours	Fees @ $200/hour	Fees @ $80/hour
Initial Office Conference with Client	1	$200	
Prepare Complaint and Related Documents	1	$200	
Information Cover Sheet Child Support Guidelines	2		$160
Scheduling Conference	1	$200	
Facilitation	2	$400	
Discovery	3	$600	
Expert Witness Statements Interrogatories Request for Documents Request for Admissions	6		$480
Respond to Other Side's Discovery	5	$1,000	
Interrogatories Request for Documents Request for Admissions	10		$800
Telephone Conferences and Letters	10	$2,000	
Prepare for and Appear at Hearing	7	$1,400	
on Temporary Support	8		$640
Conferences with Witnesses and Experts	20	$4,000	
Prepare for and	20	$4,000	
Take Depositions	20		$1,600
Legal Research	10	$2,000	
	10		$800
Prepare Pretrial Statement	1	$200	
	2		$320

continued

Pretrial Settlement Conference	3	$600	
Trial Preparation	40	$8,000	
	40		$3,200
Trial (two days at 10 hours/day)	20	$4,000	
Totals:	**242**	**$27,800**	**$7,680**

In addition to legal fees, you will have to pay costs as follows:

Filing Fee	$100
Process Server	$35
Expert Witnesses	$5,000
Deposition Transcripts	$2,500
Copies, Faxes, Overnight Delivery Service,	$500

Courier, etc. (These seemingly small expenses can add up to a lot over the course of a contested case, because your lawyer will be producing a lot of letters, pleadings, etc. that are copied and then couriered to the court, opposing counsel, you, and other participants.)

Total:	**$8,135**
Total fees and costs:	**$43,615**

Schedule

In most jurisdictions, the court will enter a scheduling order in your case. These orders set the date and time of the various hearings and conferences for your case, and set deadlines for such things as completing discovery, designating experts, and filing witness and exhibit lists. Sometimes the schedule ends with the pretrial conference, and your actual trial date is set at that time. Sometimes you will have two scheduling orders—one for custody issues, and one for financial and grounds issues. You will want your lawyer to tell you at the outset of the case approximately when these things will happen and approximately when your case will be over (assuming no appeals or postdivorce litigation).

In general, the longer your case goes on and the more court-ordered events there are in the case, the more your case will cost. You will undoubtedly find that there is a flurry of activity immediately before each hearing, conference, or court-ordered deadline. Do not worry about this. It does not mean your lawyer is disorganized. Your lawyer or law firm has many cases and lots of work, and things are done when they need to be done—and usually not much before then. Each conference hearing or deadline means the adversaries are communicating, and each is an opportunity for settlement. In evaluating or making offers, keep in mind that the next scheduled event will result in another flurry of activity and more expenses.

Reevaluate Your Attorney

If you have been negotiating through counsel or involved in an alternative dispute resolution process before the litigation, you will have an existing relationship with your attorney at the outset of the divorce litigation. Now is the time to decide whether you want to stick with him or her for the rest of the case. This may be an easy decision if you have a good relationship and have been impressed with your lawyer's skills and effectiveness. If the decision is not obvious, you should thoroughly reevaluate your choice using the process discussed in Chapter 8. You may want to switch if your experience to date has shown that you do not have the right lawyer for your case or the right lawyer for you. In deciding what to do, you should keep in mind that you will be incurring the extra expense of bringing a new lawyer up to speed on the case if you decide to switch. However, this extra expense will only increase if you change lawyers later in the case.

Working with Your Lawyer During Your Case

Keep completely up-to-date on your case. Know what is going on. When you receive a communication from your lawyer asking for your response or input by a given date, respond by that date or let your lawyer know when you will respond, and make sure the delay is not a problem. Expect your lawyer to keep his or her promises about when tasks will be performed, responses will come, and so on.

If your lawyer sends you a document for review, review it. Remember, he or she does not know the facts as you know them, even if you have told him or her several times. Always carefully review documents that will be filed or sent to your adversary for accuracy with respect to the facts.

Do not micromanage your lawyer's work during the case. It will not significantly improve the service you receive—in fact, it could detract from effective service—and it will significantly increase your costs. For example, do not worry too much about how complaints, answers, and countercomplaints read. Just make sure the dates, names, and other facts are accurate. Your lawyer will make sure that the pleading meets the legal requirements. You cannot win the case in the pleadings, so this is not the place to worry too much about persuasive argument.

On the other hand, motions, pretrial memoranda, and correspondence to the opposing party and other players in the case are or can be persuasive documents that move the case toward (or away from) resolution, or otherwise affect the litigation. You always want to be sure that your positions on the issues are known to your lawyer and accurately set forth.

Discovery

Formal discovery is the process by which litigants learn about their adversary's case using court-sanctioned procedures, such as interrogatories, requests for production of documents, request for admission, depositions, and mental or physical examinations. Informal discovery is less expensive and potentially more powerful. See the methods discussed in Chapter 3.

You probably cannot win your case in discovery, but you can most certainly lose it. Rules and philosophy about discovery vary widely around the country, so it can be difficult to generalize. Most lawyers will tell you that the discovery process is where your efforts can make an important difference in your costs and potentially in the outcome.

The first stage is paper discovery. Interrogatories are written questions that must be answered in writing, and signed under oath and penalty of perjury. Requests for documents are just that—you describe all the categories of documents you believe your adversary has or may have, and request that the documents be produced for inspection and copying. You can also set forth a series of statements and ask your adversary to admit that they are true in a *request for admissions.*

As you might expect, it is a lot easier (and cheaper) to ask all these questions than it is to answer them. It is the practice in many family law firms to get the paper discovery out early, sometimes with the complaint for divorce. Predictably, the other side's discovery requests are promptly served in self-defense. If you have done a thorough job of informal discovery, you may want to discuss with your lawyer whether any formal discovery is necessary. If it is, ask more focused questions instead of sending out all the standard ones.

Responding to discovery requests is primarily your job. If you have questions, this is a good time to get to know the paralegal or other staff working on your case at your lawyer's office. Responses are generally due between twenty-one and thirty days from the date of service. Read the requests carefully. There will probably be about four or five pages of instructions and definitions before the actual discovery requests. You can skim that part. Answer the interrogatories truthfully and completely without rambling, and send the answers to your lawyer by the requested date. Your lawyer will edit your draft answers and make appropriate objections where available.

In responding to the request for production of documents, for each request state whether or not you have documents called for by the request. Gather the requested documents and provide them to your lawyer, organized by request. You may have to request documents from third parties, such as your bank, credit card issuer, or telephone company, if you no longer have the document. If you are in doubt about how far to go, ask your lawyer.

This is a time-consuming, labor-intensive process. Nobody knows the facts or has access to the documents like you do. Discovery is a necessary evil on the road to divorce. If you are not responsive to your lawyer during discovery, it will cost you a substantial amount of money in needless discovery disputes, and it may put you at a disadvantage in litigation.

You also have an important role with respect to your spouse's discovery responses. Generally, you should do the initial review of the document production and flag documents that seem important or surprising. You should also carefully review your spouse's answers to interrogatories and send your lawyer comments, if appropriate. Your review and your feedback will help your lawyer understand the significance of the documents and answers, and to determine whether your spouse has responded fully as required by the rules. With your knowledge of the marriage and your spouse, you are best positioned to find those bits of information that can be useful at trial.

Taking the deposition of your adversary's witnesses is another discovery tool. In your divorce case, you may want your attorney to take your spouse's deposition. The advantage of taking a deposition over interrogatories is that questions are oral and must be answered orally on the spot, with a court reporter recording it all. Both interrogatories and deposition questions must be answered under oath—not many people will tell outright lies in either situation. However, at deposition, your spouse will not have time to reflect and discuss his or her answer with counsel, and he or she may ramble and say more than is necessary (maybe something that is helpful to you). Your lawyer will be able to ask follow-up questions, and will be able to evaluate your spouse as a witness and advise you accordingly. In short, the deposition is a powerful discovery tool.

Whether to take your spouse's deposition is an important tactical and financial decision in a divorce case. A deposition is the most expensive discovery tool. It requires a significant amount of the lawyer's time to prepare for and take an important deposition, such as the deposition of the spouse in a divorce case. When your lawyer gives notice that he or she is taking your spouse's deposition, you can expect that your spouse's lawyer will give notice to take yours. Once depositions are noted, they are likely to go forward. It is an expensive procedure (your lawyer taking your spouse's deposition) and a relatively unpleasant one (your spouse's attorney taking yours).

Depositions of the opposing parties take the case to another level financially and can also make the case more adversarial than it is already. You will want to make sure that the stakes and the situation warrant a deposition before you take this action. Discuss the cost and the objectives of the deposition thoroughly with your lawyer. If you decide to go forward, you may want to suggest areas of inquiry to your lawyer.

You can depose other witnesses as well. A frequent tactic in divorce cases is to depose your spouse's paramour. This can be a dramatic, yet relatively cost-effective way to obtain evidence of adultery and waste of marital funds. Noting the paramour's deposition can add to the pressure on your spouse to settle. If you do not have a paramour, it has the added advantage of being a tactic to which your adversary cannot respond in kind. If you are the spouse with the paramour, do not be surprised if your spouse serves him or her with a subpoena to appear at deposition.

Depositions often turn into settlement conferences. See the discussion on page 249 about settlement discussions immediately before trial. To a lesser extent, the same principles apply to the informal settlement conference before depositions.

Conferences

Most courts hold at least a scheduling conference at the outset of the case. The court may also schedule a settlement conference, a pretrial conference shortly before trial, and possibly status conferences during the case. Speak to your lawyer before the conference to find out the purpose and what he or she expects will happen. Appear for conferences on time and appropriately dressed. Listen carefully and follow your lawyer's lead. The court will not hear evidence at conferences and you cannot win your case at a conference. Nonetheless, these conferences are important. Both sides are in the same place at the same time after some preparation. All conferences represent opportunities to show your adversary that you are prepared to go forward or to have settlement discussions.

Pendente Lite Hearings

At hearings on *pendente lite* issues, the court can rule on spousal and child support, use of property, visitation, and access to the children during the case, and can order a pendente lite contribution to attorney's fees. In some jurisdictions, the court will decide physical custody at pendente lite hearings.

Motions Hearings

The parties can file motions to ask the court to enter an order deciding certain legal issues that can be decided before trial, and the court can hold hearings on these issues. Motions can challenge the court's jurisdiction to decide the case, test a party's grounds for divorce, or deal with more minor issues.

Trial Preparation

If your case has not settled by thirty days to one week before trial, depending on the size and complexity of the case, you and your lawyer will begin intensive trial preparation. Trial preparation is the process of planning and preparing the introduction of evidence in your case, and planning the attack on the evidence your adversary will introduce. It is time-consuming and expensive. As a general rule, it takes about three times as much time as the trial. Expect to be billed for about three days of trial preparation for a one-day trial.

It is a good idea to have a last round of settlement negotiations before the parties spend the money required to prepare for trial.

You can aid the process and keep your costs down by cooperating with your lawyer and responding to questions and requests for information. Now is the time that your lawyer will need every witness's current address and telephone number, a more detailed chronology of the marriage, an updated financial statement, and answers to interrogatories. Depending on your case, a fair amount of legwork may be involved in preparing for trial. If your own schedule permits you to devote a substantial amount of time to the case, have a discussion with your lawyer about what trial preparation tasks you can effectively do for yourself.

Get a good estimate of your trial preparation and trial costs, and if possible, pay in advance from marital property and reflect the payment on your amended financial statement. The court will divide what is left after payment of your attorney's fees. It is not a good idea to have your attorney worrying about payment of his or her fees. You want your lawyer's undivided attention on your case, and it is only human for him or her to have the issues of fees on his or her mind if they are not paid.

Things will probably get somewhat hectic before trial. You may get calls or emails late in the evening asking for information you think your lawyer already knows or should have known. Do not worry about things being hectic. It does not generally mean your lawyer is disorganized or unprepared. It is just the nature of the process.

Last-Minute Settlement

Cases sometimes settle on the courthouse steps. You should be prepared for this possibility. A couple of days before trial, review your spouse's last offer, if one was made. If none, review your last settlement proposal. Decide how much better than your spouse's last offer or how close to your proposal a settlement would need to be. Recognize that you are probably not going to recoup all the attorney's fees and other costs wasted in the litigation because of your spouse's refusal to be reasonable until the last minute. A late settlement is still better than a trial. You may find that your attorney, who has been a major proponent of settlement since the day you walked into his or her office, is now counseling to reject the offer. This is only natural. He or she has been preparing for trial for days or weeks and is ready for trial, and it is more difficult to analyze the offer at this point. Being prepared in advance for a late settlement proposal will help you to objectively evaluate it.

It is probably not a good idea to start a settlement discussion in the moments before trial or to make major changes in your settlement position, unless you have been thoroughly unrealistic prior to this time and it is clear that the trial outcome is very likely to be worse (for you) than your last offer. If this is the case, you are in a bad position. However, it is best to go ahead and modify your offer. It is better to make a reasonable settlement proposal late than to compound your error by forcing a trial you may lose because you never made a reasonable offer.

Trial

Your attorney's office should properly staff your trial. If two lawyers are appropriate because of the stakes, because the two lawyers worked on the case throughout and the knowledge of both is needed at trial, or for any other good reason, then you should have and pay for two trial lawyers. However, if one lawyer is there primarily for training purposes, you should not have to pay for that second lawyer. Discuss this in advance with your lawyer. In deciding whether to make an issue of the costs of a second lawyer, keep in mind that if a lawyer in the second chair is going to be helpful, the incremental cost, viewed as a percentage of the entire costs of the case, is probably worth it. This is not the time to be penny wise and pound foolish.

If you are represented by counsel, you can best watch your money in divorce litigation by being reasonable in setting objectives, clearly communicating those objectives, and following your lawyer's lead as to litigation strategy and tactics.

Chapter Twenty-Two

Postdivorce Issues

Just when you think it is all over, there is more to consider. Postdivorce issues include finances, the difficult former spouse, changes, bankruptcy, and more.

Check the following list of action items to be sure you have handled all of the postdivorce issues.

POSTDIVORCE CHECKLIST

❏ Complete pension fund transfers and arrange rollovers
❏ Prepare and record deed for real estate transfer, or sell property
❏ Transfer automobile titles
❏ Transfer bank accounts and close joint accounts
❏ Transfer stock and close joint accounts
❏ Transfer household items
❏ Cancel joint credit cards or remove ex-spouse's name
❏ Send letters to creditors and reporting agencies if your spouse has agreed to pay debt
❏ Notify the IRS and state tax authority if you have a new address (IRS Form 8822)
❏ Change beneficiaries on insurance policies and pension plans
❏ Convert health insurance under COBRA by the deadline
❏ Notify children's schools of addresses of both parents for mailing records
❏ Revise will

Finances

After the divorce, you and your ex-spouse will have two separate households. You will have to maintain those two homes on the money with which you have previously maintained one. Two cannot live as cheaply as one.

Difficult Former Spouse

If your spouse has been a difficult person all of his or her life, it is very unlikely that going through a divorce will make him or her a less difficult person. After the divorce you may be separated, but you are still connected by visitation, child support, alimony, or debt payments. In that case, you will still have to deal with the problems together. If your spouse has always been difficult, then no matter how hard you try, your spouse will probably still be difficult.

Changes

If you and your spouse agree to change the terms of a court order (such as a temporary support order or final decree), you must change it with another order. If your spouse says you do not have to pay alimony for the next year if you take the children to Disneyland this summer, you must get it in writing and entered in court for it to be binding on your spouse, and to protect you from *contempt.*

If you need to change child support or certain types of alimony, you can petition the court for a change. If you show a change of circumstances, then the court may modify those provisions. The changes of circumstances that most impress the court are those changes that are unexpected, such as losing your job because the company went bankrupt. The courts are less sympathetic to people who do not want to work as hard as they previously worked. Sometimes changes that everybody knew were coming are not considered a change of circumstances, such as the fact that when children become teenagers, they became much more expensive. This should have been anticipated.

Records

It is very important that you keep records of payments you make or receive for alimony and child support. If you are paying, pay by check and keep all canceled checks. If you cannot prove you paid it, you might as well have not paid it. If you are receiving payments, keep a running account in a permanent place. If you cannot prove what you have received, the court might not believe you when you testify about what you did not receive. It is easier for both parties, and sometimes required by law, to have payments deducted from the paycheck of the person who is paying.

Appeals

If your case is heard by a judicial officer who is not a full-fledged judge, you may have a less formal avenue of review of that person's decision. Usually, the judicial officer's title is something like commissioner, master, or magistrate, and the result of the hearing is a report of findings and recommendations that are filed with the court for action by the judge. A party who is not satisfied at this stage may file objections or exceptions, and may take the matter to a full-fledged judge. You may or may not be entitled to have the judge hear all of the evidence again.

You may be able to appeal the decision in your case if you are not satisfied with the outcome. If the trial judge made an error in finding the facts or applying the law that affected the outcome, your appeal may be successful. If not, appealing to a higher (appellate) court probably will not do you any good.

The appellate courts do not rehear all the evidence. They decide, based on the record of the trial court hearing, whether the trial judge made one or more mistakes, and if so, whether they were important enough to warrant changing the decision or sending the case back to the trial judge.

If you want to appeal the decision of the trial court judge in your divorce case to the appellate court, you must generally file a notice of appeal in the trial court and the appellate court, and mail a copy to the opposing party or counsel. You must also obtain a transcript of the trial. The other party can file a cross-appeal if he or she is also unsatisfied with some aspect of the trial court decision.

Once your appeal has been noted, you will have a certain amount of time under the rules or briefing schedule set by the appellate court in your case to file an appellant's brief, setting forth the errors made by the trial court and arguing for reversal. Your adversary, referred as the *appellee,* is entitled to file an opposing brief.

Sometimes the initial or second level of review is not an appeal, but is a petition that can be granted or denied. In this case, you must argue not only that the decision was wrong, but also that your case involves an important point of law that should be resolved for the benefit of all litigants. If the court grants your petition for review, the case then proceeds like a regular appeal.

At the end of your trial, you may end up with a result that you are not satisfied with and a firm conviction that the trial court has made an error. If so, you may appeal your case. You should be aware, though, that the great majority of trial court decisions are affirmed—not reversed—on appeal.

Chapter Twenty-Three

Bankruptcy

Bankruptcy law is federal law that gives overburdened debtors certain relief from payment of their debts. Divorce law and bankruptcy law frequently intersect. In this credit-driven society, family budgets are often based on two incomes supporting one household. When that one household becomes two, income can become insufficient, resulting in eventual bankruptcy. The *Bankruptcy Abuse Prevention and Consumer Protection Act of 2005* has made important changes to bankruptcy law that can affect your divorce. This chapter discusses the effect of current bankruptcy law in divorce cases. At the end of the chapter, there is a brief discussion of the former bankruptcy law, which applies to bankruptcy cases filed before October 17, 2005.

Chapter 7 Bankruptcy

The person who files bankruptcy is called the *debtor*. The persons or businesses owed money are called *creditors*. In a Chapter 7 bankruptcy (liquidation), the debtor gives up his or her nonexempt property, and receives a discharge of the obligation to pay his or her dischargeable debts. In theory, creditors are paid from the debtor's nonexempt assets, but in consumer cases, there are almost no nonexempt assets. The debtor has to file sworn schedules listing all of his or her property and assets, all debts, current income and expenses, and various facts about his or her financial affairs. All of the debtor's creditors receive notice of the bankruptcy filing. The debtor has to attend a bankruptcy meeting conducted by the bankruptcy trustee and answer the trustee's questions under oath. Creditors can also attend this meeting and question the debtor. In the six months preceding the bankruptcy filing, the debtor must attend a briefing that outlines the opportunities for credit counseling.

Discharge

Discharge means that the debtor does not have to pay the debt and the creditor cannot take action to collect it. Generally, if the debtor is eligible and has completed all of the debtor's duties, he or she will be granted a discharge in the bankruptcy case. The 2005 Act created a new requirement that debtors complete a financial management course before they receive a discharge.

Debts owed to a spouse or former spouse for support, property division, or debts based on allocation of marital debt are not dischargeable in a Chapter 7 bankruptcy. This means the debtor former spouse must pay the obligation despite the bankruptcy, and the creditor former spouse can take legal action to collect. The creditor spouse does not need to take any action in the bankruptcy case to preserve the right to collect the debt. The debtor spouse's ability to pay support will probably be improved by the discharge of his or her obligation to pay other creditors. It is not clear whether and under what circumstances the debtor's obligations to a former spouse's attorney can be discharged.

Automatic Stay

The filing of a bankruptcy case operates as an *automatic stay* of all other litigation involving the debtor. Judgments, decrees, and orders entered in violation of the stay are generally void. Most court actions that happen in a divorce case are exceptions to the automatic stay. This means if your spouse files bankruptcy during your divorce case, you do not have to go into bankruptcy court to have the stay lifted so that the divorce courts orders will be valid, and you do not have to delay action in the divorce case until the bankruptcy case is over, unless your case involves issues that are not exceptions to the stay. Examples of actions that are exceptions to the bankruptcy stay are actions to establish paternity, determine or modify child support, determine child custody and visitation, obtain relief in domestic violence cases, or obtain a divorce. Examples of actions that are subject to the stay are division of marital property, earnings withholding orders to collect support, and interception of an income tax refund. If there is any doubt, the only safe courses are to go into bankruptcy court to have the stay lifted to allow your divorce court action to proceed, or to wait until the conclusion of the bankruptcy case.

Chapter 13 Bankruptcy

In a Chapter 13 bankruptcy, the debtor files a plan that provides for payment of the debts, usually from future income. Chapter 13 plans are subject to various rules regarding the treatment of creditors. One such rule is that the plan must provide for full payment of *priority* claims. Domestic support obligations are *first priority* claims. Also, a Chapter 13 plan cannot be confirmed if the debtor is not current with all post-petition domestic support obligations.

A Chapter 13 bankruptcy case may be dismissed or converted to a case under Chapter 7 if a debtor is not timely making post-petition domestic support payments. Prepetition domestic support obligations owed to an individual must be paid in full as a priority claim in a Chapter 13 plan. However, if the obligations are to be paid to a governmental unit, the plan can provide for less than 100% payment if the debtor proposes to pay all of his or her projected disposable income into a five-year plan.

The debtor in a Chapter 13 case is granted a discharge of the obligation to pay his or her prefiling debts at the conclusion of payments under the plan. In cases involving support, the bankruptcy court will not grant a discharge until the debtor files a certificate that pre-bankruptcy domestic support obligations provided for in the plan have been paid, and that domestic support obligations that came due during the case have all been paid. As previously stated, the 2005 Act created a new requirement that debtors complete a financial management course before they receive a Chapter 7 or 13 discharge.

The Chapter 13 discharge is broader than the discharge under Chapter 7. The one exception to the rule that divorce obligations are not dischargeable is that divorce obligations that are not *domestic support obligations* can be discharged in a Chapter 13 case if the debtor makes all payments required under the plan. Examples of nonsupport debts are property settlement payments and indemnification agreements. In *indemnification agreements*, your spouse agrees that he or she will pay a debt you both owe, then he or she files a Chapter 13 bankruptcy, makes all the payments required under the Chapter 13 plan, and receives a discharge of the obligation to the joint creditor. These marital debts are not automatically excepted from the debtor spouse's discharge. The creditor spouse has to file a timely complaint in the bankruptcy case. The bankruptcy court may or may not decide that the marital debt should be excepted from the debtor's discharge, depending on the relative financial circumstances of the two spouses.

If the debtor does not complete the plan, but the failure to complete the payments is not due to the fault of the debtor, he or she will be granted a hardship discharge, which has about the same effect as a Chapter 7 discharge. Debts owed to a spouse or former spouse for support, property division, or debts based on allocation of marital debt are not covered by a hardship Chapter 13 discharge.

In a Chapter 13 case, the creditor spouse must file a proof of claim in the bankruptcy court to be paid under the Chapter 13 plan. If the creditor spouse does not file, the debtor spouse can file a claim for the creditor spouse. The debtor may want to do this, especially if domestic support obligations are involved. It is in the debtor's interest to ensure that as much of the money paid into the plan as possible goes to the creditor spouse, because whatever is not paid in the plan will remain due after the Chapter 13 case.

If bankruptcy is filed by your or your spouse as a result of the divorce (or for other reasons), you may be ineligible for Chapter 7 and may have to file a Chapter 13 bankruptcy if your income for the past six months exceeds the average income for your family size in your state. In this case, your Chapter 13 bankruptcy plan would have to provide for full payment of all debts, or if that is not possible, devote all of your disposable income to payment of claims for five years.

Joint Bankruptcy

In cases in which it appears that bankruptcy is inevitable for both spouses, the possibility of a joint bankruptcy should not be overlooked. The spouses must still be husband and wife to be eligible to file a joint bankruptcy case, so the bankruptcy petition would have to be filed before entry of the divorce decree.

Marital Settlement Agreements

In appropriate cases, the prospect of bankruptcy should be kept in mind when negotiating and drafting the separation agreement. It is not sufficient to simply say that the husband or wife agrees not to file bankruptcy, or agrees that all debts to the creditor spouse shall be nondischargeable.

The best protection for the creditor spouse is a lien against property of the debtor spouse, if there is substantial equity in the property. Another strategy is for the agreement to state (and perhaps show by means of financial statements) that debts that do not sound like support really are support. In cases in which the debtor spouse is likely to file bankruptcy, a simpler strategy may be for the agreement to provide for more support, and less or no property settlement.

These anti-bankruptcy strategies are a lot less important than they were before the 2005 bankruptcy legislation increased the protection for former spouses in bankruptcy.

If Your Former Spouse Files Bankruptcy

If you are the creditor spouse, your legal position is secure in Chapter 7 and secure with respect to support obligations in a Chapter 13. Nevertheless, you should carefully review all pleadings and notices and consult counsel early in the process if the stakes are high and there is any doubt about what you must do to preserve your rights. If your former spouse files a Chapter 13, owes you obligations that are not for support, and provided for less than full payment of that debt in the Chapter 13 plan, you should act promptly to minimize the chance that the unpaid balance of the debt will be discharged at the conclusion of the Chapter 13 bankruptcy case. Unless the stakes do not justify it, it is best to consult an experienced bankruptcy lawyer in these circumstances.

If You Are Considering Bankruptcy

If you are the debtor spouse, you may find that your postdivorce or mid-divorce circumstances require you to seek bankruptcy relief. Your former spouse is holding a lot of cards, especially if support debts are involved. Your interests and your spouse's are not necessarily directly adverse in the bankruptcy case. This is not the divorce, where every dollar one of you gets, the other one has to give up. Your former spouse's and your children's economic interests are protected in bankruptcy in a way that other creditors' interests are not. If most of your debt is owed to persons other than your former spouse, and most of your debt is not joint with him or her, your bankruptcy is probably not a bad thing for your former spouse. In these circumstances, it may be wise to give him or her advance notice, explain what you are doing and why, and persuade your former spouse that it is in his or her economic interest not to interfere with your obtaining bankruptcy relief.

Former Law

As far as divorce goes, the most important change made in the 2005 bankruptcy reform legislation was the almost complete elimination of the distinction that formerly existed between support obligations and other divorce-related debt. Former law applies to bankruptcy cases filed prior to October 17, 2005.

Under former law, support obligations were not dischargeable, and the creditor spouse did not need to take any action in bankruptcy court to preserve the debt. However, nonsupport marital debts, such as property settlement payments and indemnification agreements, were not automatically excepted from the debtor spouse's Chapter 7 discharge. The creditor spouse had to file a timely complaint in the bankruptcy case, then the bankruptcy court may or may not have decided that the marital debt should be excepted from the debtor's discharge, depending on the relative financial circumstances of the two spouses.

Conclusion

In general, bankruptcy does not afford any relief from divorce-related debt. However, divorce law and bankruptcy law are both complicated. The overlap of these two bodies of law, though simplified by the 2005 bankruptcy legislation, can still be tricky for both debtor and creditor spouses.

Conclusion

When you come to the end of your divorce, which may or may not be the date the judgment or decree of divorce is signed, you will find that life has changed. You are now single. You may be a single parent or have the new role of a noncustodial parent. You have been through the breakup of your old family, and now you have a new family situation.

You probably have a new residence and may have different employment—maybe even your first employment out of the house in a while. Your assets are less than the joint assets you and your spouse owned. Your financial obligations are different. You even had an introduction to the legal system.

If you look back over the past year, you will probably recall various choices you had to make. Those choices influenced your current personal, family, and financial situation. Everybody makes mistakes, but hopefully you avoided making any serious or costly ones. Hopefully this book was helpful to you.

Now you are at a time of new beginnings. You have to start and build a new personal, social, and financial life. If you have any children, you have to raise them. You will probably have to develop or maintain a working co-parenting relationship with your former spouse.

You have to get on with the important business of living the rest of your life. At the beginning of this book, it was mentioned that you must have a plan for your divorce and work your plan. Life is like that, too. You must have a plan for your life and work your plan—but you have to leave some room for spontaneity. After all, you're single now.

Glossary

401(k) account. A defined contribution retirement plan set up by an employer so that employees can set aside money for retirement on a pretax basis. Employers may match a percentage of the amount that employees contribute to the plan.

A

abandonment. A spouse's unjustified departure from the marital home. Generally grounds for limited divorce immediately and for absolute divorce after a waiting period. *See desertion.*

absolute divorce. A completed divorce that dissolves the bonds of matrimony and permits the parties to marry again.

accrual basis. An accounting method under which expenses are booked when they accrue and income is booked when it is earned.

adultery. Sexual intercourse by a married person with a person other than his or her spouse.

alimony. Spousal support paid by one spouse or former spouse to the other.

alimony factors. The factors a court considers in setting alimony. They are set by statute in many states.

annuity. A contract under which the annuity payer pays the annuitant a set amount monthly for life.

annulment. Judicial recognition that a purported marriage was a nullity.

alternative dispute resolution. Any process by which legal adversaries reach a decision other than bringing the matter to trial for a judge's decision. In divorce cases, it usually refers to mediation.

appeal. Procedure by which a trial court decision is brought before a higher court for review.

assets. Items of property owned by the person in question.

B

balance sheet. A summary of assets, liabilities, and equity at a point in time.

budget. A statement showing projected income and target expenses by category for a future period.

buy-sell agreement. An agreement among the owners of a closely held business entity, usually to set a procedure restricting sales of interests in the entity and the price at which the interests will be sold between existing owners.

C

cash basis. An accounting method under which expenses are booked when they are paid and income is booked when it is received.

cash flow. Cash income less cash expenses.

child support. The payment the noncustodial parent pays to the custodial parent for support of the parties' children.

child support guidelines. The charts used to determine the amount of child support to be paid. In most states, the guidelines take account of objective economic factors, which generally include the number of children, the custodial parent's income, the noncustodial parent's income, the alimony payable between the parties, the cost of health insurance, the cost of day care, and support obligations with respect to other children who are not children of both parties.

collaborative family law. A settlement process in which the lawyers contract to withdraw if one of the parties decides to litigate the divorce.

community property. Property acquired by one or both spouses during the marriage, except property acquired by gift from a third person or inheritance, or property excluded from community property by a valid agreement.

constructive desertion. A spouse's withdrawal from spousal duties and the marital relationship without leaving the marital home. Generally grounds for limited divorce immediately and for absolute divorce after a waiting period. The spouse who has left the marital home often alleges constructive desertion against the other spouse.

contested divorce. A divorce in which the parties do not agree on one or more issues and must bring the case to court for a contested divorce hearing.

contested divorce hearing. The hearing or trial in a divorce case in which the parties do not agree on one or more issues.

corroboration. Additional proof. Many states' laws require corroboration of a party's testimony to the facts entitling him or her to a divorce.

counselor. Mental health professional trained in counseling; usually not a psychiatrist or psychologist.

courts of general jurisdiction. Trial courts that hear cases not under the jurisdiction of some specialty court like tax court, workers' compensation court, or in some states, family law courts.

credit bureau. An agency that researches the credit history of consumers and maintains an accessible database that lenders use to make decisions about granting of loans.

credit rating. An evaluation of a person's creditworthiness, done by credit bureaus.

credit report. A report on a consumer's financial history and creditworthiness by a credit bureau.

cruelty. One spouse's mistreatment of the other that is so serious that it is grounds for divorce. Cruelty usually includes physical violence.

custody. The legal right to act as parent to the children, have the children live with you, and make decisions about their welfare and upbringing. In a divorce case, unless the parties reach an agreement, the court decides which parent will have custody of the children.

custodial parent. The parent who has custody of the children.

D

decree of divorce. The court's decision concluding a divorce case in those states that retain a distinction between law cases and equity cases. Where this distinction still exists, in procedure or sometimes just in terminology, divorce cases are equity cases.

deductions. Items deducted from income in computing income tax (short for tax deductions).

defined benefit plan. A traditional employer-provided pension plan that provides a lifetime annuity at retirement.

defined contribution plan. An employer-provided retirement plan where the amount the employer contributes is set by the plan, but the benefit the employee receives is not; for example, a 401(k) plan.

dependents. Persons you support. In income tax parlance, persons you are entitled to claim as an exemption on your tax return.

deposition. A discovery procedure. A party to litigation can compel the other party or other witnesses to submit to oral questions under oath before a court reporter.

desertion. A spouse's unjustified departure from the marital home. Desertion is grounds for absolute divorce, usually after a waiting period of one year. *See abandonment.*

direct examination. A party's (or his or her attorney's) questioning of a witness that the party has called as part of his or her case in a trial or hearing.

discovery. A variety of pretrial procedures that can be used to discover facts from the other party. The most common methods are depositions, interrogatories, requests for production of documents, and requests for admission.

divorce. Judicial dissolution of the bonds of matrimony between married persons.

divorce hearing. In an uncontested case, the hearing at which the spouse who filed a complaint for divorce presents evidence of the facts constituting grounds for divorce and facts relevant to any other issue, such as the parties' separation, the property settlement agreement, or the amount of child support to be paid.

domestic violence. Violence against a spouse or a person in another family or romantic relationship. Many states' laws provide special expedited procedures to meet the security and financial needs of victims of domestic violence.

E

equitable distribution. The process of identifying, valuing, and equitably dividing marital property, or ordering a compensatory payment from one spouse to the other.

equity line of credit. A secured preapproved credit arrangement that allows the borrower to borrow up to the limit of the line automatically. The usual security is a second or lower mortgage or deed of trust against real property.

evidence. The proof presented at trial. A witness's answer under oath, documents, or other tangible things presented by a party are accepted as evidence by the court.

exceptions. Procedure by which a judicial officer's (not a full-fledged judge) report or findings and recommendations are brought before the judge for review.

exemptions. An amount you can deduct from income in computing income tax. You can claim an exemption for yourself and for each of your dependents. Shorthand for tax exemptions.

exhibit. In trial jargon, a document offered in evidence.

expense budget. A statement showing target expenses by category for a future period.

F

family court. In some states, there are special trial courts that hear divorce and other family law matters.

family division. In some states, there are special divisions of the trial court that hear divorce and other family law matters.

family home. In some states, if there are minor children, the spouse with custody can be awarded exclusive use and possession of the family home, furniture, and automobile during the case, and often for some period of time after the case.

filing status. Under the tax code, your tax is determined by applying the rates in one of four tax schedules to your taxable income. The schedules are determined by your filing status: single; married, filing jointly; married, filing separately; and, head of household.

financial planner. A finance professional who assists individuals with long- and short-term financial goals.

findings and recommendations. The title of the judicial officer's report to the court after hearing evidence.

G

goodwill. The part of a business's value that is attributable to its value as a going concern and not its identifiable assets.

grounds for divorce. The legal basis for granting a divorce.

guardian ad litem. An attorney (usually) appointed to act as the child's or children's advocate in a divorce case.

I

income and expense statement. A statement of income earned or received, and expenses incurred or paid, over a period of time.

income statement. A statement of income earned or received over a period of time.

incorporated but not merged. The term used to mean that the parties' agreement is part of the court's judgment or decree, and that failure to perform will be a violation of a court order punishable by contempt. The agreement also remains a private contract that can be enforced by suit for breach of contract.

indefinite alimony. Alimony that is payable until death of either party, remarriage of the payee, or further order of court. Usually, the court retains jurisdiction to modify or terminate indefinite alimony, and may do so if a party shows that there has been a material change in circumstances since the order setting alimony, and the change warrants modifying or terminating alimony.

individual retirement account (Roth). An account that qualifies for special treatment under the tax code. Contributions are not deductible but the earnings are not taxable. The principal and accumulated earnings are not taxed when they are withdrawn.

individual retirement account (traditional). An account that qualifies for special treatment under the tax code. Contributions are deductible for qualifying individuals up to certain limits and the earnings are not taxable. The principal and accumulated earnings are taxed when they are withdrawn.

interrogatories. A discovery procedure. A party's written questions to the other party that have to be answered in writing and under oath.

irreconcilable differences. A no-fault ground for divorce in many states.

J

judgment of divorce. The court's decision concluding a divorce case in states that do not retain a distinction between law cases and equity cases.

jurisdiction. The power of a court to hear and decide the matter that is before it, and bind the parties by its decision.

L

legal custody. The right to make long-term parenting decisions about the child's upbringing, health, education, religion, and so on.

liabilities. Debts or financial obligations.

limited divorce. Judicial recognition of the separate status of the parties. It is a divorce for tax and many other purposes, but it does not permit the parties to marry again. Also called legal separation and divorce from bed and board.

line of credit. A preapproved credit arrangement that allows the borrower to borrow up to the limit of the line automatically.

M

marital property. The property that the court will equitably divide between the parties in a divorce, or that it will consider in ordering any compensating payment (monetary award) from one party to the other. Generally, marital property is property acquired by one or both spouses during the marriage, except property acquired by gift from a third person or inheritance, or property excluded by a valid agreement.

marital residence. The home where the spouses last lived together. If the divorcing couple has minor children, depending on state law, the custodial parent is often awarded title to the marital residence or exclusive use and possession for some period of time.

marital settlement agreement. Spouses' agreement settling the issues arising in their separation and divorce. The agreement may cover such matters as the spouses living separately, child custody and support, alimony, division of property, allocation of responsibility for debt, insurance, and allocation of tax benefits.

mediation. A process by which the parties meet to discuss the disputed issues with a skilled neutral person who guides the process and helps the parties reach agreements on the issues in the case.

minority discount. A percentage reduction in value, applied to a less than controlling interest in a closely owned corporation because such interests cannot generally be sold for a price that is equal to the percentage of ownership times the value of the entire business.

monetary award. The compensatory payment the court may order one spouse to pay another as an adjustment of their respective equity in marital property.

motion. A party's request, written or stated orally in open court during trial, asking the court to make an order and stating grounds for the order.

N

nesting. A custodial arrangement under which the children remain in the marital home, and the parents move in and out on an agreed schedule.

noncustodial parent. The parent who does not have custody of the children, or if custody is shared, the parent who has less custody.

nonmarital property. Property that is not marital property, generally because it was owned by a spouse prior to the marriage, it was acquired by gift or inheritance from a third person, or it is excluded from marital property by a valid agreement. *See separate property.*

O

objection. A party can use this procedure at trial to attempt to keep out a piece of evidence offered by the other party. Objections are made orally and grounds must be stated. The objection to a question must be made before the witness answers it, and an objection to a document must be made before that court admits the document into evidence.

P

parenting classes. Court-sponsored classes on the negative impact of divorce on children and how to minimize it, as well as related subjects that the court may order parties to attend in contested custody cases.

pendente lite. During the litigation; temporary until the trial.

pendente lite alimony. Alimony ordered to be paid until the final hearing. Pendente lite alimony is usually only an amount sufficient to pay for necessities.

pendente lite relief. Court orders regarding support or other matters entered during the litigation to allow the parties to maintain the status quo until the final hearing.

pension plan. An employer-sponsored retirement plan, usually used to refer to a defined benefit plan that provides a lifetime annuity at retirement.

physical custody. Refers to the home in which the children primarily reside. The parent who lives in that home has physical custody of the children.

pleadings. Papers filed with the court, such as the complaint, answer, and counterclaim.

prayer for relief. The last section of a pleading where the party tells the court what the party wants the court to do.

pretrial conference. Final conference with the court before trial. The parties may have to file joint or separate statements of marital property, as well as a pretrial statement regarding such things as identification of witnesses, documents, and pending motions.

property settlement agreement. An agreement under which the spouses divide marital property.

psychotherapist. A mental health professional who assists an individual through psychotherapy, a technique used to encourage communication of conflicts and insight into problems, with the goal of relief of symptoms, improved functioning, and growth.

Q

Qualified Domestic Relations Order (QDRO). A judgment or decree issued under domestic relations law that divides the rights and benefits of a qualified retirement plan between the plan participant (the employee spouse) and the alternate payee (the nonemployee spouse).

Qualified Medical Child Support Order (QMSCO). A judgment or decree issued under domestic relations law that designates the child as an alternate under the employee spouse's health plan, and allows the child or the child's custodian to deal directly with the health insurance carrier.

qualifying order. A judgment or decree issued under domestic relations law that divides the rights and benefits of a government employee pension between the plan participant (the employee spouse) and the alternate payee (the nonemployee spouse).

R

rehabilitative alimony. Alimony for a stated term to permit a party to become self-supporting.

request for production of documents. A discovery procedure in which one party writes a request to the other party to produce documents for inspection and copying.

retirement plan. Generally, an employer-sponsored arrangement under which funds are set aside during active employment to be drawn or paid out over the employee's retirement.

S

scheduling conference. First court appearance at which the court schedules various hearings depending on the issues in the case, and may schedule mediation or order the parties to attend parenting classes.

separate maintenance. Spousal support paid by one spouse or former spouse to the other.

separate property. Property that is not marital property, generally because it was owned by a spouse prior to the marriage, it was acquired by gift or inheritance from a third person, or it is excluded from marital property by a valid agreement. *See nonmarital property.*

separation agreement. Spouses' agreement regarding the terms of their separation. In addition to the agreement that the spouses shall live separately, it will often cover matters such as child custody and support, alimony, division of property, allocation of responsibility for debt, insurance, and allocation of tax benefits.

shared custody. The noncustodial parent has custody a significant amount of time, and therefore, child support is calculated under the shared custody child support guidelines.

split custody. Each parent has physical custody of one or more of the party's children.

spousal support. *See alimony.*

stock option. A contract under which the holder has the right to buy a number of shares of a particular stock at a stated price over a defined period of time.

suit money. Litigation costs the court can order one spouse to pay to another, comprised of attorney's fees, court costs, and other litigation costs, such as expert witness fees.

survivor benefit plan. A feature of some pensions that continues payment of a reduced annuity to a named survivor for his or her life after the pensioner's death.

T

tax credits. Items deducted directly from tax in computing income tax.

tax deductions. Items deducted from income in computing income tax.

tax exemption. Each taxpayer can deduct an amount from income in computing income tax for him- or herself and each of the person's dependents.

therapist. *See psychotherapist.*

time-sharing. The noncustodial parent's time with the children. Also often referred to in agreements and orders as *visitation.*

trial. The hearing at which the parties to litigation present witnesses, documents, and other evidence about the facts bearing on the contested issues in the case.

U

uncontested divorce hearing. The hearing at which the spouse who filed a complaint for divorce presents evidence of the facts constituting grounds for divorce and facts relevant to any other issue, such as the parties' separation and property settlement agreement, or the amount of child support to be paid.

use and possession. Term used in those states where a spouse with custody of a minor child or children of the parties can be granted exclusive use and possession of the family home, furniture, and automobile.

V

visitation. The noncustodial parent's time with the children. Sometimes referred to in agreements and orders as *time-sharing.*

Appendix

Child Support Agencies

Contact your state child support agency with questions about your situation. For those states that do not show a mailing a street address, please refer to the state's website for local office locations.

**Alabama Department
  of Human Resources
Child Support Enforcement
  Division**
P.O. Box 304000
Montgomery, AL 36130
www.dhr.state.al.us
334-242-9300
334-242-0606 *(fax)*

**Alaska Child Support
  Services Division**
550 West 7th Avenue
Suite 310
Anchorage, AK 99501
www.csed.state.ak.us
907-269-6900
907-269-6650 *(fax)*

**Arizona Division of Child
  Support Enforcement**
3443 North Central Avenue
Suite 100
Phoenix, AZ 85012
www.de.state.az.us/dcse
800-882-4151

**Arkansas Office of Child
  Support Enforcement
  Division
Central Office Customer
  Service**
400 East Capitol
P.O. Box 8133
Little Rock, AR 72203
www.arkansas.gov/dfa/child_
  support
501-371-5349
501-682-6002 *(fax)*

**California Department of
  Child Support Services**
www.childsup.cahwnet.gov
866-249-0773

**Colorado Child Support
  Enforcement**
1575 Sherman Street
5th floor
Denver, CO 80203
www.childsupport.state.co.us
303-866-4300
303-866-4360 *(fax)*

**Connecticut Department of
Social Services**
25 Sigourney Street
Hartford, CT 06106
www.dss.state.ct.us/svcs/csupp.htm
800-842-1508

**Delaware Division of Child
Support Enforcement**
P.O. Box 904
84A Christiana Road
New Castle, DE 19720
www.dhss.delaware.gov/dhss/dcse
302-577-7171
302-326-6239 *(fax)*

**District of Columbia Child
Support Services Division**
441 4th Street, NW
Suite 550N
Washington, DC 20001
www.csed.dc.gov/csed
202-442-9900

**Florida Department of Revenue
Florida Child Support
Enforcement
State Program Office**
P.O. Box 8030
Tallahassee, FL 32314
http://myflorida.com/dor/
childsupport
800-622-KIDS (5437)

**Georgia Office of Child Support
Enforcement
State Customer Service Unit
OCSE Administration**
2 Peachtree Street NW
20th Floor
P.O. Box 38450
Atlanta, GA 30334
https://services.georgia.gov/dhr/
cspp/do/public/Welcome
800-227-7993

**Hawaii Child Support
Enforcement Agency**
601 Kamokila Boulevard
Suite 251
Kapolei, HI 96707
www.state.hi.us/csea/csea.html
808-692-8265
888-317-9081

**Idaho Department of Health
and Welfare
Child Support Services**
450 West State Street
Boise, ID 83720
www.healthandwelfare.idaho.gov
800-356-9868

**Illinois Child Support
Enforcement**
www.ilchildsupport.com
800-447-4278

**Indiana Child Support Bureau
Division of Family and Children**
402 West Washington Street
Room W360
Indianapolis, IN 46204
www.in.gov/dcs/support/index.html
800-840-8757

**Iowa Department of Human
Services**
https://childsupport.dhs.state.ia.us
888-229-9223

**Kansas Child Support
Enforcement**
www.srskansas.org/cse/iwo
785-296-4687

Kentucky Cabinet for Health
and Family Services
Division of Child Support
P.O. Box 2150
Frankfort, KY 40602
http://chfs.ky.gov/dcbs/dcs
502-564-2285
800-248-1163 *(Child Support Hotline)*
502-564-5988 *(fax)*

Louisiana Department of Social
Services
Office of Family Support
Enforcement Services
530 Lakeland Avenue
Baton Rouge, LA 70804
www.dss.state.la.us
225-342-4780
225-342-7397 *(fax)*

Maine Division of Support
Enforcement and Recovery
11 SHS Whitten Road
Augusta, ME 04333
www.maine.gov/dhhs/bfi/dser
207-287-3110
207-287-2334 *(fax)*

Maryland Child Support
Enforcement Program
Child Support Enforcement
Administration
311 West Saratoga Street
Baltimore, MD 21201
www.dhr.state.md.us/csea
800-332-6347

Massachusetts Department of
Revenue
Child Support Enforcement
Division
Office of the Advocate
P.O. Box 9552
Boston, MA 02114
www.cse.state.ma.us
800-332-2733
617-660-1234
617-887-7540 *(fax)*

Michigan Department of
Human Services
Office of Child Support
P.O. Box 30037
Lansing, MI 48909
www.michigan.gov/dhs
866-540-0008

Minnesota Department of
Human Services
Child Support Enforcement
Division
444 Lafayette Road
St. Paul, MN 55155
www.dhs.state.mn.us
651-296-2542 *(Twin Cities
metro area)*
800-657-3954 *(toll-free)*

Mississippi Department of
Human Services
Division of Child Support
Enforcement
750 North State Street
Jackson, MS 39205
www.mdhs.state.ms.us/cse.html
800-345-6347

Missouri Department of Social Services
Child Support Enforcement
221 West High Street
P.O. Box 1527
Jefferson City, MO 65102
www.dss.state.mo.us/cse
573-751-4815

Montana Department of Public Health and Human Services
Child Support Enforcement
3075 North Montana Avenue
P.O. Box 202943
Helena, MT 59620
www.dphhs.mt.gov/aboutus/
divisions/childsupport
enforcement
800-346-KIDS *(in Montana)*
406-444-9855
406-444-1370 *(fax)*

Nebraska Department of Health and Human Services
Child Support Enforcement
P.O. Box 94728
Lincoln, NE 68509
www.hhs.state.ne.us/cse
402-441-8715
877-631-9973 *(toll-free)*

Nevada Department of Health and Human Services
Division of Welfare and Supportive Services
1470 East College Parkway
Carson City, NV 89706
www.welfare.state.nv.us/child.htm
775-684-0500
775-684-0646 *(fax)*

New Hampshire Department of Health and Human Services
Division of Child Support Services
129 Pleasant Street
Concord, NH 03301
www.dhhs.state.nh.us/DHHS/DCSS
603-271-4745

New Jersey Department of Human Services
Office of Child Support Services
www.njchildsupport.org
877-NJKIDS1

New Mexico Child Support Enforcement Division
P.O. Box 25110
Santa Fe, NM 87504
https://elink.hsd.state.nm.us/clink
800-288-7207 *(toll-free from within New Mexico)*
800-585-7631 *(toll-free from outside New Mexico)*

New York Division of Child Support Enforcement
https://newyorkchildsupport.com
888-208-4485

North Carolina Division of Social Services
Child Support Enforcement
P.O. Box 20800
Raleigh, NC 27619
www.dhhs.state.nc.us/dss/cse/
index.htm
800-992-9457 *(toll-free)*
252-789-5225 *(in the Martin County Area)*

North Dakota Department of Human Services
Child Support Enforcement Division
1600 East Century Avenue
Suite 7
P.O. Box 7190
Bismarck, ND 58507
www.state.nd.us/humanservices/
   services/childsupport
701-328-3582
701-328-6575 *(fax)*

Ohio Office of Child Support
30 East Broad Street
32nd Floor
Columbus, OH 43215
http://jfs.ohio.gov/ocs
800-686-1556
614-752-6561
614-752-9760 *(fax)*

Oklahoma Department of Human Services
Child Support Enforcement Division
P.O. Box 53552
Oklahoma City, OK 73152
www.okdhs.org/childsupport
405-522-2273 *(Oklahoma City Metro)*
918-295-3500 *(Tulsa Metro)*
800-522-2922 *(toll-free)*

Oregon Department of Justice
Division of Child Support
1495 Edgewater Street NW
Suite 170
Salem, OR 97304
www.dcs.state.or.us
503-986-6090
503-986-6297 *(Fax)*

Pennsylvania Department of Public Welfare
Bureau of Child Support Enforcement
www.humanservices.state.pa.us/csws

Puerto Rico Departmento de la Familia
Adminstracion para el Sustento de Menores
Oficina Regional
Carr. #2 Km 121.5
Bo. Caimital Alto—Sótano
P.O. Box 970 Victoria Station
Aguadilla, PR 00605
www.gobierno.pr/Familia/Agencias/
   ASUME
787-891-6250
787-891-6270 *(fax)*

State of Rhode Island Child Support Enforcement
77 Dorrance Street
Providence, RI 02903
www.cse.ri.gov
401-222-2847

South Carolina Child Support Enforcement
P.O. Box 1469
Columbia, SC 29202
www.state.sc.us/dss/csed
800-768-5858

South Dakota Department of Social Services
Division of Child Support
700 Governors Drive
Pierre, SD 57501
www.state.sd.us/social/DCS/
   index.htm
800-286-9145

Tennessee Child Support Services
400 Deaderick Street
15ᵗʰ Floor
Nashville, TN 37248
www.state.tn.us/humanserv/
   child_support.htm
800-838-6911
615-253-4394

Texas Office of the Attorney General
Child Support Division
P.O. Box 12548
Austin, TX 78711
www.oag.state.tx.us/child/
   index.shtml
512-460-6000
800-252-8014 *(24-hour hotline)*

Utah Department of Human Services
Office of Recovery Services
Child Support Services
P.O. Box 45011
Salt Lake City, UT 84145
www.ors.utah.gov

Vermont Agency of Human Services
Office of Child Support
103 South Main Street
Waterbury, VT 05671
www.ocs.state.vt.us
800-786-3214

Virginia Department of Social Services
Department of Child Support Enforcement
7 North Eighth Street
Richmond, VA 23219
www.dss.state.va.us/family/
   dcse.html
804-726-7000

Washington Division of Child Support
Division of Child Support
P.O. Box 11520
Tacoma, WA 98411
www.dshs.wa.gov/dcs
800-442-KIDS

West Virginia Bureau of Child Support Enforcement
Central Office
350 Capitol Street
Room 147
Charleston, WV 25301
www.wvdhhr.org/bcse
304-558-3780
304-558-4092 *(fax)*

Wisconsin Department of Workplace Development
Bureau of Child Support
www.dwd.state.wi.us/bcs
608-266-9909

Wyoming Department of Family Services
Child Support Enforcement
http://dfsweb.state.wy.us/cse_
   enforce.html
307-777-6948

Index

About the Authors

James J. Gross is cofounder and managing partner of the law firm of Thyden Gross and Callahan in Chevy Chase, Maryland. He has practiced family law and business law for thirty years. He has represented hundreds of fathers in their efforts to secure their parental rights.

Mr. Gross received his Masters of Laws in Taxation from Georgetown University in 1982; a Juris Doctor from the University of Missouri in 1975; and a Bachelor of Science in Chemical Engineering from the University of Missouri in 1970.

Mr. Gross was named as one of the top divorce lawyers by *Washingtonian Magazine* in 2004. He appears frequently on television and radio in connection with fathers' rights. He is the author of *Fathers' Rights* and coauthor of *File for Divorce in Maryland, Virginia or the District of Columbia*. Mr. Gross writes the columns "The Daily Answer Desk" and "In the Courts." He is the Maryland legal expert for DivorceInfo.Com. Mr. Gross also has online blogs, including "The Maryland Divorce Crier," "Not Just Every Other Weekend," and "Married Guy, Single Guy."

Mr. Gross teaches divorce classes at the Montgomery County Commission for Women and presents programs for other family lawyers through the Montgomery County Bar Association. He was recently a copresenter on *Shame as a Tactic in Divorce Trials* at the Association of Family Courts and Conciliators.

He is on the Board of Directors of Affiliated Community Counselors, Inc. and the D.C. Capitols Track and Field Club. He is a member of the Family Law Sections of the American, District of Columbia, Maryland, and Montgomery County Bar

Associations. Mr. Gross is a trained mediator and collaborative lawyer. He is the cofounder and president of the Collaborative Law Society of Maryland, Virginia, and the District of Columbia and past president of Metropolitan Washington Mensa.

Mr. Gross, formerly in-house counsel to Satellite Business Systems and an attorney with the Federal Communications Commission, is rated *AV* by his fellow attorneys—the highest rating in Martindale-Hubbel.

He lives with his wife, Holly and two sons, Jake and Nicholas in Chevy Chase, Maryland. He may be contacted at **tgclawyers@smart.net** or by calling 301-907-4580. His website is **www.MdDivorceLawyers.com**.

Michael F. Callahan, formerly with the Internal Revenue Service, has practiced for eighteen years in the areas of family law, civil litigation, business law, tax controversies, and bankruptcy. He received his Juris Doctor from Georgetown University in 1987, and his Bachelor of Science in Marketing from University of Illinois at Chicago in 1974.

Mr. Callahan is a member of the Georgetown Chapter of Order of the Coif. He practices family law in Maryland, Virginia, and the District of Columbia. Mr. Callahan has written and lectured on divorce law for many years, and he is the coauthor of *File for Divorce in Maryland, Virginia or the District of Columbia*.

Mr. Callahan was selected as one of the top divorce lawyers in the Washington area by *Washingtonian Magazine*, March, 2004 issue, and one of Washington's top lawyers by *Washingtonian Magazine*, December, 2004.

He lives in Arlington, Virginia with his wife, Madelyn; son, Max; and daughter, Nora. Contact Mr. Callahan at **callahan@smart.net** or by calling 301-907-4580.